Writing Poetry through the Eyes of Science

Frameworks for Writing
Series Editor: Martha C. Pennington, Georgia Southern University

The *Frameworks for Writing* series offers books focused on writing and the teaching and learning of writing in educational and real-life contexts. The hallmark of the series is the application of approaches and techniques to writing and the teaching of writing that go beyond those of English literature to draw on and integrate writing with other disciplines, areas of knowledge, and contexts of everyday life. The series entertains proposals for textbooks as well as books for teachers, teacher educators, parents, and the general public. The list includes teacher reference books and student textbooks focused on innovative pedagogy aiming to prepare teachers and students for the challenges of the 21st century.

Published

The College Writing Toolkit: Tried and Tested Ideas for Teaching College Writing
Edited by Martha C. Pennington and Pauline Burton

The "Backwards" Research Guide for Writers: Using Your Life for Reflection, Connection, and Inspiration
Sonya Huber

Writing Poetry through the Eyes of Science: A Teacher's Guide to Scientific Literacy and Poetic Response
Nancy S. Gorrell with Erin Colfax

Forthcoming

Exploring College Writing: Reading, Writing, and Researching across the Curriculum
Dan Melzer

Tend Your Garden: Nurturing Motivation in Young Adolescent Writers
Mary Anna Kruch

Becoming a Teacher Who Writes: Let Teaching be Your Writing Muse
Nancy S. Gorrell

Writing from the Inside: The Power of Reflective Writing in the Classroom
Olivia Archibald and Maureen Hall

Arting, Writing, and Culture: Teaching to the 4th Power
Anna Sumida, Meleanna Meyer, and Miki Maeshiro

Seriously Creative Writing: Stylistic Strategies in Non-Fictional Writing
Sky Marsen

Reflective Writing for English Language Teachers
Thomas S. C. Farrell

Writing Poetry through the Eyes of Science

A Teacher's Guide to Scientific Literacy and Poetic Response

Nancy S. Gorrell

with Erin Colfax

equinox

SHEFFIELD   OAKVILLE

Published by Equinox Publishing Ltd.

UK: Unit S3, Kelham House, 3 Lancaster Street, Sheffield S3 8AF
USA: DBBC, 28 Main Street, Oakville, CT 06779

www.equinoxpub.com

First published 2012

© Nancy S. Gorrell 2012

ISBN   978-1-84553-439-4   (hardback)
        978-1-84553-440-0   (paperback)

British Library Cataloguing-in-Publication Data

A catalogue record for this book is available from the British Library.

Library of Congress Cataloging-in-Publication Data

Gorrell, Nancy.
  Writing poetry though the eyes of science: a teacher's guide to scientific literacy and poetic response / Nancy Gorrell, with Erin Colfax.
     p. cm. – (Frameworks for writing)
  Include bibliographical references and index.
  ISBN 978-1-84553-439-4 – ISBN 978-1-84553-440-0 (pbk.) 1.
Poetry–Study and teaching (Secondary) 2. Creative writing–Study and teaching (Secondary) 3. Science–Poetry. 4. Science in literature. 5. Language experience approach in education. 6. Interdisciplinary approach in education. I. Colfax, Erin. II. Title.
  PN1101.G68 2010
  428.0071'2—dc22
                            2010000018

Typeset by S.J.I. Services, New Delhi
Printed and bound in the UK by the MPG Books Group

For my mother,
Lillian Marian Schwartz,
the first naturalist in my life
who taught me by example
to see, name, and love the world;

and

for my father,
Robert Morris Schwartz,
(1920–2008)
the first scientist in my life,
who taught me by example
how to measure the immeasurable.

Contents

SECTION TWO: FUNDAMENTALS

BASIC LESSONS FOR SCIENCE POETRY WRITING

SECTION THREE: FUSION

ADVANCED LESSONS FOR SCIENCE POETRY WRITING

SECTION FOUR: FORGING COMMON GROUND

INTERDISCIPLINARY CURRICULUM

APPENDICES

Acknowledgments

I wish to thank Erin Colfax, my science partner, colleague, contributing author and friend, who shared with me her scientific eye, indomitable spirit, expeditions, and emerging science poetry. Without her creativity, passion, and collaboration, this book would not have been possible.

I wish to thank Steven Handel, my science mentor and friend, for sharing with me his personal and professional wisdom, his passion for science, and his enthusiasm for poetry, art, and nature. Thank you for sharing with me the scientific scholarship central to this book.

I wish to thank Jennifer Furphey, my English colleague, for opening her classes to my science poetry visitations and for collaborating with me in developing a science poetry unit for A.P. English Language and Composition classes.

I wish to thank the Morristown High School English and science students, whose creativity, intelligence, and adventurous spirit produced the bounty of science poems that adorn the pages of this book. To them, I am eternally grateful.

I wish to thank the Science Academy of Morristown High School, and in particular, Jill Magidson, for supporting my participation in the summer science poetry expeditions.

I wish to thank Janyce Trampler, my science colleague, for sharing with me her summer expedition science poetry and for contributing to the pages of this book.

I wish to thank scientists Roald Hoffmann, Lei Bao, and Steven Handel for granting me thought provoking interviews on the subject of science and poetry.

I wish to thank Steve Larsen and the Orange County Great Park Corporation and Great Park Studio for granting permission to reprint the photographs of their park development.

I wish to thank Stanley Moss, my uncle, for his enduring poetic inspiration and invaluable poetic counsel over the years.

I wish to thank Ben Herzberg, who led me to the exact source of the Marcel Proust quote.

I wish to thank my editor, Martha Pennington, who literally birthed the idea for this book, nurtured it from its inception, and guided its development from the first page to the last. I am grateful for her enduring faith in me as an author, her patience to allow my writing to unfold, and her gift of collaborative editing. Thank you for helping to make my first book a labor of love.

I wish to thank my father, Robert M. Schwartz, the first scientist in my life, and my mother, Lillian M. Schwartz, the first naturalist in my life.

I wish to thank my daughters, Sara and Elizabeth, who remind me always to see through the eyes of the child.

Lastly, I wish to thank my husband, Joe, whose love, patience, and support has proven once again that "in the know of your eyes/ I am me."

Grateful acknowledgment is made to the following for permission to reprint copyrighted material:

"Cascadilla Falls" from *Collected Poems 1951–1971* by A. R. Ammons. Copyright © 1972 by A. R. Ammons. Used by permission of W.W. Norton & Company, Inc.

"Genetic Sequence" (originally entitled *26*). The poem originally was published in *The Monarchs: A Poem Sequence* (Louisiana State University Press, 1997). Copyright © 1997 by Alison Hawthorne Deming. The work appears with permission of the author.

"In Broken Images" from *The Complete Poems of Robert Graves* by Robert Graves edited by Beryl Graves. Reprinted by permission of Carcanet Press Limited.

"Fluorite" from *The Sciences* 28 Sept. Oct. 1988 by Roald Hoffmann. Copyright © 1988 by Roald Hoffmann. Reprinted by permission of the author.

"Giving In" from *The Paris Review* 33(121) 1991 and *Memory Effects* (Calhoun Press, 1999) by Roald Hoffmann. Copyright © by Roald Hoffmann. Reprinted by permission of the author.

"Tsunami" from *Soliton* (Truman State University Press) by Roald Hoffmann. Copyright © 2002 by Roald Hoffmann. Reprinted by permission of the author.

"The Wellfleet Whale" from *Passing Through: Later Poems New and Selected* by Stanley Kunitz. Copyright © 1985 by Stanley Kunitz. Used by permission of W.W. Norton & Company, Inc.

"Parents" from *Search for a New Land: History of Subjective Experience* by Julius Lester. Copyright © 1969 by Julius Lester. Used by permission of the author.

"In Memoriam James Joyce" from *Complete Poems 1920–1976* VOL II by Hugh MacDiarmid edited by Michael Grieve and William Russell Aitken. Copyright © 1978 by Christopher Murray Grieve. Lines reprinted by permission of Carcanet Press Limited.

"Tsunami Song" from *Rejoicing New and Collected Poems* by Stanley Moss. Copyright © 2009 by Stanley Moss. Used by permission of Anvil Press Poetry for the UK and Commonwealth and from the author for the USA and Canada.

"Figures of Thought" from *The Collected Poems of Howard Nemerov* (University of Chicago Press) by Howard Nemerov. Copyright © 1977 by Howard Nemerov. Used by permission of Margaret Nemerov.

"Learning the Trees" from *The Collected Poems of Howard Nemerov* (University of Chicago Press) by Howard Nemerov. Copyright © 1977 by Howard Nemerov. Used by permission of Margaret Nemerov.

"What If We Were Alone?" from *An Oregon Message* (Harper & Row) by William Stafford. Copyright © 1987 by William Stafford. Reprinted by permission of The Estate of William Stafford.

Grateful acknowledgment is made to the following for permission
to reprint non-copyrighted material:

"Activities of a Bricklayer, The" by Colin Hostetter. Reprinted by
permission of Colin Hostetter.

"Agate Springs" by Catherine Chu. Reprinted by permission of
Catherine Chu.

"Amber" by Meghan Crippen. Reprinted by permission of Meghan
Crippen.

"Amber" by Nancy Gorrell. Reprinted by permission of Nancy
Gorrell.

"American Dream, The" by Karley Murphy. Reprinted by permission of Karley Murphy.

"An Arabesque" by Sarah Ryan. Reprinted by permission of Sarah
Ryan.

"Aquamarine" by Maggie McArdle. Reprinted by permission of
Maggie McArdle.

"Beyond Configuration" by David Pitt. Reprinted by permission
of David Pitt.

"Bones" by Maya Blades. Reprinted by permission of Maya
Blades.

"Butterfly and Me, The" by Sarah Ryan. Reprinted by permission
of Sarah Ryan.

"Butterfly Theory, The" by Jessica McKinley. Reprinted by permission of Jessica McKinley.

"Commentaries" by Jennifer Furphey. Reprinted by permission of
Jennifer Furphey.

"Cricket in the Amber, The" by Nancy Gorrell. Reprinted by permission of Nancy Gorrell.

"Dances with Stars" by Nancy Gorrell. Reprinted by permission
of Nancy Gorrell

"Dancing in the Sky" by Ashish Gupta. Reprinted by permission
of Ashish Gupta.

"DNA" by Karley Murphy. Reprinted by permission of Karley
Murphy.

"Gjainfoss" by Erin Colfax. Reprinted by permission of Erin
Colfax.

"Gasp" by Anne Schwartz. Reprinted by permission of Anne Schwartz.

"Grasshopper, The" by James Murphy. Reprinted by permission of James Murphy.

"Geothermal Energy" by Paige Diamond. Reprinted by permission of Paige Diamond.

"Humming Bird Gone" by Erica DeLaney. Reprinted by permission of Erica DeLaney.

"Icelandic Mystique" by Erin Colfax. Reprinted by permission of Erin Colfax.

"Interview" by Steven Handel. Reprinted by permission of Steven Handel.

"In the Botanical Gardens" by Erin Colfax. Reprinted by permission of Erin Colfax.

"Land of Laki, The" by Erin Colfax. Reprinted by permission of Erin Colfax.

"Lonely Old Man with Wings" by Janyce Trampler. Reprinted with permission by Janyce Trampler.

"Look Up" by Theresa Gold. Reprinted by permission of Theresa Gold.

"Love Song, A" by Ben Levenson. Reprinted by permission of Ben Levenson.

"My Geode" by Cori Connolly. Reprinted by permission of Cori Connolly.

"Nerves" by Alex Davis. Reprinted by permission of Alex Davis.

"O Asymptote" by David Pitt. Reprinted by permission of David Pitt.

"O. hannah" by Kaity Duffy. Reprinted by permission of Kaity Duffy.

"Old Faithful" by Eric Villhauer. Reprinted by permission of Eric Villhauer.

"Pathways of a Plant" by Maggie McArdle. Reprinted by permission of Maggie McArdle.

"Plate Tectonics" by Rachel Needle. Reprinted by permission of Rachel Needle.

"Pumice" by Anna McCabe. Reprinted by permission of Anna McCabe.

Grateful acknowledgment is made to the following for permission to reprint non-copyrighted images:

Cover Design: By permission of Michael Kravit.

Chapter 1

Photograph: The Present, El Toro Marine Airbase. Reprinted with permission of the Orange County Great Park Corporation/ Great Park Design Studio.

Artist Rendering #1: The Future, Orange County Great Park. Reprinted with permission of the Orange County Great Park Corporation/ Great Park Design Studio.

Artist Rendering #2: Orange County Great Park Natural Panorama. Reprinted with permission of the Orange County Great Park Corporation/ Great Park Design Studio.

Artist Rendering #3: Orange County Great Park Transportation System. Reprinted with permission of the Orange County Great Park Corporation/ Great Park Design Studio.

Chapter 8

Photograph (Opening illustration): Weather data collection at Seljalandsfoss, Iceland. Reprinted with permission of Erin Colfax.

Photograph (Illustration for poem, "Geothermal Energy"): Nesjavellir Geothermal Power Plant, Iceland. Reprinted with permission of Erin Colfax.

Chapter 11

Photograph (Opening illustration) Science Objects Pastiche. Reprinted with permission of Nancy Gorrell.

Photograph (Illustration for poem, "Red Panda"): Red Panda at the Bronx Zoo. Reprinted with permission of Cori Connolly.

Photograph (Illustration for poem, "Lonely Old Man with Wings"): Stork at the Bronx Zoo. Reprinted with permission of Cori Connolly.

Editor's Preface

Historically, science was built as a new kind of activity in the world, with its own unique ways of seeing and knowing, and its own unique form of discourse. Science opened up a new space for seeing and knowing about the world, and for expressing that new vision through a new, *scientific* kind of language – a language of high precision and explicitness, of clear observation and description, of logic and theory. In almost opposite ways, poetic forms evolved as ways of knowing, seeing, and expressing through *poetic* language – a pared down mode of expression focused on aesthetics and evocation, on rhythm and music, on implicit and associative meaning. These two languages, the language of science and the language of poetry, each speak on a different plane from ordinary language, making a space for creating new meaning. The language of science, when married to poetic form, expands both the scientist's and the poet's semiotic repertoire into vast new realms of linguistic potential.

Writing Poetry through the Eyes of Science: A Teacher's Guide to Scientific Literacy and Poetic Response, in breaching the disciplinary boundary between English class and science class, is a great gift to educators, providing a new place for knowledge to be created and expressed. This work, a unique marriage between a prize-winning English teacher and poet, Nancy Gorrell, and a prize-winning science teacher, Erin Colfax, opens new territory for creative interdisciplinarity and shows teachers the way to build learning opportunities in this new interdisciplinary space. In so doing, science poetry offers exciting curriculum resources for teachers of English as well as science that can help students make connections between what they are learning in different parts of the curriculum and stretch themselves creatively and intellectually.

Writing Poetry through the Eyes of Science is an inspired and inspiring work. It grew from Nancy Gorrell's inspiration, which comes across on every page, transmitting the author's energy and excitement in opening up the world of science poetry in her own life and the lives of her students, and in sharing the expertise she acquired through learning and teaching science poetry in her own classes in partnership with Erin Colfax. The book offers a comprehensive introduction to the topic with lesson material for English or science teachers wishing to introduce their students to writing poetry in a new way, through the eyes of the scientist, or to writing science in a new way, through the eyes of the poet. In exploring educational opportunities in a merged creative space between poetry and science, this work illustrates the potential for education to form disciplinary linkages that expand opportunities for students to realize their full expressive potential on the leading edge of knowledge.

– Martha C. Pennington
Series Editor, Frameworks for Writing

Both the known and the unknown, the two worlds of our ances-tors, nourish the human spirit. Their muses, science and the arts, whisper: Follow us, explore, find out.

    – Edward O. Wilson, *Consilience: The Unity of Knowledge*

             (Wilson, 1998: 233)

Prolegomenon
(What Is Being Said First)
Connections
Bridging the Cultural Divide

CONNECTIONS

This book is about making connections of the visible with the invisible, the material with the immaterial, the possible with the impossible, the finite with the infinite. It's about what our eyes simply see, and how, when we least expect it, something not so simple as it seemed, returns, but now, so much more complex, and freighted with the universe. Yet the question remains: The universe *of what*? Sense, if we're lucky, nonsense if we are not, and poetry, if we are enlightened.

   This book is about making connections between poetry and science. Although there was a time when poetry and science walked naturally hand in hand in the verse of the ancient bards, in recent times the academy has separated the world of poetry from the world of measurable facts. This view of "two cultures," one science, the other the arts and humanities, in practice has been challenged all along by poets who have looked to science, and scientists who have looked to poetry, to both inform and inspire their work.

This book is about making connections to find the common ground. It asks you to consider: Why do scientists and mathematicians speak of elegance in their experiments and equations? Why do poets resort to scientific data – the physical, the concrete, and the observable – to create metaphors? Why do scientists resort to metaphor – visualized "thought experiments" – to explain their facts, concepts, and theories? And why do both poets and scientists dwell in the universe of ambiguity?

Above all else, **this book is about making connections** – your own connections – as you enter the universe of science poetry.

BRIDGING THE CULTURAL DIVIDE

Debates in academia about the relationship of science, poetry, and the arts – the "schism that occurred probably in the 18th century, leaving a wide crack down the center of western intellectual life" (Brown, 1998: xiv) – continue to this day to concern many on both sides of the "cultural divide." This divide found its most controversial expression in 1959 when C. P. Snow, English physicist turned novelist, delivered a landmark lecture identifying an unbridgeable gap between the "Two Cultures," one the science culture, and the other, the arts or literary culture (Snow, 1959). Certainly, the complexity and depth of this debate is well beyond the scope of this book, and yet, our science and arts students and our teaching compel us to take a clear position. For this divide, despite all efforts to bridge it, despite all movements for cross-curricular and interdisciplinary teaching, reflects without a doubt the state of pedagogy in the vast majority of high schools in the United States and abroad today – that is, a clear divide between the arts, the sciences, and poetry.

This divide is so institutionally pervasive that it is rarely challenged and barely noticed by high school students and teachers alike. Yet it promotes a world view in which science and poetry are divided into two distinct and separate realms: the first, material, tangible, measurable, and real: the second, immaterial, intangible, unquantifiable, and imaginary (Morris, 2006: 147). In such a dichotomous world, stereotypes prevail. Scientists are perceived as logical, rational, objective, unemotional, and detached while poets are perceived as passionate, intuitive, subjective, emotional, engaged, and humanistic. Science is based on reason, on factual, verifiable truth; poetry is based on passion, on imagined or personal truth. As with all stereotypes, these are partly rooted in reality, but as generalizations, they are inherently untrue and destructive to scientists, poets, and renaissance students alike who may wonder how they can pursue both science and poetry at the same time.

Writing Poetry through the Eyes of Science poses a direct challenge to the cultural divide. As high school teachers, my science partner, Erin Colfax, and I firmly believe that such a divide is antithetical to the creative, critical, and divergent thinking we strive to foster in our students. Philosophically, we believe that diversity of perspectives and the cross-fertilization of disciplines enriches our experience, inspires innovation, and expands knowledge. In this sense, we view this book as a crossover work, one that bridges for our students scientific and poetic ways of seeing, knowing, and understanding.

We recognize that our tool for this "bridging" – science poetry writing – is not a panacea. It will not solve the problems of current education or remedy alone the prevailing two-culture division of the arts and sciences. But on an individual level, student by student, it can be transformational, opening the eyes of that student to a world where the arts and sciences, together, form a synergy of limitless possibility. In just this way, we as science and English teachers may be helping to create the future Roald Hoffmanns of the world.[1] Bridging the cultural divide for high school students through science poetry remains the core objective of this work.

Note

1. Roald Hoffmann is a Nobel prize-winning chemist (1981) who has written four books of science poetry. He is the Frank H. T. Rhodes Professor of Humane Letters and Professor of Chemistry at Cornell University. Hoffman's science poem, "Tsunami," models the art form in this book's signature lesson: *What is Science Poetry?* (Chapter 4). For other lessons using Hoffmann's science poems as models see Chapters 6 and 10.

Prologue

"Dances with Stars"
How I Wrote My First Science Poem

As a child, I had an encounter with the mystery of the universe that has stayed with me to this very day. That mystery has come to inform my personal and professional life, allowing me to know myself and the world through many eyes. Now I see that experience as a guide, leading me – through the eyes of poetry and the eyes of science – to further inspiration, insight, and ultimately, to the writing of this book. It happened this way.

One dark summer night (it was probably dusk, but as a child I remember it being very dark), I walked down to the beach, pail in hand, to look for shells. I was an insatiable collector, and this night was no different from any other night. But it was. I looked out at the waves. They seemed a yellow-green color, somewhat glowing. I looked down at my feet. They were glowing too. I walked. I left a trail of sparkles in the sand. I ran down by the water. It was filled with sparkles. I splashed. Stars sparkled through my fingers into the air. I danced for joy

I have no memory of going back to the beach house to tell my mother what I saw. If I did, there was no reaction, explanation, or response. The mystery of that moment was like a star that fell from the sky and planted itself inside my soul. That sparkle I like to think of today as the seeker in me, the part of me that wants to know, learn, and discover. As a child, I wanted to experience the sparkles again and again. Every night thereafter, I went back to the beach to see the glowing waves. But there were none. Not then. Not ever.

In my young adulthood, I became an English teacher and began teaching a new elective at Morristown High School, Creative Writing. At the time I knew about as much about teaching creative writing as I knew about the stars of my childhood. But I was a seeker, and my teaching led me to new knowledge. One day I discovered the poetry of the Cree Indians of North America, in particular, their naming poems. Written in the third person, the community names or renames a person after they have come to know that person's inner spirit or personality. I thought to myself, what a wonderful introductory lesson for creative writing. And so, writing Cree naming poems became the first lesson of day one in creative writing.

Now it wasn't long before one of my students asked, "Ms. Gorrell, what is your Cree name?" My memory sparkled. I knew instantly what I would rename myself. "Dances with Stars," I said, and that night I attempted to write the poem:

Dances with Stars
        (Jersey shore, circa 1959)

it happened only once
in the night of summer darkness
when the great salt waters turned
so still their voice could not be heard,
some say the wind called to her
and she answered with small feet
on the warm soft sand, walking
with her head down, down as always,
looking for shells, in the black of weeds,
looking for crabs to put in her pail,

looking for a fish she might bring
home to father

the truth is she did not know
she left her feet behind,
until she looked back
and saw a trail glowing in the sand,
as they tell it, her feet glowed too,
a yellow-green as bright as the stars
in the moonlit night, and then she heard
the song of the sand, and let the grains
sparkle through her hands, sparkle
through the dark night air, sparkle
like stars onto her glowing toes

this is how it began for her
that summer of the great darkness
when the lava waves turned *fluorescent*
and she heard the beat and danced
with the light of her feet splashing
stars back into the starry sky

they say the spirit spoke to her that night
although she did not know it,
her name tells it so
it happened only once
though we can see her still
waiting by dark waters

                    – Nancy Gorrell

Although I have shared this poem with my creative writing classes countless times, I have never considered it finished. At the time of writing, I struggled literally and figuratively with the language of the unknown – how to describe that sparkle, those waves; and what actually did I see – Sparkles? Glowing waves? The color was fluorescent, but I never liked that word. It seemed too artificial, man-made, for a moment so filled with naturalistic wonder and mystery. So I settled on *yellow-green* and then finally, in stanza four, I acquiesced in my search for language, and wrote, *fluorescent*. I had a total of ten drafts, none of which pleased me. The Cree Indians, I thought, would not have spoken of the experience in terms of fluorescence.

It never occurred to me to look to science to inform my poem. Although I was an inveterate naturalist as a child, checking my trusty *Golden Guides* each time I came home with a new finding of shells, butterflies, insects, or flowers, I knew of no golden guide to explain this mystery. And perhaps that was the point, or the poetic truth of it all. Perhaps subconsciously I didn't want to find out the answer; perhaps I wanted to hold onto the moment of mystery – the joy of not knowing – the pleasure of the quest to make the unknown, known. That joy was not so much the literal sparkles, but the sense of profound awe I felt at that moment.

But as luck would have it, there are all kinds of guides. And so one came to me in my 36th year of teaching – Erin Colfax, science research teacher, and my team-teacher in Science Academy English. I had never taught Science Academy English before. On a whim, I decided to introduce the course with the Cree naming poem lesson. After sharing "Dances with Stars" with my students, I asked them to try writing their own naming poems as introductions. While the students were busily writing and Erin and I were circulating, I whispered to Erin, "You know, I still don't know what I saw." Erin looked up at me and said, quite matter-of-factly, "Bioluminescent algae! Phytoplankton." The thought of an actual answer to my question stunned me. How profound was my lack of scientific knowledge! That night I researched and rediscovered the tiny free floating sea creatures of my childhood, *dinoflagellates*, one cell algae with plates of armorina, 20 micro meters or 1/1250th of an inch of sparkle, most likely *Pyrodinium Bahamense (Dinophyceae)*. I also learned that this tiny creature, guided by its biological clock, will produce luminescence only at night. Yes, bioluminescent algae – that was certainly what I saw.

That same night, **through the eyes of science**, I was able to "finish" the poem. I discarded the troubling word, *fluorescent*, and substituted the word, *luminescent*, a word that reveals a greater truth: it was scientifically true to the phenomenon of bioluminescent algae, but it was also poetically true to the language of that experience, *luminescent* connoting an ever-expanding sense of light (literally) and enlightenment (figuratively) that was true for me at the time and would shine true for me for years to come. For if the final draft of "Dances with Stars" remains in the spirit of Cree naming poetry, it must say something about the subject's (my) inner spirit or soul. And this, I think it does. I would become a seeker, a patient observer, *waiting by dark waters*. Although I remain in the poem a child in awe of the mystery, embedded in the poem is the "answer" as yet to be discovered. In time, I would move from seeing the literal light on those waves to greater enlightenment as an adult informed by science. In this sense, I see my enlightened draft as my first science poem.

Seeing through the eyes of science gave me two gifts: the gift of more precise, accurate, and scientifically true language to express and inform my experience, and the gift of knowledge, one answer to the mystery. *Luminescent* – it is the perfect word, at once poetically beautiful and more scientifically accurate. I even liked its sound and alliterative ring: *when the lava waves turned luminescent*. And yet, I wonder, have I lost anything in the process? Has my newfound scientific knowledge taken all the mystery and awe out of the encounter? Now that my eyes are open, now that I'm seeing with new eyes, what will I see when I wait by dark waters? Will I see the *sparkles* of my childhood or the *dinoflagellates* of my mature years? And will I still revel in the mystery of the universe?

For me, science and poetry are equally informative guides to knowledge and enlightenment, their fusion a natural consequence of the quest to make the unknown, known. And so, in my research, I discovered that bioluminescent algae is most commonly found in tropical waters, in particular, Puerto Rico and Florida. Why then did I see the phenomenon at the Jersey shore of my youth? Why at that time and at that place? The answer remains for me a mystery. My new found scientific knowledge has not diminished my pleasure in the natural world. I have yet to see another occurrence of bioluminescent algae. But I am still waiting, still seeking, still going down to the waves at night to look for the stars.

* * *

Yes, there are all kinds of guides. "Dances with Stars" has served as a prophetic one, leading me to discover how science can inform poetry, and how poetry can inform science. I am as captivated by this process as I was captivated by the waters of my childhood. *Writing Poetry through the Eyes of Science* offers a teacher's guide to this captivating universe – the universe of science poetry – one that will open your eyes and your students' eyes to new ways of seeing, knowing, creating, and experiencing. I invite you and your students to go down to dark waters, wherever they may be for you, and dance with your stars.

Introduction
Entering Common Ground
Let Science Poetry Lead the Way

The only true voyage of discovery, the only really rejuvenating experience would be not to visit strange lands but to possess other eyes, to see the universe through the eyes of another, of a hundred others, to see the hundred universes that each of them sees.

– Marcel Proust[1]
"The Captive" in *Remembrance of Things Past*, Vol. III
(Proust, 1982: 259–260)

OVERVIEW: THIS BOOK AT A GLANCE

The aim of this book is to introduce to you readers, my respective English and science colleagues, a little known but quite remarkable teaching tool, **science poetry**. This tool fuses the knowledge, precision, and language of science with the voice, vision, and language of poetry to produce something unique, the **science poem**. If you are an English teacher reading this book, you might think that science poetry is another type of poetry to teach in your literature or writing classes. This is true, of course, but only a small part of the objective. If you are a science teacher reading this book, you might think that science poetry is another way to teach science more creatively. This is also true, but only a small part of the objective. Science poetry is not about science or poetry per se; it is not about teaching scientific facts or knowledge alone, or about teaching another type of poetry to add to an already rich poetry curriculum.

Science poetry is about entering new terrain, poetically speaking, a universe of a different kind, but more literally, an *interdisciplinary universe*. In this universe, students fuse the knowledge, methods, procedures, language, and ways of seeing and knowing of one discipline, *science*, with another discipline, *poetry*. In doing so, they learn to transfer their knowledge and skills from one discipline to the other. Such transfer challenges students' critical, analytical, imaginative, and creative thinking, requiring them to turn to both science and English, and science and English teachers, as their guides. The result creates a powerful and exciting synergy. As a subject, science poetry's value, utility, and potential is limited. As a tool, its value, utility, and potential is limitless. The aim of this book is to put this remarkable teaching tool in your hand and let you and your students soar.

For myself, teaching science poetry has become a true voyage of discovery. But in this voyage, I was not alone. I had a guide, my science colleague, partner, and contributing author to this book, Erin Colfax. Together, we began the voyage team-teaching Science Academy English III at Morristown High School, Morristown, New Jersey. With newfound eyes we created in our Science Academy classroom a universe of a different kind, the interdisciplinary, cross-curricular universe of science poetry teaching. This common ground began as we came together in one classroom, taught one science poetry lesson, and dialogued with our students, through the multiple eyes of our disciplines, the meaning of a science poem. Later in our separate voyages, when I as an English teacher taught science poetry in English classes, or when Erin as a science teacher taught science poetry in science classes and expeditions, we each began to discover the expansive meaning of Marcel Proust's "true" voyage of discovery.

This book is a record of that voyage, a map so to speak, one you can follow as you create your own voyage of discovery. For both of us, it has been a voyage of joy as much as it has been a voyage of creative challenge, intellectual and philosophical enlightenment, personal fulfillment, and just plain fun. In this sense, the ultimate goal of this book is transformational, to encourage you to embark on your own "true" voyage of discovery, exploring with your students the vast potential of science poetry to inspire, inform, and ignite imagination, inventiveness, and creativity.

If such a lofty goal makes you hesitant to embark on the voyage alone, consider for a moment: you are not alone. This book will serve as your guide, your colleagues will serve as your guide, your students will serve as your guide, and most certainly, science poetry will serve as your guide. It will engage your imagination, it will provoke your thinking, it will prompt you to ask questions, and it will cause you to stand in wonder of the universe. If you are an English teacher, my science partner and I encourage you to seek out a like-minded science colleague for cross-curricular dialogue, for scientific information and materials, and for guest lecturing in your classes. Conversely, if you are a science teacher, we encourage you to do the same with a like-minded English colleague. For us, nothing has been more exciting than when we sat down, science teacher, English teacher, and student-poet together, to ponder the meaning of the image, *azimuthal spin*, in the science poem-in-progress of one of our students, David Pitt (see Chapter 4). Such interdisciplinary conversations and collaborations form the heart of this book as well as the heart of the voyage of discovery.

As with all voyages of discovery, there is paradox: you are not alone, but you must make the voyage on your own; otherwise, it would not be "true." Keeping this in mind, this book is adaptable, flexible, and portable, based on extensive teaching in science and English classrooms as well as in the field, including botanical gardens, science museums, zoos, parks, and science poetry expeditions to places as different as Iceland and New York City (see Chapters 8 and 11). This book offers practice exercises, poetry writing activities, individual lesson plans, unit lesson plans, and science poetry expedition plans for you to adapt to your particular students, school setting, preferences, and curriculum. The poetry writing exercises are inquiry-based, activity-oriented learning fusing the best practices and methodology of both disciplines. Most importantly, these exercises are sequential in complexity and scale, moving from foundation exercises preparing students to write science poetry (Section One), to fundamental science poetry writing exercises (Section Two), culminating in advanced science poetry writing exercises (Section Three), in which students strive to achieve the *perfect fusion* that is the essence of the art form. Whether in the English classroom, the science classroom, or in the field, students read and write science poems within the framework of a larger inquiry:

- *How is the poem inspired and informed by science?*
- *What questions does the science poem raise for science and poetry?*
- *What is the common ground between science and poetry?*
- *What is the ultimate nature of science poetry?*

All of the exercises in this book teach students how to read and write science poetry. In your hand and in your classroom, this remarkable teaching tool may also lead to other discoveries or terrain. Why? Because the purpose of writing a poem is not just to inform or provoke thinking, but to evoke the deepest emotions, inspiring students to enter what John Burnside, poet, calls *the mystery*: "while science at its best seeks to reduce our ignorance, it cannot – and should not seek to – eliminate mystery. The more we know, the more the mystery deepens" (Burnside, 2006: 95).

The ultimate hope of this book is that by *writing poetry through the eyes of science*, you and your students will engage in some small way in "the mystery." And when it comes to engagement with mystery – the unknown, unseen, or unforeseen – there is no better port of entry than poetry. Who knows where the voyage will lead? But one point is certain: by teaching science poetry with your students and colleagues, you will be helping to launch a new literacy and a new pedagogy for the 21st century.

A CLOSER LOOK

What is Science Poetry? One English Teacher Finds New Eyes

The Secret Sits

We dance round in a ring and suppose,
But the Secret sits in the middle and knows.

– Robert Frost
"The Secret Sits"
(Frost, 1969: 362)

Thirty years ago, when I first came across Frost's poem, I thought I understood it. I imagined the personified *Secret*, sitting *in the middle* on a chair with all of us dancing around it in a never-ending circle or ring of ignorance and confusion. *We*, the speaker of the poem, could be any individual or the collective "we." The poem seemed to work either way. And who was the *The Secret*? Or, what was *The Secret*? I did not actually know. And that, I thought, was the point of the poem. I saw *The Secret* as the personification of the answer to the questions that puzzle and plague us about any unknown. That was, of course, all before I began to teach science poetry, and all before I came across, "Atomic Poetry: Using Poetry to Teach Rutherford's Discovery of the Nucleus" (Abisdris and Casuga, 2001: 59). Thinking of the atom from my rudimentary science background, I immediately saw the science–poetry connection in Frost's couplet. Written in 1936, Frost was alluding to the Rutherford-Bohr model of the atom: the speaker of the poem, *we*, the electrons; the *ring*, the orbit; and the *middle,* where *the Secret sits,* the nucleus. Now, through the eyes of science, Frost's tone seemed to perhaps mock the scientists of his time struggling to understand the mysteries of the atom.

"The Secret Sits" caused me to question: Was Frost significantly influenced by the science of his time? The answer, not commonly known, is a resounding "yes." Apparently, in 1923, Frost had attended two lectures at Amherst College given by Neils Bohr on atomic structure and quantum physics. He read *Scientific American,* was aware of the scientific discoveries of his day, and developed a profound interest in the structure of the atom (Abisdris and Casuga, 2001: 59). With his philosophical mind and poetic sensibility, it is not surprising that he used the language of science to inspire and inform his poetry. But it was not until 1992 that Frost's "miscel-laneous" science poems came to the attention of the disciplines with the publication of "Robert Frost and the Poetry of Physics," by Coletta and Tamres (1992), two professors from the departments of English and physics at the University of Wisconsin at Stevens Point, respectively. Coletta and Tamres (1992: 360) confirm Frost's interest in physics, noting how Frost continues the Anglo-American tradition of capturing scientific themes in pithy couplets.[2]

Ironically, Frost's poem was leading me to recognize the "secret" of my own blindness: I just had to see the poem with new eyes. In the past I had asked of a poem: what does it say about the poet, about society, about the social context, politics, race, gender, and ethnicity? I had never before asked: *What does the poem say about science*? In other words, I had never before read poetry *through the eyes of science*. In a sense, I was scientifically illiterate; that is, I was not applying my scientific knowledge, eye, or sensibility to the understanding of literature and life.

Teaching science poetry has become for me a true voyage of discovery. Today my eyes are opened. I see science literally everywhere – in the literature I read, in the poems I write, in the lessons I teach, and in the natural world I inhabit. For me, teaching science poetry unearthed a latent passion for science long buried in my childhood. Similarly, teaching science poetry has opened my science partner's eyes as well. Now Erin sees poetry everywhere – on her expeditions, in her research classes, and in her observations of the natural world.

Science Poetry: A Working Definition

Now that the "secret" is out, the question still remains: *What, more precisely, is science poetry*? This book offers a working definition, one my science partner and I developed together and present to our students after they engage with "The Secret Sits."

Any poetry inspired and informed by scientific facts, phenomena, principles, theories, questions, observations, and experience may be considered **science poetry** if it includes all or most of the following elements:

- *Utilizes both quantitative and qualitative data in a poem;*
- *Utilizes scientific facts, information, or experience to prompt or begin a poem;*
- *Utilizes science, scientific theories, or phenomena as allusion in a poem;*
- *Utilizes science, scientific theories, or phenomena as metaphor in a poem;*
- *Utilizes science, scientific theories, or phenomena as imagery in a poem;*
- *Utilizes specific scientific and technical vocabulary in a poem;*
- *Utilizes science as the subject or theme of a poem.*

In sum, we tell our students that a science poem must have two parts: **a science part** (*quantitative data*) and a **poetry part** (*qualitative data*). We emphasize that the science poet strives to artfully fuse these parts together. Furthermore, in developing a working definition, we wanted to distinguish the little known science poem from the more common nature, pastoral, or lyrical poem so familiar to our students. Therefore, for pedagogical purposes, we would not consider nature poems students might write to be science poetry, unless those poems met the stated criteria – in particular, employing more technical vocabulary, quantitative data, and/or science. We also wanted clear criteria upon which we could evaluate students' poems, and we wanted to challenge our students to demonstrate their scientific knowledge and technical vocabulary in poetic form.

In our reading and research, we tested our working definition against noted science poems currently anthologized in Kurt Brown's *Verse and Universe: Poems about Science and Mathematics*, and in virtually all cases, these model poems support our working definition. Most importantly, our students understood the definition and wrote inspired and scientifi-cally informed poetry that we could assess and evaluate with constructive feedback. Some authorities, like Kurt Brown, distinguish between science and technology, the former from the Latin, *scire*, "to know," the latter from the Greek, *techne*, meaning "skill, craft, or art" (Brown, 1998: xiii). Brown limits science to "the pure study of the universe and all it contains for the sake of knowledge and understanding alone" (p. xiii). For him, *technology* is the "application of scientific principles for practical, and economic, ends" (p. xiii), and therefore, he defines medicine as "technology in action" (p. xiii). As a consequence, Brown's collection includes only poems of "pure" science. Other authorities like Robert Crawford, *Contemporary Poetry and Contemporary Science* (Crawford, 2006), regard science in their collections in a much broader sense, including poetry informed and inspired by technology, virtual realities, medicine, psychology, and the social sciences. For pedagogical purposes, we have adopted a broad definition of science to include technology, medicine, and virtual realities in our teaching of science poetry.

A Word About Terminology: *Poet, Science Poet, Scientist-Poet*

To clarify, this book distinguishes among the following:

Poet: a writer recognized as a poet by practice and profession who may write occasional science poems; for example, Billy Collins, Rita Dove, Robert Frost, Stanley Kunitz, Stanley Moss, John Updike.

Science Poet: a writer recognized as a poet by practice and profession who generally writes science poems or is widely recognized for his or her science poetry; for example, A. R. Ammons, Alison Hawthorne Deming, Hugh MacDiarmid, Edwin Morgan, Howard Nemerov.

Scientist-Poet: a writer recognized first and foremost as a scientist by practice and profession but who also writes poetry, generally science poetry, but not necessarily exclusively science poetry; for example, Loren Eiseley, Roald Hoffmann, Miroslav Holub.

On Mathematics, Numbers, and Mathematical Poetry

In the language of mathematics, equations are like poetry.
– Michael Guillen, *Five Equations that Changed the World: The Power and Poetry of Mathematics* (Guillen, 1995: 2)

Without a doubt, mathematics is an integral part of science and scientific inquiry, and yet, it remains a separate but related discipline, with separate but related methods, procedures, pedagogy, and professional organizations. Although it is beyond the scope of this book to consider the relation between mathematics and poetry in terms of ways of knowing, thinking, seeing the universe, and pedagogy, my science partner and I include mathematics in our working definition of science poetry. Science poets readily include mathematical concepts, theories, themes, and subjects in their poetry. Theorists and critics in both the sciences and the arts demonstrate significant common ground uniting mathematics and poetry.

Kurt Brown's *Verse and Universe* (Brown, 1998) includes stellar examples of mathematics as inspiration, as subject, and as metaphor: for example, Lisel Mueller's "Reasons for Numbers," Sue Owen's "Zero," William Bonk's "Boolean Algebra: $X^2 = X$," and Pattiann Rogers' "A Fractal Pattern." Michael Guillen, in *Five Equations that Changed the World: The Power and Poetry of Mathematics* (Guillen, 1995), adopts poetry as a metaphor to explain mathematics and the math-poetry connection:

> *In the language of mathematics, equations are like poetry: They state truths with a unique precision, convey volumes of information in rather brief terms, and often are difficult for the uninitiated to comprehend. And just as conventional poetry helps us to see deep* within *ourselves, mathematical poetry helps us to see far* beyond *ourselves – if not all the way up to heaven, then at least out to the brink of the visible universe.* (Guillen, 1995: 2; emphasis in original)

For Guillen, equations *are* poetry. He clarifies: "While the equations represent the discernment of eternal and universal truths, however, the manner in which they are written is strictly, provincially human. That is what makes them so much like poems, wonderfully artful attempts to make infinite realities comprehensible to finite beings" (Guillen, 1995: 6).

Similarly, Jonathan Holden's provocative essay, "Poetry and Mathematics" (Holden, 2001), convincingly demonstrates the math-poetry connection in terms of the concept and application of *measurement*: "The function of poetry, like the function of mathematics, is measurement; and 'measurement' presumes there is something to measure" (Holden, 2001: 93). Holden poses and answers a critical question: "What then does a good poem attempt to measure? And how seriously can analogies between poems and 'certain pages of algebra' be drawn?" (p. 93). He then answers the question by demonstrating mathematical measurement in the poem, "Anecdote of the Jar," by Wallace Stevens:

> *The poem, like a mathematical demonstration, escorts us through a sequence of linear transformations. Moreover, like a mathematical*

demonstration, in each of its steps it succeeds, through its specialized language, in expressing 'something' that, without this language, would have remained inexpressible and, because it was inexpressible, scarcely perceptible at all. It is this issue of 'inexpressibility' that should enable us to appreciate fully the analogy between poetry and mathematics. (Holden, 2001: 96–97)

Clearly, mathematics and poetry find common ground in shared concepts and application of measurement as well as the struggle to express the inexpressible. Yet, despite the recognition of the integral importance of mathematics and numeracy in science poetry writing, this book necessitates narrowing the subject and scope of inquiry. Therefore, in teaching science poetry, my science partner and I have limited this book to teaching in science and English classes, as well as limiting the pedagogical issues, concerns, and strategies to the disciplines of science and English exclusively.

The Goals of This Book

The goals of this book are:

- To introduce to the disciplines of English and science a unique teaching tool for interdisciplinary literacy: **science poetry**.
- To demonstrate the value of scientific methods, processes, and literacy which inform as well as inspire poetic response.
- To demonstrate the value of poetic methods, processes, and literacy which inform as well as inspire scientific inquiry, knowledge, and creative thinking.
- To afford students in the English classroom the opportunity to engage in an alternate literacy, **scientific literacy**, and the use of quantitative data (cognitive domain) for poetic response.

- To afford students in the science classroom the opportunity to engage in an alternate literacy, **poetic literacy**, and the use of qualitative data (affective domain) to inspire and express feelings, attitudes, and opinions.
- To demonstrate creativity and the creative process as common ground for both poetry and science.
- To challenge myths and stereotypes regarding science, poetry, and the "cultural divide" between the arts and sciences.
- To forge a new, interdisciplinary literacy for the 21st century.

On Science Poetry, Literacy, and Pedagogy

The teaching of science poetry with its fusion of two disciplines – science and poetry – fuses as well two of the most important movements in 21st century pedagogy – the movement for literacy in general, in the field of English, and the movement for scientific literacy, in particular, in the field of science. Originally meaning "to read and write," the use of the term *literacy* has expanded to embrace not only the skills of reading and writing, but the skills of listening, speaking, viewing, media literacy, thinking, and most recently, technology. On February 15, 2008, the National Council of Teachers of English (USA) adopted a position paper, "Toward a Definition of 21st Century Literacies," as follows:

> The 21st century demands that a literate person possess a wide range of abilities and competencies.... These literacies – from reading on-line newspapers to participating in virtual classrooms – are multiple, dynamic, and malleable. Twenty-first century readers and writers need to
>
> - *Develop proficiency with the tools of technology.*
> - *Build relationships with others to pose and solve problems collaboratively and cross-culturally.*
> - *Design and share information for global communities.*

- *Manage, analyze and synthesize multiple streams of simultaneous information.*
- *Create, critique, analyze, and evaluate multi-media texts.*
- *Attend to the ethical responsibilities required by these complex environments.*

(NCTE, 2008)

Science poetry finds its logical home in the wider literacy movements of the 21st century, supporting NCTE's statement in language and spirit. Science poetry is dynamic, malleable – (and I would add, portable) – involving multiple literacies and multimedia texts, collaboration, problem solving, analysis, synthesis, evaluation, creativity, and technology. Most importantly, science poetry, with its use of poetic language to express the emotive aspects of thought, feeling, and opinion, provides a highly powerful tool to communicate ethical responsibilities and issues in a global world. Enter the science poem as protest poetry, as political advocacy, as cross-cultural communication, and as a mode to wrestle with the consequences of human action in the delicate balances of our natural world.

Most importantly, the movement for scientific literacy holds particular promise for the inclusion of science poetry in science education. In *The New Science Literacy: Using Language Skills to Help Students Learn Science*, Marlene Thier argues convincingly that "tremendous synergies are possible between the disciplines of science and language literacy because, in essence, they seek to develop reciprocal skills in students – skills that complement and strengthen each other" (Thier, 2002: 6). Her study draws on the scholarship of the last decade to demonstrate that "Good science – and effective teaching and learning in science – is dependent upon strong language skills" (Thier, 2002: 8). Based on her work and research, she advocates for literacy-enhanced, inquiry-based science instruction: "Understanding science – being able to use it to make informed personal and societal decisions and having the literacy skills to communicate and learn concepts – is what the new science literacy is all about" (Thier, 2002: xvi).[3]

For purposes of this book, my science partner and I view *language literacy* as incorporating not only specific vocabulary and communication skills, but also a world view, or way of seeing, knowing, experiencing, or finding meaning which becomes the primary "eyes" or lens of that literacy. Therefore, we define *scientific literacy* as more than the acquisition and application of scientific knowledge, but in addition, to include the ability to see the multiple universes of literature, life, and self through **the eyes of science**. Similarly, we define *poetic literacy* as more than just the acquisition and application of poetic knowledge, its content or forms, but in addition, to include the ability to see the multiple universes of literature, life, and self through **the eyes of poetry**. For both disciplines, those "eyes" incorporate an awareness that each has its own particular language for communication – the *language of science* and the *language of poetry* (see Chapters 2 and 3).

The teaching of science poetry is therefore, a unique and challenging endeavor for students, requiring *interdependent* and *reciprocal* ways of seeing, ways of knowing, ways of learning, and ways of expressing (writing and speaking), not just what they know, but also how they feel about what they know. And here is where poetry, and, more specifically, the teaching of science poetry, comes in. For scientific literacy – through journaling, field note observations, personal narratives, reflections, and science poetry – opens the door to how students feel about science in the classroom and in the laboratory; and when it comes to feelings, poetic response provides a natural and logical alternative mode of expression. Mike Watts, of the University of Surrey (United Kingdom), an ardent proponent of poetry in the science classroom, argues: "All of learning (and science is no exception) has an affective dimension. Feelings and emotions shape attitudes, tastes, moods, and motivations for learning…either creating hostility and aversion to learning…or enabling learners to achieve, even to become excited by the richness of scientific knowledge available to them" (Watts, 2001: 201).

For both science and English teachers, the teaching of literacy becomes the fundamental common ground uniting the two disciplines. In this sense, science poetry is not an oxymoron, science representing "objective" reason and poetry representing "subjective" passion, but rather, a fusion combining the essence of both worlds, leading to the understanding of how science needs poetry and how poetry needs science. It is this understanding that will finally bridge the cultural divide, enabling the creation of a new, all-embracing literacy – *interdisciplinary literacy.*

How This Book Began: Team-Teaching Science Academy English

Writing Poetry through the Eyes of Science traces its origin to the Science Academy of Morristown High School, Morristown, New Jersey, United States.[4] In the fall of 2006, I was assigned, quite unexpectedly, to teach something new – one section of Science Academy English to high school juniors (grade 11). For a moment I paused to think of my qualifications for such an assignment. My formal training in science ended with 12 credits on the college level in courses for non-science majors. Not only was I heavily schooled in literature, poetry, and the creative arts, but I had never team-taught an entire course before, let alone team-taught with a colleague outside my discipline. Although I had been teaching in the same school for 36 years, I rarely frequented the science wing, which was literally at the opposite end of the building. I knew most of the science teachers from meetings and in-service workshops, but I had never actually talked with any of them specifically about science or their science teaching, nor had I ever had the opportunity to share with them the heart and art of my discipline, English.

There was much I did not know: I did not know my assigned team-teacher, Erin Colfax, a relative newcomer to the high school; I did not know formal science; and most importantly, I did not know anything about the first unit we would be team-teaching together

– *science poetry*. In fact, I did not even know if such poetry existed. It was just a spontaneous thought, a suggestion made by Erin in our first planning session. Similarly, there was much Erin did not know as well. Having tested out of English in college, she took only one three-credit English course, and her poetry experience was limited to her high school education. And that, of course, may have been the point. Our lack of shared knowledge and background in each other's disciplines intrigued us, prompting our desire to learn, to discover something new, and to teach something new, together.

As we embarked on our voyage of discovery, we asked the questions that would frame our inquiry approach:

- *What is science poetry?*
- *How does scientific literacy inspire and inform poetry?*
- *How does poetic literacy inspire and inform science?*
- *What is the common ground between poetry and science?*

Framing the questions, we realized that each of us possessed authority over some of the answers. I looked to Erin, the scientist, for scientific knowledge, while she looked to me, the poet, for poetic understanding and meaning-making. Gradually, we began to view our endeavor as a partnership, referring in class to each other as "science partner" or "poetry partner." In our planning and subsequent teaching, we formed a synergy rooted in the essence of each of our respective disciplines: *science* from the Latin word for "knowledge" and *poetry* from the Greek word for "making." Together with our students, we created a different universe in room 213 – the *universe of science poetry* – where the multiple perspectives of science and poetry informed, guided, and inspired learning, understanding, and appreciation of a different kind.

In the beginning, we were completely unaware of the uniqueness of our voyage. If we had thought about it, we might have readily recognized the physical separation of the sciences and the arts in our own high school – the science wing housed at one end of the building and the English wing at the other – as a reflection of the historic and entrenched "cultural divide" in academia, one hotly debated ever since C. P. Snow proposed the idea of the *Two Cultures* (Snow, 1959). Our ignorance, perhaps, was fortuitous, for we welcomed the diverse perspectives of our disciplines and relished the search for new knowledge and common ground. In fact, it was our ignorance of each others' disciplines that excited us the most and launched us into the dialogue which ultimately resulted in the creation of this book.

In retrospect, it was also fortuitous that we both possessed qualities well-suited for the voyage, for each of us was personally and professionally acquainted with the spirit of the unknown. As a poetry teacher, I appreciate the presence of ambiguity in every poem I read and teach; in fact, it is the wonder of mystery that propels my own poetry writing. Similarly, Erin revels in the uncertainty of adventure, undertaking with her research science students expeditions to Mt. Kilimanjaro, Antarctica, and Iceland to gather data for future scientific research. We both felt that spirit of adventure when we began our planning, the first week of school, for Science Academy English III.

Erin informed me that the Science Academy English curriculum requires students to read the same core literature as other English students, with the distinction that the Academy English students explore the science within each text, choosing a scientific idea, question, or problem for inquiry, investigation, and projects. Each unit of study centers on a piece of literature, usually a novel, with an eye to science. She shared with me the established American literature curriculum, incorporating the teaching of the *Grapes of Wrath*, *The Great Gatsby*, and *Death of a Salesman*. After reviewing the core curriculum, Erin said quite spontaneously, "I know you really like poetry. What do you think about teaching a poetry unit? No one's ever done that before in the Academy." I'm certain she must have seen the surprise on my face. The possibility of teaching poetry in a science class had never crossed my mind.

"You know I love to teach poetry," I responded with hesitation, "...but wouldn't the poems have to relate to science?" Erin's reply launched our voyage.

"Ok. We'll just have to teach science poems."

And so began an intensive search for science poems we could teach to our students. While Erin investigated pedagogy on the teaching of science poetry, I began asking colleagues, librarians, poetry publishers, and poet-friends if they knew anything about science poetry.

"Science poetry? What's that?" was the most common reply to my inquiries. I quickly learned that science poetry was not a well-known genre, even among noted poets and teachers. It was not listed in Ron Padgett's noted *Teachers and Writers Handbook of Poetic Forms* (Padgett, 2000), nor in any of the other common reference works I consulted. Finally, I decided to call one of the most knowledgeable poetry resources in the State of New Jersey, James Haba, former Director of the Waterloo Poetry Festival. If anyone would know of a scientist-poet, it would be James. I'll never forget his words when I asked him.

"Well, there is a noted science poet," he answered, "a Nobel prize-winning chemist at Cornell University. Do you know of the work of Roald Hoffmann?" To this day I am grateful to James Haba for introducing me to Roald Hoffmann, whose science poem, "Tsunami," would provide the model for our first science poetry writing lesson (see Chapter 4, "What is Science Poetry?").

"No," I replied. That night I conducted an Internet search and discovered through Roald Hoffmann's website a treasury of science poems and articles on science and poetry. My preliminary research led to four other exceptional resources in the field: *Verse and Universe: Poems about Science and Mathematics,* an invaluable anthology edited by Kurt Brown (Brown, 1998); *The Measured Word: On Poetry and Science*, a collection of essays and criticism also edited by Kurt Brown (Brown, 2001); *Contemporary Poetry and Contemporary Science*, a cross-over collection of essays and criticism edited by Robert Crawford offering rare dialogues between scientists and poets (Crawford, 2006); and *Cross Pollinations: The Marriage of Science and Poetry*, an inspiring collection of scientific field work essays by Gary Paul Nabhan demonstrating how science needs poetry and poetry needs science (Nabhan, 2004). I was struck by the discovery. There was science poetry – beautiful, awe inspiring, thought provoking, serious, and provocative poetry – poetry written not only by noted poets, but poetry written by noted scientists as well. I was most amazed to find that these English-language poems were widespread and global, created by scientists and poets on both sides of the Atlantic.

The following day in school I could not contain my enthusiasm as I burst into the Science Academy classroom and exclaimed to Erin, "There are science poems – great ones – and now we just have to figure out how to teach them!" For one semester in Science Academy English, my science partner and I did just that, exploring with our students the genre of science poetry. When the voyage was over, the students had written not only inspired and informative science poetry, but insightful commentary attesting to the value of our cross-curricular, interdisciplinary approach. The science-minded Academy students began to see with new eyes, fusing the worlds of scientific literacy and poetic expression.

As a result, that summer, Erin led a scientific expedition to Iceland to collect naturalistic, sensory data for writing science poems. While in the field, she and her Science Academy students wrote science poems prompted by the environment. In the fall, her Research Science class experienced the Icelandic data hands on and wrote additional environmental science poetry. The students' science poem responses were universally startling, beautiful, and inspired. Surprisingly, the poems written by the students in the field were as informative and inspired as the poems written by the students back in the classroom. Jeff Keith, primary guide and leader of the expedition, was amazed when he heard the Icelandic science poems shared in our reading circle: "They're all so inspired. You can't tell who went to Iceland and who did not!" (see Chapter 8, "Into the Field: It's Only Natural").

My science partner and I were also amazed. We began to consider the potential application and portability of our teaching methods for other English and science classes. We knew that scientific field work would always be an instructive and inspirational basis for serious, scientific inquiry, but we also knew, from a practical standpoint, that science as well as English teachers may not always have the opportunity to conduct extensive field work for each and every lesson or class. The Icelandic data confirmed to us that teachers could gather their own field data, or data from other teachers and sources, to provide an equally effective hands-on approach to inspired poetry writing in class as well as in the field.

We decided the time had come to share our work with our colleagues. In the fall of 2007 we presented a workshop on *Poetry Writing through the Eyes of Science* at the annual convention of the National Council of Teachers of English (NCTE) in New York City. As fortune would have it, our editor, Martha Pennington, observed the presentation and asked if we would consider writing a book on teaching science poetry. And so, phase two of the project began in earnest by expanding our science poetry teaching to include additional science and English classes at Morristown High School.

How This Book Evolved: Expanding the Universe of Science Poetry

In year two, I began by teaching science poetry lessons in Advanced Placement (AP) English Language and Composition classes and in Creative Writing elective classes. My science partner began by teaching science poetry lessons in Honors Biology and Research Science classes. Then she developed and applied for grants to conduct summer science poetry expeditions: the first, to Iceland in the summer of 2007; the second, to various science venues in New York City in the summer of 2008. In the process, we considered several ongoing pedagogical issues:

- *How would literature teachers respond to teaching science poetry in their literature classes?*
- *How would science teachers respond to teaching science poetry in their science classes?*
- *How would English students respond to learning about science in English class?*
- *How would science students respond to learning about poetry in science class?*
- *What is the value of teaching science poetry in high school?*

Points of View

What Teachers Say about Science Poetry

Teaching science poetry opens up a world of connection to the students. It also makes the science teaching better. It brings out the emotional level. Students today are faced with difficult decisions – choosing between artistic and expressive interests and professional, scientific ones. Science poetry shows you can do both.

– Roald Hoffmann
Interview (Gorrell, 2008)

In the course of our teaching in non-Academy English and science classes in Morristown High School, we discovered the exceptional portability, adaptability, and relevance of science poetry writing for diverse English and science students. English teachers who invited us into their classes to share lessons or unit plans were amazed how science poetry writing supported and enriched their programs of study. At the conclusion of each of our lessons, we asked our colleagues for comments. Jennifer Furphey, an AP English Language and Composition teacher, confirms the value of science poetry for her students and curriculum:

For the first time in my teaching experience I think that my students actually saw the importance of science in literature, and how one can fuse two subjects that usually seem at such different ends of the spectrum into one. My students enjoyed their experience with science poetry because they saw that they could be scientific and creative at the same time. It was interesting to watch them reluctantly begin the process with this new type of poetry and then quickly dive into the poetry writing after studying only a few scientific poems introduced by Ms. Gorrell. Many of my weaker analytical writers developed strong voices in this unit, emerging as the best creative writers, which was exciting and surprising for me.

– Jennifer Furphey, teacher

Our science colleague, Janyce Trampler, biology teacher and chaperone on the summer science poetry expedition (see Chapter 11) also confirms the value of science poetry for not only her students and curriculum, but for herself, personally and professionally:

Science poetry was a whole new concept to me. Was it possible that the emotional and scientific parts of my brain (two very active parts) could be stimulated simultaneously? On the summer science-poetry expedition, I was inspired to write my first science poem. Since then I have written three others and have ideas in my head for several more. It has become a new intellectual and emotional outlet for me. I now realize that science poetry may be a whole new way to reach my students while teaching science. I am so eager to try out my ideas during this coming school year in my biology classes!

– Janyce Trampler, teacher

What Students Say about Science Poetry

At the conclusion of the unit of study, I asked Ms. Furphey's AP English Language and Composition students to evaluate their experience with science poetry. Their comments confirmed how science poetry opened their eyes to new ways of seeing themselves, their studies, and their learning.

As a poet, I now delve into science with a newfound curiosity and rigor to discover pattern and meaning, realizing now that meaning I had always associated with art exists in science as well.

– David Pitt, student (see Chapters 4, 9, and 10 for David's science poems)

I was impressed with what I learned about science from poetry. I had figured since I am pretty knowledgeable about the phenomena of science that the poems would not teach me much, but I was quickly proved wrong.

– Karley Murphy, student (see Chapters 6 and 7 for Karley's science poems)

I have definitely become more appreciative in regard to the connection between science and English, which is often overlooked. Now when I look around me, my scientific observations take on a greater meaning. I not only analyze them as they are, but how they may be poetically viewed.

– Jessica McKinley, student (see Chapter 7 for Jessica's science poem)

I found that writing science poetry solidified my knowledge of the scientific principles used in the poem. Part of that is the reinforcement and expansion of knowledge that comes from application. For example, prior to writing my first science poem, "The Second Law of Thermodynamics," I understood the concept of the heat death of the universe, but now I can recite the predicted timeline. I had read the timeline before, but since I had to know and understand it well enough to use it in a poem, I will not forget it.

– Alex Davis, student (see Chapters 4 and 10 for Alex's science poems)

Science Poetry: The Power to Transform Students

For most of the students, science poetry clearly opened their eyes to a different universe. But for a select group of science students planning science careers, like Alex Davis and Meghan Crippen, that opening became profoundly transformational. Alex describes his transformational realization: he can do <u>both</u> science and poetry writing.

My interest in writing and my interest in science seemed so far apart that I would wonder if I could ever be successful in either if I continued to devote thought to both. Science poetry changed my viewpoint. Through science poetry, I learned that my interest in science can inform my interest in poetry. Thought devoted to science is not wasted when my mind turns to poetry.... I loved the science poetry unit. It commanded my attention in a way that school rarely can.

– Alex Davis, student

Meghan describes her engagement with the art form transforming how she views education as a whole.

As a science person, I find comfort in what is logical, rational, and concrete. When I was first introduced to science poetry, I was uneasy and apprehensive for several reasons. First, I was uncomfortable with the abstract and emotional qualities of poetry. I also believed it is impossible to combine rationality of science with the indefinable aspects of poetry. I will admit that I held a relatively negative attitude. However, I was pleasantly surprised to find that science and poetry blended in a fairly simple manner, and this new style of writing, in fact, increased my understanding of science.

After this unit, my views of both science and poetry have been transformed. On a deeper level, this new understanding has transformed the way I view education as a whole. Science and poetry at first seemed like polar opposites, but in writing science poetry, I developed ways to bridge the gap between the two; my original skepticism was eliminated. This has encouraged me to cross unlikely disciplines in the future.

– Meghan Crippen, student (see Chapters 5 and 6 for
Meghan's science poems)

What is Unique about This Book

This book is unique in several ways:

- First, it is directed to a dual audience, both science and English teachers. This dual audience is intentional, grounded in the author's advocacy for interdisciplinary, cross-curricular literacy and education.
- Second, as a consequence of a dual audience, this book speaks in multiple voices: the author's primary voice; the voice of contributing author, Erin Colfax; and the voices of several colleagues and many student poets.
- Third, this book offers a practical, effective, and engaging strategy for bridging the cultural divide between the arts and sciences in high school and beyond, which is: *science poetry*.
- Fourth, this book offers a single, pedagogical tool that supports at once the movements for educational reform in both the language arts and the sciences in the United States and abroad – in particular, the movements for literacy, scientific literacy, interdisciplinary literacy, environmental education, ecological literacy, inquiry-based science education, and humanization of science.

Organization and Contents of This Book

This book includes a section of Preliminaries giving background and setting the stage for the chapters to come and is then divided into four main sections that build lessons sequentially from the background foundation, to the fundamentals, and then to the more advanced lessons fusing science and poetry together in the essence of the art form. The final section demonstrates forging common ground in the field, beyond the classroom, and in the pedagogy of our disciplines.

- Section One: Foundation
- Section Two: Fundamentals
- Section Three: Fusion
- Section Four: Forging Common Ground

Each of the chapters in this book offers both theory and practice in the understanding, appreciation, and teaching of science poetry. All chapters include lessons and activities relevant to both the science and English classrooms, and all chapters include student responses, commentary, and model student science poems.

Preliminaries

- **Prolegomenon** ("What is Being Said First - Connections: Bridging the Cultural Divide") introduces the connections that can be made between science and poetry.
- **Prologue** ("'Dances with Stars': How I Wrote My First Science Poem") describes my first experience with science poetry, which grew from a felt need for language to describe an observed phenomenon in a poem. The quest for knowledge and language to describe what I had seen led to my science partner, Erin Colfax, who readily supplied the scientific knowledge I lacked and just the right word to describe what I had seen.
- **Introduction** ("Entering Common Ground: Let Science Poetry Lead the Way") offers a general introduction to the book and an overview of chapters and appendices.

Section One: Foundation

Principles, Issues, and Pedagogy

- **Chapter 1** ("Hide and Seek: Multiple Ways of Seeing Trees") begins building the foundation with three activities and a science closure poem that prepare students to "see" through multiple eyes; that is, through the eyes of art, nature, science, and poetry. Once students have acquired the sensibility of multiple perspectives, they are prepared to engage with science poetry writing.

- **Chapter 2** ("What is Poetry? Developing the Poetic Eye") continues building the foundation with four activities that explore and answer the question: *What is poetry?* Designed to be relevant for both science and English students, these activities develop students' poetic eyes, assessing their attitudes toward poetry and their poetic literacy. For science teachers in particular, this chapter offers a creative and engaging science textbook reading strategy.

- **Chapter 3** ("What is Science? Developing the Scientific Eye") answers the question: *What is science*? Designed to be relevant for both English and science students, the three activities in this chapter develop students' scientific eyes, assessing their attitudes toward science and their scientific literacy. For interested teachers, chapter 3 offers several model poems for explication exploring attitudes toward science and the nature of science and the scientific method.

- **Chapter 4** ("What is Science Poetry? A Tsunami of Possibility"), this book's signature lesson, answers the question: *What is science poetry?* Designed as a model lesson of definition, Chapter 4 demonstrates for science and English teachers how to teach their first science poetry writing lesson. This chapter includes several model student responses.

- **Chapter 5** ("How to Teach Science Poetry Writing: Teacher as 'Chemical Artist'") concludes Section One by offering for the science and English teacher alike a compendium of practical tips, strategies, methods, and handouts useful for science poetry teaching and writing.

Section Two: Fundamentals

Basic Lessons for Science Poetry Writing

- **Chapter 6** ("It's a Gem! Rocks and Minerals") begins the fundamentals with two basic activities in writing science poetry on the subject of rocks, minerals, and gemstones relevant to the earth sciences.
- **Chapter 7** ("What's Buggin' You? Insects and Other Living Things") continues the fundamentals with two basic activities in writing science poetry on the subject of insects and other living things relevant to the life sciences.
- **Chapter 8** ("Into the Field: It's Only Natural") moves the fundamental lessons from the classroom to the field, offering a discussion of a teacher-led expedition to Iceland to gather field data for poetic response. This chapter includes an expedition protocol and model lessons using the field data gathered in Iceland back in research science and English classrooms. The chapter ends with suggestions for replication and adaptation of the Icelandic expedition model for science and English classroom use.

Section Three: Fusion

Advanced Lessons For Science Poetry Writing

- **Chapter 9** ("Writing from Awe, Wonder, Reverence, and Empathy") begins the advanced lessons in science poetry writing that require the more artful fusion of science and poetry. In this chapter, students write science poetry prompted by the emotions of awe, wonder, reverence, and empathy. Student poems in this chapter demonstrate movement from academic to more personally authentic science poetry.

- **Chapter 10** ("Writing from Outrage, Protest, Perplexity, and Speculation") continues the advanced lessons in science poetry writing that require the more artful fusion of science and poetry. In this chapter, students write science poetry prompted by the emotions of outrage, protest, perplexity, and speculation. Student poems in this chapter continue to demonstrate movement from academic to more personally authentic science poetry.

Section Four: Forging Common Ground

Interdisciplinary Curriculum

- **Chapter 11** ("Walking in This World with Our Students and Colleagues") demonstrates teachers and students forging common ground in the urban "fields" of museums, zoos, and botanical gardens. This chapter confirms the transformative power of walking in this world with students and colleagues through the genre of the walk poem.
- **Chapter 12** ("How to Assess Student Science Poetry: The Art of Response") offers for the science and English teacher alike individual and collaborative tips and strategies for responding to student science poems in progress as well as methods of assessment and grading based on best practices in the discipline of writing.
- **Conclusion** ("Toward a New Interdisciplinary Literacy") summarizes the common ground between science and poetry and offers four good reasons for teaching science poetry.
- **Epilogue** ("What is Being Said Last") returns to the introductory theme of making connections.

Appendices

- **Appendix A** ("Recommended 'Timely' Course Designs") provides practical advice and lesson strategies for English teachers (including AP, composition, and creative writing teachers) and science teachers in different subject areas.
- **Appendix B** ("Recommended Two-Week Unit Plan") presents a day by day plan for a two-week unit with additional optional activities.
- **Appendix C** ("Science Poetry Resources for the Teacher") lists websites, weblogs, and contests related to science poetry.
- **Appendix D** ("Further Reading for the Teacher") lists books, chapters, poetry collections, reference works, and anthologies related to science poetry.

How to Use This Book

Some "Timely" Suggestions for the Teacher

I hope that by this point you are intrigued and inspired enough to want to experience the universe of a different kind in your respective science or English classrooms. Yet given the unique challenge of science poetry writing, you might feel overwhelmed, especially by that singular most critical nemesis to all educational change and innovation – *time*. Having taught myself for 36 years in the secondary school classroom, I know what it means to teach under the demands of time. So with respect to your time constraints, and with the recognition that most teachers will not have time enough to read this book from cover to cover, I offer the "timely" reading and teaching suggestions for the science and English teacher who is hard-pressed for time but desires to teach some science poetry, in "Recommended 'Timely' Course Designs," Appendix A. For the teacher with more time to devote to science poetry, see "Recommended Two-Week Unit Plan," Appendix B.

A Final Word to Science and English Teachers

Just Imagine...

You can do it, too. All you need is imagination. Perhaps you have already experienced curricular collaborations within your discipline; for example, inter-arts projects involving poetry and music, or poetry and art, or poetry and history, or science research projects drawing on math, chemistry, physics, or biology. Now imagine crossing the cultural divide. Consider, for example, *Chemistry Imagined*, a collaboration by Roald Hoffmann, chemist and poet, with visual artist, Vivian Torrence, to use poetry and artwork to inform chemistry (Hoffmann and Torrence, 1993). Or imagine walking on a lava flow, gathering scientific data with your students, while pausing to write a poem (see Chapter 8). Or imagine walking in a botanical garden, gathering botanical data with your students while writing a walk poem (see Chapter 11). Once again, imagine crossing the cultural divide. You can do it, too. Just let science poetry lead the way.

Notes

1. I am indebted to Andre Benhaim, Assistant Professor of French, Princeton University, for the source of this commonly known and liberally paraphrased passage from Marcel Proust's "The Captive" in *Remembrance of Things Past:*

    > A pair of wings, a different respiratory system, which enabled us to travel through space, would in no way help us, for if we visited Mars or Venus while keeping the same senses, they would clothe everything that we saw in the same aspect as the things of Earth. The only true voyage of discovery…. (Proust, 1982: 259–260)

2. Coletta and Tamres reference Alexander Pope's famous couplet dating from 1730: "All nature and her Laws lay hid by Night/ God said, Let Newton be: And all was light!" (Coletta and Tamres, 1992: 365). The authors also identify and discuss the following physics-related science poems by Frost: "All Revelations" (1938) and "A Never Naught Song" (1962), poems informed by the quantum nature of atoms, and "For Once, Then Something" (1920), a poem dealing with Bohr's complementary principle and the Heisenberg Uncertainty Principle. Gil Abisdris and Adele Casuga, in "Atomic Poetry: Using Poetry to Teach Rutherford's Discovery of the Nucleus" (Abisdris and Casuga, 2001), teach two science poems by Frost: "The Secret Sits" and "Version."

3. Although most of Thier's language literacy strategies center on the use of note taking, field journals, observations, reports, descriptions, and essay writing, she does include poetry writing as part of the "new science literacy" – in particular, suggesting nature poetry, haiku, the cinquain, and the poem, "Birches," by Robert Frost (Their, 2002: 134–136). It is interesting to note that Thier includes naturalistic haiku poetry and Frost's "Birches" in her discussion of the "new science literacy" under the heading, "The Human Side of Science," reflecting the view that poetry in the science classroom "humanizes" science instruction.

4. The Science Academy, a school-within-a-school program, was founded in 2003 through a unique partnership between the New Jersey Department of Education, the Morris School District, and the Pfizer Corporation. The Academy's mission is to serve the average to above-average science-minded student by offering an interdisciplinary program of studies in the humanities and the sciences. The Academy selects students who have "demonstrated a passion in science, math, and technology" and who anticipate a career in science or the medical arts. The students – who span grades 9, 10, and 11 – take their core subjects together: Academy English, Academy history, Academy language, and Academy science.

Section One: Foundation

Principles, Issues, and Pedagogy

SECTION OVERVIEW

Section One offers four foundation lessons to prepare science and English students to write their own science poetry followed by a fifth chapter for the teacher on how to teach science poetry writing. Each student foundation chapter is framed by an inquiry question designed to engage students of all abilities to enter the mindset, literacy, and language of poetry, science, and ultimately, science poetry:

- Chapter 1: *What is it to see through multiple eyes?*
- Chapter 2: *What is poetry?*
- Chapter 3: *What is science?*
- Chapter 4: *What is science poetry?*

Chapter 1 begins establishing the foundation by asking students to exercise their powers of observation. Students observe the subject *trees* through the eyes of the artist, the naturalist, the scientist, and, as closure, the science poet. In the process, they engage with a painting, a nature essay, an interview, a park design, and a science poem. In Chapter 2, students define poetry, experimenting with found poetry to discover the poetic potential in non-literary and scientific texts. In the process, they write their own science found poem based on their reading of scientific texts. In Chapter 3, students define science, engaging with activities to further their scientific literacy and understanding of the scientific method and ways of knowing. In Chapter 4, students define science poetry and engage in writing their first science poems.

Section One concludes with Chapter 5, "How to Teach Science Poetry Writing." Directed to both science and English teachers alike, Chapter 5 offers an effective and highly instructive method for teaching science poetry writing to students of all levels and abilities.

SUGGESTIONS FOR USING THIS SECTION

Although the four student foundation lessons proceed in a sequential order, they may be taught as individual lessons and in any order appropriate for particular science or English courses of study. For example, teachers who have students well-acquainted with *what is poetry* and *what is science* may prefer to move directly from the foundation lesson in Chapter 1, "Hide and Seek," to the foundation lesson in Chapter 4, "What is Science Poetry?" To facilitate this transition, Chapter 1 ends with a reading of Howard Nemerov's science poem, "Learning the Trees." This poem serves a dual purpose: a closure for Foundation Lesson One and an envoy to Foundation Lesson Four.

1   Hide and Seek

Multiple Ways of Seeing Trees

What you see is what you get.
> – Annie Dillard, *Pilgrim at Tinker Creek*
> (Dillard, 1974: 16)

OVERVIEW: FOUNDATION LESSON ONE

The aim of Foundation Lesson One is to prepare students to enter the universe of science poetry. In order to do so, students must find new eyes – to see the world of art, nature, science, and poetry through multiple perspectives and complementary lenses. Such seeing requires the skills of close observation, heightened sensory awareness, metaphoric viewing, and imaginative and creative thinking. Most importantly, such seeing requires an attitudinal shift from eyes "wide shut" to eyes "wide open," from seeing unaware to seeing keenly aware, from not knowing to knowing: *what you see is what you get*. In this sense, Foundation Lesson One encourages, inspires, and models the transformation necessary to engage in the interdisciplinary endeavor of writing science poetry.

In "Seeing," from *Pilgrim at Tinker Creek,* Annie Dillard describes her nature walks as a game of hide and seek: "It's all a matter of keeping my eyes open. Nature is like one of those line drawings of a tree that are puzzles for children: can you find hidden in the leaves a duck, a house, a boy...? Specialists can find the most incredibly well-hidden things" (Dillard, 1974: 18). Lesson One introduces students to four specialists – a visual artist, Pavel Tchelitchew; a naturalist, Annie Dillard, a botanist, Steven Handel; and a poet, Howard Nemerov – and how those specialists see a singular subject, *trees*, from different yet complementary perspectives, resulting in different yet comparable creations: a painting, a naturalistic essay, a park design, and a science poem, respectively. That Lesson One begins teaching multiple ways of seeing by focusing on an aspect of nature and the natural world is intentional. For if there is one ground where both science and poetry naturally come together, it is in nature and the natural world. Thus, the ultimate aim of Lesson One is to:

- *Open students' eyes;*
- *Raise their awareness of interdisciplinary connections; and*
- *Heighten their appreciation for all disciplines within the arts and sciences.*

Foundation Lesson One consists of four parts incorporating three activities followed by a science poem for closure, "Learning the Trees," by Howard Nemerov, and Part Five giving suggestions for further student written responses. The chapter closes with a reflection on the value of teaching different perspectives and ways of seeing.

Foundation Lesson One at a Glance

<u>Part One</u>: Art
Activity #1: The Painting, *Hide and Seek,* by Pavel Tchelitchew

<u>Part Two</u>: Nature
Activity #2: Excerpts from the nature essay "Seeing" by Annie Dillard

<u>Part Three</u>: Science
Activity #3: An Interview and park design by Steven Handel

<u>Part Four</u>: Poetry
Closure Science Poem: "Learning the Trees" by Howard Nemerov

<u>Part Five</u>: **Student Written Response**
Foundation Lesson One Prompts
Model Student Response: Poem, "Rings" by Anne Schwartz

Why Teach Ways of Seeing and Multiple Perspectives?

Students first view Pavel Tchelitchew's painting, *Hide and Seek*, a biological metamorphosis of a tree that explodes with metaphoric seeing. They "play" the game of "hide and seek," discovering the pleasure of surprise that comes from seeing through the eyes of the artist. Then, in Activity #2, they compare Tchelitchew's painting of a tree to excerpts from Annie Dillard's essay, "Seeing" (Dillard, 1974), a remarkable synthesis of all ways of seeing, culminating in the ultimate way of seeing – seeing, for the first time, as a newly sighted person would see. In *the tree with the lights in it* passage Dillard blends at once scientific fact, naturalistic observation, personal experience, and poetic inspiration. As such, "Seeing" serves a dual purpose. First, the essay illustrates for students the fusion of science and poetry in prose form; in fact, many of Dillard's passages exemplify prose poetry at its best. Second, Dillard – herself, a poet, writer, and naturalist – models the renaissance sensibility that my science partner and I want to encourage in our students. This sensibility encompasses:

- *The ability to transfer learning from one discipline to the other;*
- *The ability to synthesize that learning and skill to produce interdisciplinary creations; and*
- *The ability to recognize and value the common ground between the arts and sciences.*

Activity #3 further opens students' scientific eyes with this author's interview with Steven Handel, botanist, as he discusses his view of trees and his work in restoration and park design and ecology. The chapter ends with a science poem for closure, "Learning the Trees," by Howard Nemerov. Nemerov's poem affirms for students the value of dual ways of seeing – through the eyes of science <u>and</u> the eyes of poetry.

Materials Needed

Painting: *Hide-and-Seek,* 1940–42, oil on canvas, by Pavel Tchelitchew available for viewing in the online collection of the Museum of Modern Art, New York or available for purchase;[1]
Nature Essay: Excerpt from "Seeing" by Annie Dillard (provided)
Interview: Botanist, Steven Handel (provided)
Park Design: Botanist, Steven Handel (provided)
Science Poem: "Learning the Trees" by Howard Nemerov (provided)

SUGGESTIONS FOR USING THIS LESSON

As an opening lesson establishing the mindset necessary for writing science poetry, Foundation Lesson One is appropriate for any high school literature, science, or creative writing class. English teachers will find lesson one useful, practical, and portable for teaching multiple perspectives and ways of seeing that are necessary for literary analysis and criticism. I have used the painting, *Hide-and-Seek,* to teach observation skills, metaphoric seeing, and the creative process in Science Academy English, creative writing classes, and poetry workshops. Science teachers will find Lesson One particularly applicable in biology, botany, environmental science, and ecology courses. Steven Handel's interview demonstrates the passionate and creative side of a scientist's work while Annie Dillard's *Pilgrim at Tinker Creek* provides a wealth of scientific data from the natural world as well as poetic and philosophical inspiration. Science teachers will also find Howard Nemerov's poem, "Learning the Trees," a creative "field guide" to plant kingdom identification.

Both science and English teachers engaging in field work with their students will find Dillard's naturalistic journal writing an instructive model for students to emulate. Dillard's essay is an ideal source for teaching scientific literacy – the ability to read, comprehend, and speak about scientific facts, discoveries, ideas, phenomena, and investigations with authority and passion. Foundation Lesson One naturally prompts creative writing responses, preparing students to write science poetry in the subsequent chapters with greater confidence, authority, and skill. My science partner and I encourage both science and English teachers to consider creative uses of all the activities as they relate not only to science poetry writing in particular, but writing, literacy programs, and interdisciplinary teaching in general.

Suggested Time Allocations

Time allocations for each activity will vary depending upon the level of students, length of follow-up discussion and writing responses, and curriculum needs. Recommended guidelines:

    Activity #1 (30 minutes)
    Activity #2 (20 minutes)
    Activity #3 (30 minutes)
    Closure Science Poem (20 minutes)

PART ONE: ART

ACTIVITY #1: THE PAINTING, HIDE AND SEEK, BY PAVEL TCHELITCHEW, VISUAL ARTIST

First Seeing

Display the painting, *Hide-and-Seek*, preferably in poster form, so that all students in the room can see the details as clearly as possible. Let students remain in their assigned seats for the first seeing. This is important because you are going to point out how different vantage points result in different observations, reactions, and realities. In addition, do not tell students the title of the painting. Later, you will ask your students to imagine and speculate on what title the artist has given his work. This too will ultimately change perspectives and points of view. Tell your students that they are going to learn about observation and multiple ways of seeing through their first viewing of the painting. Withholding the title of the painting, tell them the name of the artist, his nationality (Russian), and that he painted the work over the course of several years. Then instruct your students to view the painting, observing as much as they can from their individual vantage points. Call their attention to the following artistic elements: lines, color, value, shapes, textures, patterns, movement, mirror images, and the focal point of the painting.

Freewriting

After students have observed for a few minutes, tell them they may begin writing in their journals to one of the following prompts whenever they feel ready and inspired. Distribute or project the following writing prompts:

Freewriting Prompts Based on the Painting

1. What emotions does the painting evoke for you? What mood? Freewrite a description that captures the feeling or mood of the painting for you.
2. Study the colors. Freewrite a short prose piece or poem using the colors as prompts.
3. What memories does the painting evoke for you? Freewrite what the painting recalls for you, or freewrite what the painting makes you think about.
4. Observe the central figure in the trunk of the tree. Imagine what the figure is doing or about to do. Imagine what the figure is feeling or thinking. Write an imaginary story or poem based on this figure.
5. What science do you see in this painting? Freewrite about the science you see in the painting in any form you prefer – prose, poetry, or essay. You may focus on one part or aspect of the painting.

Post-Writing Seeing

After your students have finished freewriting, open their eyes to multiple ways of seeing by taking them on a visual journey through the painting. Begin with their initial "seeing" from their seats. Start with the back of the room or back rows, pointing out that students, far away, have a more *macro* view of the painting. Students at a distance generally see a dark, massive area that they identify as a tree. Sometimes they also notice heads and profiles in the branches, leaves, and skeletal outlines in the lower right hand corner. Ask students close to the painting what they see in their more *micro* view. These students will generally point out that the base of the tree looks like a foot, and that at the top of the tree, the branches look like the back of a right hand. At this point, most students become rather excited. They start to look again and see images they did not see the first time. Some see a central figure – what appears to be a young girl, possibly in a red dress, clutching the bark of the trunk of the tree. Now, more observant, some students begin to notice the embryo at the base of the trunk and a profusion of apparitional children branching out in the upper right quadrant of the painting. They also may see the young girl in the center of the tree surrounded by many images of naked children, most likely younger ones, embedded in the outlines of the trunk of the tree. Point out for students how some of these images become mirrors of the others. Trace with a pointer the outline of the left side of the trunk. Show students how the inside of the profile line appears to be a body or figure of a child. Then point out the right side of the trunk of the tree. Show students how the right profile also reflects a body or figure, this time of an older child on the outside of the profile line.

Re-Seeing: Changing Point of View

At this juncture, tell students that you want them to change their point of view to see something they had not seen the first time. Before students move from their seats, suggest to them areas that they should observe more closely. Tell them that no space in the painting truly exists; that what is normally space in reality (the negative space between branches or fingers, or the space on either side of the trunk of the tree), is filled by the artist with anthropomorphic images, many of them, ghost-like and apparitional. Encourage them to keep focusing and narrowing their viewing of these negative spaces, getting closer and closer to the images until finally they can notice minute details like the shadowy figures in the fingers of the arm in the upper left hand quadrant of the work, or the shadowy figure of a blind girl in the cheek socket of the right profile.

After students have had the opportunity to view from multiple vantage points, they will have undoubtedly observed the painting's metamorphosis – in particular, the girl in the upper left quadrant whose left arm is a branch, the images of the caterpillar and the butterfly as well as the entire image of the tree transforming from naturalistic images to human images and vice versa.

Multiple Ways of Seeing

Lead a discussion identifying with students all of the ways to observe and engage with the painting. Ask students to compare what they observed when they were looking at the painting through *micro* versus *macro* eyes. Ask how the discipline of science uses the terms *micro* or *microcosm* and *macro* or *macrocosm*, and how these different ways of seeing affect perspectives and interpretations.

Then ask students to look at the painting *through the eyes of science* – as they imagine a scientist might view the painting. Most students in high school have enough scientific literacy to notice a profusion of natural and scientific images in the painting: the suggestion of seasons and evolution, metamorphosis of the tree itself, the propagation of plants, seedlings, the dandelion flower and its "puff," the suggestion of an embryo, bodies in fetal positions, possible stages of human life, and the suggestion of human anatomy, blood, veins, capillaries, bones, skeletal, and X-ray inspired images. Suggest that the painting may be viewed on two scientific levels: the internal system of the human body (*microcosm*) and the energy and matter of the universe (*macrocosm*). For students schooled in biology, ask them to speculate why some art critics call this painting a *biological* or *nature fantasias* (Bourdon, 1995: 65).

Last, ask students to look at the painting *through the eyes of* literature, poetry, or English. What do they see or think they see? Literature students often point out symbols or symbolic meanings: the apple (replete with symbolism in Western literature) in the upper center of the work and the doves (a symbol of peace) in the upper left corner. Students often suggest that the tree and the apple allude to the Garden of Eden in the Old Testament of the Bible. Although some mention that the painting does not look like Paradise, others speculate that the painting could be a depiction of the Garden of

Eden after Eve had eaten the apple. At this point some students may also mention metaphoric or figurative "seeing," how the painter personifies the tree with anthropomorphic images of hands, feet, and faces as well as the multiple human forms throughout.

Imagining the Title of the Painting

Ask your students to imagine the title Tchelitchew gave to his painting. If they seem to struggle, suggest they divide the painting into four quadrants, each quadrant representing one of the seasons. Generally, students will see the four quadrants as representing the change of seasons: the lower left, spring; the upper left, summer; the upper right, fall; and the lower right, winter. With this observation in mind, students often offer the following possible titles: *The Four Seasons*, *The Tree of Life*, *Life Cycles*, or *Metamorphosis*. Historically minded students often note the time period and social context of the painting, speculating that the title may have something to do with World War II, the Holocaust, or children hiding. In all the years I have taught this lesson with high school English students, I have never had a student come close to the actual title of the painting: *Hide and Seek*.

Interpreting the Meaning of the Title, *Hide and Seek*

Now tell students that the title of the painting is *Hide-and-Seek*. Students usually respond with outbursts of recognition. "Oh!" Often they see the figure of a girl in the center of the tree as literally playing the game of hide and seek. Guide students to go beyond literal interpretations of hide and seek by asking:

- *What do you think Tchelitchew might be saying about seeking?*

- *What do you think he might be saying about what is hidden, what we see, and what realities we observe?*

Suggest to students that the title may be saying something more about how we observe or see rather than about how we understand the literal subject, tree. Students soon come to see the larger meaning of the title and the hide and seek metaphor: *things are not what they seem*. Encourage your students to seek additional interpretations, sharing your own as well.

I tell my students that Tchelitchew wants us to pause, to question, and to play the game of hide and seek, seeing the world more fully, with new eyes, using all of our powers of observation. I suggest that when we see the painting through the eyes of the artist, we re-create its meaning as our eyes re-trace each line and stroke of the artist's brush. By engaging us to seek with our eyes what is hidden, Tchelitchew not only challenges us to play the "game," he makes us *co-creators* in his surrealistic vision. Tell your students this is what all artists and poets want from their creations – to have the viewer or reader look again, more deeply, and to enter the work imaginatively. At this point, I usually share with students that this painting is part of the permanent collection of the Museum of Modern Art in New York City, and that I have seen crowds of strangers gathered around the painting spontaneously seeking the hidden within, enjoying the surprise of each and every observation and discovery.

Metaphoric Seeing

To conclude Activity #1, ask students to imagine how Tchelitchew sees the literal vision of a *tree*. If necessary, identify for students the concept of *metaphoric seeing*: looking at one thing and seeing another. Point out that this way of seeing is inherently poetic – the artist looks at the tree but sees something human – personifying the natural world. I like to suggest to my students that all creators, whether they be artists or scientists, begin with a void – a blank canvas, a blank page, or the unknown – and then they intuit or formulate an image, an idea, a theme, a thesis, or a hypothesis which serves as a prompt – a beginning – for their creation.

PART TWO: NATURE

ACTIVITY #2: NATURE ESSAY, "SEEING" BY ANNIE DILLARD, NATURALIST

Seeing "Free Gifts" from the Universe

To synthesize all of the ways of seeing, have your students engage with two excerpts from Annie Dillard's Pulitzer Prize winning *Pilgrim at Tinker Creek*. In her work, Dillard records, over the course of one year, her poetic nature walks in the Roanoke Valley of the Blue Ridge Mountains. Part science, part poetry, part philosophy, part mysticism and spirituality, "Seeing" becomes a model of interdisciplinary prose style, where all disciplines blend together artfully, informing and inspiring each other. More able English and science students may be assigned this remarkable naturalistic essay to read overnight in its entirety, for it is as an exemplary way of developing students' scientific literacy as well as their appreciation of nature.

Keeping with the subject, trees, Activity #2 focuses on two critical passages excerpted from "Seeing" where Dillard observes trees and the hidden secrets within. The first passage, the *Osage orange tree*, occurs early in her essay; the second, *the tree with the lights in it,* concludes her essay. I tell my students about Dillard's first experience where she describes how nature reveals and conceals: "now-you-don't-see-it, now-you-do" (Dillard, 1974: 18). One day she walks up to an Osage orange tree to "investigate the racket" only to see at first a "whisk of color" and then a flight of a "hundred birds." The birds disappear downstream. She stands in awe: "These appearances catch my throat; they are the *free gifts* the bright coppers at the roots of trees" (Dillard, 1974: 18; emphasis added, NG).

Sharing "Free Gifts"

After explaining the brief *Osage orange tree* passage, ask students to recall if they have ever experienced an awe-inspiring sight, a "free gift" from the universe? Share your own memories with your students. I often share my encounter with the luminous waves of my childhood (see Prologue). My students respond by sharing memories of mysterious sunsets, surprising rainbows, and awe-inspiring canyons and snowstorms. After sharing, remind students how Dillard describes nature as a puzzle, using the hide and seek metaphor previously attributed to her in the opening of this chapter. But now, ask students to go further in their understanding of seeing, to recognize that seeing, as in the *Osage orange tree* passage, is more than a game of hide and seek when it inspires, raises questions, and arouses curiosity, entering the realm of the spiritual and mystical.

Transformative Seeing or Seeing for the First Time

Dillard concludes her essay with the second passage, *the tree with the lights in it,* a description of the ultimate way of seeing – seeing that transforms – which, more often than not, is seeing for the first time. This type of seeing moves beyond finding hidden puzzles, uncovering unexpected surprises, or inspiring feelings of awe and spirituality. This kind of seeing involves deeply personal connections and insights which ultimately transform the viewer, allowing the viewer, for the first time, to see the world and the world of self with new eyes.

Reading *The Tree with Lights in It* Passage

Distribute to students *the tree with the lights in it* passage. Set up the reading by explaining that Dillard describes the case of a little girl, blind at birth by cataracts. Read to students: "When her doctor took her bandages off and led her into the garden, the girl who was no longer blind saw *the tree with the lights in it*" (Dillard, 1974: 35). Tell students that Dillard then describes how she searches for years to see something similar to *the tree with the lights in it*, until finally one day, she does. Read aloud to students Dillard's experience with seeing for the first time.

The Tree with the Lights in It Passage

> *...I was walking along Tinker Creek thinking of nothing at all and I saw the tree with the lights in it. I saw the backyard cedar where the mourning doves roost charged and transfigured, each cell buzzing with flame. I stood on the grass with the lights in it, grass that was wholly fire, utterly focused and utterly dreamed. It was less like seeing than like being for the first time seen, knocked breathless by a powerful glance.... I had been my whole life a bell, and never knew it until at that moment I was lifted and struck. I have since only very rarely seen the tree with the lights in it. The vision comes and goes, mostly goes, but I live for it, for the moment when the mountains open and a new light roars in spate through the crack, and the mountains slam.* (Dillard, 1974: 35)

Post-Reading Discussion

After reading *the tree with the lights in it* passage, ask students to explain what they imagine the little girl saw. Then ask them if they have ever seen anything for the first time that caused them to feel so transformed. Tell students it may be something they understood and recognized, or it may be something they did not understand, but hoped to see again. Once again, I refer to the luminous waves of my childhood (see Prologue). If students are able to respond with examples, ask them:

- *How were your eyes opened?*
- *Did you understand what you saw?*
- *Were you able to explain it through the eyes of science?*
- *Did you need to turn to poetry to express the unknown?*

Reviewing All the Ways of Seeing

After students have engaged with all four activities, conclude Foundation Lesson One with a brief review of all of the ways of seeing:

- *Microscopically*
- *Macroscopically*
- *Sensorily*
- *Metaphorically*
- *Poetically*
- *Analytically*
- *Empathetically*
- *Philosophically*
- *Experientially*

Encourage your students always to keep their eyes open, to be patient and wait, and never to give up seeking Dillard's "free gifts" of the universe.[2]

PART THREE: SCIENCE

ACTIVITY #3: AN INTERVIEW WITH STEVEN HANDEL, SCIENTIST, AND A PARK DESIGN

In order to explore how a scientist might view a tree, I interviewed Steven Handel, Department of Ecology, Evolution, and Natural Resources at Rutgers University, New Brunswick, New Jersey. In Handel's interview, students hear the voice of a botanist, passionate about his subject, trees and their environment, yet maintaining at all times the eyes of science. Handel's interview serves several, introductory purposes:

- *A first glimpse into the mind and the mind's eye of a scientist at work;*
- *A corrective to stereotypical notions that science is devoid of aesthetic appreciation, passion, and emotion; and*
- *A contrast to Tchelitchew and Dillard's ways of seeing a similar subject, trees.*

Simulating an Interview with Steven Handel

To make the interview more accessible and lively for students, I recommend simulating the interview process by assigning students the roles of interviewer and botanist, respectively. For a creative approach, students may "costume" as the botanist, Steven Handel, use props, and/or improvise for additional insights.

Interview

Q: *As a botanist, how do you see a tree?*

A: I think I see a tree physically very differently than you. I see it from the roots up, from its hidden parts to what's above ground.

The underground parts are *so* important. I don't see the tree as a "lollipop" – you know, as a trunk with a round top, a stem and top.

Q: *That's an interesting image. Can you elaborate on that?*

A: When I look at a tree I think about the root mass underground which has its own shape and function, but the above ground parts are what most see. Roots interact with other organisms in the soil. They grow in their own way. It's very complex. Most roots are waterproof; only the microscopic root hairs absorb water. They're hard to study.

Q: *So you see at once not only the visible but also the invisible parts of a tree; what's hidden and microscopic. Can you tell us more about the visible parts we are all familiar with? For instance, what do you see when you see a tree in its natural environment, in an open field or meadow?*

A: I see something that is alive, dynamic, changing its shape; how it looks different each season. Most see trees as static elements in the landscape. I see trees as shimmering, desperately trying to stay alive! Dynamic, striving; a meadow is not peaceful and serene.

Q: *Can you define for us your discipline as it might apply to trees?*

A: My field is to determine, why does the pattern of nature look like it does? What drives it? What determines what a tree looks like? Why does that tree look different from every other tree? What is it? What species is it? When I look at a tree while walking in the woods or a field, I look around. What's the history of this place? What has happened? I look for clues, a record of the dynamic of change. It's very interesting. Lots of people are blind to the information contained in a stand of trees. Trees are clues to the environment. There is no such thing as a "standard" meadow, field, or forest. Each is a result of what has happened at that specific place.

Q: *I see that you are getting very animated and excited when you talk about trees.*

A: Yes, I see nature in a much more fined-grained way. This tree has beautiful buds. Nature is a fine-scaled mosaic. I get a lot of pleasure out of. I don't just see green.

I see histories and the personalities of the trees. My impulse is to see each tree as an individual. Why is that tree shaped like that? Just because a tree is small doesn't mean it's young. I really see trees as moving, living things; they shimmer. They don't just sit there rooted in the ground.

Q: *As a botanist, how does it feel to take a nature walk? Let us see that walk through your eyes.*

A: I see Van Gogh's images of nature as the most artistically accurate. Nature is wild movement, change, things fighting each other, trying to reproduce. I look at a meadow as a battleground. I don't look at it like a bunch of posies. I see action in things standing still. I see it and it often makes me nervous. I know a tree is shaped by critters trying to eat it, its neighbors crowding it, weather acting upon it. I don't see "the pretty tree with the green leaves."

Q: *Can you explain more fully how you see seasonality?*

A: Seasonality is very important. I feel a tremendous sense of the flow of time and seasons, and how living plants respond to the flow of time. For trees, it's an enormous problem how to make it through the winter. I see "no leaves" as an incredible response to stress – trees giving up a huge amount of resources and energy to make it through the winter; spring is a burst of energy to live again. When I walk in the woods, it is not relaxing. It's not a quiet experience. It's energetic, active, and an intellectual experience. I don't go to the woods to relax. Nature is not solitude, quiet, pastoral to me; a meadow is rapid birth and death.

Q: *You most certainly feel intimately connected to nature, seasonality, and trees.*

A: Most people are separated from seasonality and the flow of time. Yet trees so clearly illustrate this connection. In my park designs I try to provide social opportunities for every season. I'm trying to get people to see the seasons. Also, nature is changing a lot. Hundreds of new plant species from Asia and Europe are coming into the United States. Things are moving so quickly now. Our forests are degraded; there is no such thing as untouched forests.

Q: *Before you tell us more about park design, can you explain some of the stresses you see on trees in our environment?*

A: Many stresses on trees result from animals in the environment. I almost immediately ask what animals are involved in its life – Birds? Flies? Insects trying to eat leaves and bark? So much of a tree is defense against enemies. Trees of different sizes have different fates and enemies. A small tree often can't grow up because it's so shaded or crowded; size and age are linked. In learning about individual tree species, each species has a different set of solutions to growing and living in its environment. Fifteen to twenty common trees equal fifteen to twenty ways of successful living. When I look at a tree, I see just as much liveliness. It doesn't move, but it grows. Its seeds and pollen move; it responds, not as dramatically as animals do, but I don't think animals are any more interesting or dynamic than plants.

Q: *Can you tell us how you use trees in your park designs?*

A: I use them to start a process – expanding patches of plants until the land is covered; becoming habitat for animals, whether birds or insects; and stands that start to re-establish the sense of place or natural heritage for a human community. I see a lot of my ecological restoration work as rebuilding links between people and the botanical world. That's a link that's been terribly invisible in our urban world. That gives me great pleasure.

(Gorrell, 2007)

Viewing a Park Design for the Orange County Great Park

In 2006 the Orange County Great Park Corporation commissioned Steven Handel to design a grand 1400-acre public park on a closed marine corps airbase in Irvine, California. By 2009, 30 acres of the park had been open to the public. Handel shared with me during our interview a photograph and three artist renderings of his park design in progress.

The Present, El Toro Marine Air Base
Original El Toro marine airbase was an active military facility since World War II. Over 600 acres of runways and over 140 buildings were removed to create new public uses. (Great Park Design Studio, Irvine, California)

Artist Rendering #1: The Future, Orange County Great Park
The design for the new facility includes cultural, natural, and athletic activities. Over 1400 acres of the old airbase will become the new park. (Artist overlay on the photograph) (Great Park Design Studio, Irvine, California)

Artist Rendering #2: Orange County Great Park Natural Panorama
Situated in the middle of an urban area, the new park must satisfy public needs as well as ecological services for a sustainable future. The principles of ecology guide the design to introduce people to their natural heritage.
(Great Park Design Studio, Irvine, California)

Artist Rendering #3: Orange County Great Park Transportation System
Situated in the middle of Orange County, access will be by mass transit as well as car.
People will come for many reasons: 160 acres are for sports; 160 acres for botanical
gardens; large areas of natural habitat; and flexible fields for public events.
(Great Park Design Studio, Irvine, California)

Post Interview and Park Design Discussion

After students have read or simulated the interview and have
viewed the park renderings, open discussion by asking them for
reactions. The following questions may guide the discussion:

- *What did you learn about trees through the eyes of science
  that you did not know before?*
- *What did you learn about botanists or scientists that you
  did not know or appreciate before?*
- *What may have surprised you or provoked your
  thinking?*

Use this brief discussion as an opportunity to unearth student
attitudes about science vis-a-vis poetry and the arts. Science
teachers in particular may want to use this discussion to introduce,
further develop, or supplement a botany lesson on trees.

Comparing Ways of Seeing: The Visual Artist, the Naturalist, and the Scientist

To conclude Activity #3, ask students: "Is there common ground between the visual artist, the naturalist, and the scientist in the way they see, engage with, and respond to the subject of trees?" High school students readily draw parallels without much prompting. Lead them, through discussion, to make connections and discover the common ground. Be sure to note with students the following similarities. All three – the artist, naturalist, and scientist – are close observers, paying keen attention to detail, the unseen as much as the seen. In this sense, all three are highly sensitive to the ambiguity of seeing and the possibility of always seeing and knowing more. The highly surrealistic painting illustrates this ambiguity as much as Annie Dillard's highly surrealistic seeing in the *tree with the lights in it* passage. The scientist is equally captivated by the invisible, the root system, and the complexity of the stress factors that determine the ultimate survival of the tree. All three seem fully aware of seeing more than the obvious, visible realities. All three make metaphoric leaps, using metaphoric seeing. All three see the tree, or the natural world it represents, in human terms, personifying or personally engaging with the sight images. The visual artist looks at one thing, a tree, and sees another – hands, feet, bodies, and human forms. The scientist, while not so literal, describes trees as having personalities; he describes them with individual characteristics almost in human terms when he speaks of their life, death, and survival. The naturalist engages personally and spiritually with the sight of the tree (nature), reacting emotionally (she is a "pilgrim"). Finally, all three express passion, emotion, and aesthetic appreciation for their subject: the tree. Similarly, the response of all three to that engagement is not just intellectual or abstract; it's concrete, creating a work of art – a painting, an essay, or a park design. Their creations underscore one of the most important of all areas of common ground between artists and scientists: their use of creative thinking and the creative process to explore, discover, and invent.

PART FOUR: POETRY

SCIENCE POEM, "LEARNING THE TREES" BY HOWARD NEMEROV

Howard Nemerov has written a science poem aptly suited to serve both as a closure to Chapter 1, "Hide and Seek," and as an envoy to Chapter 4, "What is Science Poetry?" In "Learning the Trees," students see the subject, trees through the eyes of both science and poetry. Before reading the poem as closure, ask students to imagine how a science poet might see the subject, trees. Then read Nemerov's poem aloud followed by discussion of his theme: the value and need for both scientific and poetic ways of seeing and knowing that is the essence of the science poem: *You may succeed in learning many trees / And calling off their names as you go by / But their comprehensive silence stays the same.* For Nemerov, learning the trees indoors out of books is one way to know them; learning the trees through the delight of the words themselves is another; but learning the trees through experience and engagement outdoors remains the more complex and meaningful way to learn about the *language* and *knowledge* that is *trees*.

Learning the Trees

Before you can learn the trees, you have to learn
The language of the trees. That's done indoors,
Out of a book, which now you think of it
Is one of the transformations of a tree.

The words themselves are a delight to learn,
You might be in a foreign land of terms
Like samara, capsule, drupe, legume and pome,
Where bark is papery, plated, warty or smooth.

But best of all are the words that shape the leaves –
Orbicular, cordate, cleft and reniform –
And their venation – palmate and parallel –
And tips – acute, truncate, auriculate.

Sufficiently provided, you may now
Go forth to the forests and the shady streets
To see how the chaos of experience
Answers to catalogue and category.

Confusedly. The leaves of a single tree
May differ among themselves more than they do
From other species, so you have to find,
All blandly says the book, "an average leaf."

Example, the catalpa in the book
Sprays out its leaves in whorls of three
Around the stem; the one in front of you
But rarely does, or somewhat, or almost;

Maybe it's not catalpa? Dreadful doubt.
It may be weeks before you see an elm
Fanlike in form, a spruce that pyramids,
A sweetgum spiring up in steeple shape.

Still, *pedetemtim* as Lucretius says,
Little by little, you do start to learn;
And learn as well, maybe, what language does
And how it does it, cutting across the world

Not always at the joints, competing with
Experience while cooperating with
Experience, and keeping an obstinate
Intransigence, uncanny, of its own.

Think finally about the secret will
Pretending obedience to Nature, but
Invidiously distinguishing everywhere,
Dividing up the world to conquer it.

And think also how funny knowledge is:
You may succeed in learning many trees
And calling off their names as you go by,
But their comprehensive silence stays the same.

– Howard Nemerov (1977b: 486)

PART FIVE: STUDENT WRITTEN RESPONSE

Foundation Lesson One Prompts

Foundation Lesson One offers a wide range of writing opportunities from poetry, fictional narratives, reflective essays, personal essays, and naturalistic journal writing. The following are prompts to suggest to students after they have engaged with Tchelitchew's painting, Dillard's nature essay, and Handel's interview and park design.

Foundation Lesson One Writing Prompts

1. After observing *Hide-and-Seek*, write a final poem, fictional narrative, descriptive essay, or memory piece based on your reflections, inspiration from the painting, or freewriting notes.
2. After reading Dillard's essay excerpts, write your own journal entry or poem about a time you observed or received a "free gift" from the universe.
3. After reading Dillard's essay excerpts, write your own journal entry about a time when you engaged with the "hide and seek" of nature.
4. Take your own walk in a natural setting of choice. Like Dillard, be observant, take notes in your journal, and practice seeing with dual eyes. Write a scientific and poetic reflection of your observations.
5. After reading Handel's interview, write a scientific description of a tree based on your studies or based on a field observation. Observe the tree through the eyes of the botanist or scientist. Then try writing a poem about your observation of the tree. Express your scientific observation in any poetic form you wish.

Model Student Response: The Poem, "Rings," by Anne Schwartz

Anne Schwartz responds to the writing prompts with "Rings," a poem based on four separate memories of trees she observed, encountered, and experienced in her life. Remarkably, her poem seems to take its inspiration from several of the activities in Foundation Lesson One: the painting, the hide and seek metaphor, the interview, and the overwhelming feeling of awe reflected in Dillard's passages. With *upturned eyes of wonder*, Anne juxtaposes thought provoking images of trees that "rings" only as poetry can.

Rings

"As long as there is one tree left on the Earth, there is still hope"
I thought the man,
Sitting among his plants and shaded by trees
In a Mexico full of hunger and blossoming sugar cane
Was very brave to say that.

I remember putting my small hands, not more than six or seven years old
On the cross-section of a fallen tree
To feel the rings, marking decades and centuries
A clear yet cryptic account of history
Hidden beneath the surface

It seems a lot is colored in by trees
The skeleton of branches against the sunset
A waterfall of willow
The dappled sunlight of leaves and sun
The birth of buds in spring
The blush of leaves in fall

I held up a little girl, not more than six or seven years old
To see a cardinal's nest hidden in a tree
She pushed back the branches to see a nest
A small bird staring back at her

Beneath the surface
As the rings grew

Every tree is made of leaves and branches and roots
And rings.
Rings of cells or memories,
photosynthesis or upturned eyes of wonder,
Of every one tree.

—*Anne Schwartz*, student

Anne's Commentary

When I was thinking about writing this poem, I had a lot of different memories of trees floating around in my head. My real challenge was trying to pick and choose the most interesting stories to put in the poem, and to find a way to tie them together. Each image used in the poem is something that I actually saw. The quote at the beginning comes from a man in Mexico who spoke to a visiting youth group that I was a part of. I didn't have much of a plan when I started writing, but as I went on I decided I really liked the image of rings – a tangible sign of history, made up of both small and large actions.

WHY TEACH WAYS OF SEEING AND MULTIPLE PERSPECTIVES?

Let's consider for a moment one of the foremost creative minds in science, Jonas Salk, inventor of the Salk vaccine for polio. According to Mihalyi Csikszentmihalyi, "A central theme in Salk's life was the effort to see, and to make others see, that which is hidden. At the most obvious level, this has involved bringing to light the viral processes that caused polio" (Csikszentmihalyi, 1994: 284). But as Csikszentmihalyi points out, Salk went one step further. He created the Salk Institute, assembling men and women from very different disciplines, in the hopes of making the invisible

visible through conversations that would generate new ideas and discoveries. In Salk's own words:

> *I can see this done in the form of a collective mind, by a group of individuals whose minds are open and creative and are able to bring forth even more interesting and more complex results. All of this leads me to the idea that we can guide this process – this is in fact part of the process of evolution, and ideas that emerge in this way are equivalent to genes that emerge in the course of time.*
> (Csikszentmihalyi, 1996: 284)

If we as science and English teachers heed Salk's words, we can become the guides in this evolutionary process by teaching our students to see in multiple ways, from multiple perspectives within and beyond our individual disciplines. Transfer of knowledge is essential to our task, but knowledge alone will not foster the creativity and the mindset needed to advance the culture. Opening our students' eyes will. English teachers need to encourage students to look at the world of literature and language through the *eyes of science* as much as science teachers need to encourage their students to look at the world of science through the *eyes of literature and language*. This interdisciplinary seeing and teaching is at the core of this book and the core of 21st century pedagogy.

Notes

1. Go to the Museum of Modern Art website (www.MoMa.org) and search for Pavel Tchelitchew, *Hide and Seek*. The painting is available in poster form, *The Hide and Seek Poster* (Item # 37054; full color; 31 by 30 inches) at a nominal price. The poster may also be ordered by calling customer service at the museum at 1 800 793 3167.
2. Interested teachers may at this point introduce Wallace Stevens' poem, "Thirteen Ways of Looking at a Blackbird" as an extension activity demonstrating multiple ways of looking at anything. Teachers might also

want to point out that Stevens' poetic method is similar to the ancient Persian poetic form of the *ghazal*, popular today in the work of Rumi. The contemporary ghazal is characterized by long-lined couplets, usually unrhymed, presenting mystical thoughts (Padgett, 2000: 84–85).

2   What is Poetry?

Developing the Poetic Eye

Poetry, like science, is a way of knowing. The poem: an episte-mological artifact, a musical synthesis, a layered history of ideas. A thinking dream.

– John Allman
Curve Away from Stillness: Science Poems
(Allman, 1984: x)

Poetry is the art of creativity which is the core ability we want to train our students in science and technology.

– Lei Bao
Professor of Physics, Ohio State University
Interview (Gorrell, 2009)

OVERVIEW: FOUNDATION LESSON TWO

Poetry, like a rare species of bird, refuses to be categorized or defined – that is, defined simply. We can hear its song one minute, and then lose it the next, only to find we hear it again, in a heartbeat.

Ambiguous by nature, ever playful with words, poetry conceives, receives, deceives, and believes in sound, sense, and, above all else, meaning-making. A poem may suggest a game of hide and seek, but it should never be a trick. It should offer more truth, beauty, and pleasure than what was found before, but it does not always have to; as William Carlos Williams once said: *So much depends upon* how you see. A poem may be defined by its special use of language – literary – and its special way of seeing – metaphoric – and its special way of knowing – by allowing us to participate in experience rather than by telling us <u>about</u> that experience. And so, in attempting to "catch" the elusive bird of poetry through telling words of definition, I have tried a more poetic, or engaging, approach, allowing you to hear some hidden rhyme, discover for yourself a playful pun in time, and, I hope, engaging you to imaginatively participate in the process of discovering meaning. In this sense, every poem is a universe unto itself – poised, incandescent, ready to become more with the engagement of a good reader. What is a good reader? A reader who sees *through the eyes of poetry*.

And that's the aim of Foundation Lesson Two – to make students more aware, more attuned, and more inspired seekers and finders of poetry in general, and science poetry in particular. To this end, they will have to move their vision, voices, and mindsets from the simple to the complex – from the literal, practical, informational, and scientific uses of language to the more figurative, experiential, and literary uses of language. This critical foundation is necessary if students are to appreciate the complexity resulting from the fusion of science and poetry in the form of the science poem. In this regard, the ultimate aims of Foundation Lesson Two are to:

- *Introduce students to the universe of poetry;*
- *Raise their awareness of their own poetic literacy;*
- *Develop students' poetic eyes;*
- *Define what poetry is; and*
- *Engage students in writing their own science found poems.*

Foundation Lesson Two consists of four activities divided into three parts, Part One: *Getting Started*; Part Two: *Let Found Poetry Help Your Students Find Poetry*; and Part Three, Responding to Non-Literary Texts. Part One offers two activities to begin teaching any science poetry unit plan: the first, a self-identification activity to raise personal awareness regarding poetry and science, and the second, a poetry awareness poll to explore students' poetic literacy and knowledge. Part Two offers a found poetry reading activity to develop a poetic or criteria for defining *what is poetry*, and Part Three offers a found science poem writing activity based upon scientific and non-literary texts and textbooks. In sum, Foundation Lesson Two consists of three parts, along with a final reflection, as shown in the following box.

Foundation Lesson Two at a Glance

Part One: Getting Started
Activity #1: Student Self-Identifications
Activity #2: Poetry Awareness Poll

Part Two: Let Found Poetry Help Your Students Find Poetry
Activity #3: What is Poetry? A Lesson in Definition

Part Three: Responding to Non-Literary Texts and Science Textbooks
Activity #4: Writing a Found Science Poem
Model Student Response: A Found Science Poem, "The Activities of a Bricklayer," by Colin Hostetter

The Value of Teaching Found Poetry: Developing the Poetic Eye

---

Students begin by identifying how they view themselves in terms of the disciplines of science and English; they write on index cards: *scientist, poet*, or *renaissance student*. These self-identifications will become useful for self-evaluation and teacher assessment of students' changing attitudes and growth. They will also serve as an invaluable instrument for grouping students in collaborative science poetry writing. Next students evaluate their poetic literacy by taking a poetry awareness poll. This activity serves as an ideal introduction to some of the most noted scientists and poets, both past and present, writing science poetry. After evaluating their literacy, students engage with a found poem, "Parents," by Julius Lester and develop criteria for defining poetry. Last, they read a model found science poem written by a science student based on his chemistry textbook. Informed and inspired, students respond in kind by searching through their own science textbooks as well as journal articles to find and write their own science found poems.

Materials Needed

Poetry Awareness Poll (provided)
Found Poem: "Parents" by Julius Lester (provided)
News Article: *New York Times,* "Coed Kills Herself To Spare Pet Dog Doomed by Father" (provided)

SUGGESTIONS FOR USING THIS LESSON

The activities in Foundation Lesson Two are relevant to the disciplines of both science and English. The skill of close reading, as critical in science class as it is in English class for the development of literacy, remains the primary skill developed in students' encounter with found poetry. Science teachers will find Foundation Lesson Two a creative way to engage science students in the reading of scientific texts. Similarly, English teachers will find Foundation Lesson Two a creative way to engage students in the reading of non-literary texts.

Both my science partner and I encourage you to *let found poetry help your students find science poetry.* Instruct your students to bring their science textbooks to class and have them work individually or collaboratively to discover found poetry material in their texts. For more able students, the found poetry writing prompts may be assigned as homework; for the less able, or for students needing guided writing, allow time to begin writing the found poems in class. Students enjoy playing "hide and seek" with these non-literary texts, and they produce highly instructive poems.

Suggested Time Allocations

Time allocations for each activity will vary depending upon the level of students, length of follow-up discussion, and time allotted in class for found poetry writing. Recommended guidelines:

Activity #1 (10 minutes)
Activity #2 (30 minutes)
Activity #3 (40 minutes)
Activity #4 (30 minutes)

PART ONE: GETTING STARTED

ACTIVITY #1: STUDENT SELF-IDENTIFICATIONS

Begin your science poetry classes by asking students to self-identify on an index card – *scientist*, *poet*, or *renaissance* student (both scientist and poet) – according to how they view themselves in terms of the disciplines of science and English. These self-identifications will become useful for self-evaluations and assessment of students' changing attitudes and growth. High school students often have established preferences for either the sciences or the arts. Grading systems reinforce such preferences, determining students' assessments of their "strong" subjects versus "weaker" ones based more on grades than on inherent interests. Preferably, there will be a balance of science-minded, poetry-minded, and renaissance students in your class. If not, you may need to adjust pace, expectations, and lessons according to individual class attitudes, abilities, and knowledge.

Student Self-Identification Questions

1. Do you feel most comfortable in liberal arts – English, history, languages, art, music, or drama? List courses completed in those subjects.

2. Do you feel most comfortable in the sciences – earth science, biology, chemistry, or physics? List courses completed in those subjects.
3. Do you perform better in one (arts or sciences) discipline than in another? Get better grades?
4. Do you feel equally comfortable and proficient in both the arts and the sciences, with equal success and grades?

If you identify more fully with the liberal arts, put *poet* on the top of your index card. If you identify more fully with the sciences, put *scientist* on the top of your index card. If you identify equally with both the liberal arts and the sciences, put *renaissance student* on the top of your index card. On the back of the card, write a paragraph explaining your self-identification and your attitudes towards poetry and the sciences.

Discussing Self-Identifications

By show of hands, ask students to identify themselves as *poets*, *scientists*, or *renaissance students*. Call on volunteers to share their identifications, attitudes, and experiences. Let the class assess the implications of their particular peer group breakdown.

- Are there more scientists, poets, or renaissance students in the class?
- Do they seem to value one discipline more than another?
- Does society value one discipline more than another?

Lead a discussion or dialogue challenging stereotypes about scientists and poets that might arise from the self-identification process.

Teacher Use of Self-Identifications

Self-identifications provide useful information for planning, instruction, and assessment. You can ask students to put these identifications on the top of their science poems so that you can better react to and assess their science poetry writing and progress. At the end of the unit, you can also use these identifications to evaluate a students' attitudinal change or transformation. You also may want to teach science poetry writing by pairing partners or small group collaborations. Knowing which students are poetry-friendly or experienced poets, or which students are science-minded or proficient in some field of scientific knowledge will facilitate the formation of poetry writing partners and small group collaborations for sharing and evaluating poems.

Self-identifications may also open your eyes to other sides of a student you may or may not know or appreciate. Too often we as English or science teachers tend to see our students exclusively in terms of our own subjects and disciplines. Science poetry writing and teaching will allow you to more fully see, appreciate, and teach to the whole student.

ACTIVITY #2: POETRY AWARENESS POLL[1]

For most high school students, interdisciplinary, cross-curricular learning and teaching will be a new experience. Such students will need rationales for why they are learning poetry in science class and science in English class. However the teaching of science poetry supports, supplements, or enriches your current English or science curriculum, students will benefit from an exploration of their poetic literacy. My experience has been that many high school students, regardless of ability level, are significantly lacking in knowledge when it comes to familiarity with poetry in general and science poetry in particular. In addition, few truly understand the nature of poetic language, and how it may be distinguished from other forms of language.

The aim of Activity #2 is to raise students' awareness of their poetic literacy; that is, their knowledge about poetry, their ability to read it, to speak about it, to write about it, and to share it with others. Such literacy is influenced by students' experiences with poetry in their school, home, and cultural life. By the time they reach high school, students have typically established clear attitudes as well as knowledge and possible misconceptions regarding poetry. Activity #2 exposes ignorance and dispels misconceptions about the cultural divide, thereby paving the way for the writing of science poetry.

Taking the Poetry Awareness Poll

Distribute or project the following poll to your students and have them complete the answers in writing on a separate piece of paper. If you prefer, you may dictate the questions orally, pausing after each one for written responses.

Poetry Awareness Poll

1. Name five deceased 20th century or current American or world poets.
2. Name five living 20th century or current American or world poets.
3. Name five scientists you know who write poetry.
4. Name five poets you know who write science poems.
5. Recall one poem you especially like. Identify its title. Can you remember a line from the poem? If so, write that line.
6. Can you recall a science poem you have read? Identify its title. Can you remember a line from the poem? If so, write that line.

7. Have you ever written a poem in school? What was it about? How did you feel about the process?

8. Have you ever written a poem for yourself (not assigned in school)? What was it about? How did you feel about the process?

9. Have you ever shared a poem with another person – showed them a poem you liked and discussed it together? Or have you ever given a poem to someone as a present (store-bought cards excluded)? If so, explain.

10. Have you ever heard a poet read poetry in a live performance? Explain.

11. If you wanted to hear a poet read poetry in a live performance, would you know where to go?

12. Do you have a favorite poet, excluding rock musicians? Name the poet.

13. Do you have a favorite poet/musician? Name the poet.

14. How do you feel about poetry? How do you feel about science poetry?

15. What do you think poetry is? Comment on your definition.

16. What do you think science poetry is? Comment on your definition.

Discussing the Poetry Awareness Poll Results

When students are finished taking the poll, discuss, in numerical order, the answers to each question. Students generally enjoy hearing the responses of other students. A lively and informative interchange usually ensues. Use student responses to questions #1–4 to inform and enlighten students regarding noted scientists writing poetry as well as noted poets writing science poems. Familiarize students with a few noted poets, past and present, writing poems informed and inspired by science: Roman poet, Lucretius' epic poem, *On the Nature of the Universe*; Dante's *Divine Comedy* influenced by the Ptolemaic theory of the universe;

T.S. Eliot's *The Waste Land*, influenced by theories of relativity; and Robert Frost's poems inspired by advances in 20th century physics. Similarly, familiarize students with a few noted scientists, past and present, writing science poetry: Loren Eiseley, naturalist, anthropologist, paleontologist: *Notes of an Alchemist*; Roald Hoffmann, Nobel-prize winning chemist: *Soliton*; and Miroslav Holub, biologist, immunologist: *The Rampage*.

Then elicit responses from questions #5–11. Encourage students to share their experiences, attitudes, and knowledge of poetry as well as their favorite poets and poet musicians. Once again, use the opportunity to clarify understanding and disabuse students of possible misconceptions about poetry. Last, use responses to questions #15 and 16 to open the topic, *what is poetry* and *what is science poetry*. After the airing of views, tell students that Activity #3 will help them define *what is poetry*, and ultimately, *what is science poetry*.

Evaluating Students' Poetic Literacy

The poetry awareness poll invariably uncovers the lack of knowledge most high school students have regarding poetry. At this juncture in the lesson, evaluate the results of the poetry awareness poll for your class and your students. You may do this formally or informally. In my English classes, the lack of poetic literacy is so evident and overwhelming that no formal, numerical analysis is necessary to make the point. Even advanced students are hard-pressed to name poets other than the canon English language poets taught in most American high schools: Edgar Allen Poe, Robert Frost, Langston Hughes, and, of course, William Shakespeare. Very few students can recite poetic lines or recall the names of favorite poets. Most of the poems they recall are those from early childhood and elementary school. Students are generally unaware whether a poet is alive and still writing or deceased. In the United States, the favorite poets for students seem to be Dr. Seuss and Shel Silverstein, both widely popular with children and publishers of poetry. Most students have a favorite poet/musician, although many have not considered the lyrics of such songwriters as poetry. With the advent and popularity of spoken word poetry and hip hop, some students are readily able to "rap" lines from their favorite poet/musician. Yet few are able to define poetry with any confidence or rigor.

Most importantly, the large majority of students are unfamiliar with scientists writing poetry or poets writing science poems. In all of my science poetry teaching experience, none of my English students or my science partner's science students could recall reading any science poems. With the exception of William Carlos Williams, a pediatrician from Paterson, New Jersey, and noted modernist poet who frequently taught in advanced English classes in the United States, students can name no science poets. They are universally surprised by the existence of science poetry and intrigued by the science-poetry connection. Their curiosity to learn about something so totally new and foreign establishes the positive attitude and atmosphere of wonder essential for further inquiry.

PART TWO: LET FOUND POETRY HELP YOUR STUDENTS FIND POETRY[2]

ACTIVITY #3: WHAT IS POETRY? A LESSON IN DEFINITION

What is Found Poetry?

Found poetry results when a poet "finds" hidden, poetic potential or material in a nonliterary source, such as newspapers, magazines, manuals, and textbooks, and lifts that material out of its context, re-lines the text, and then adds a title to create something new – a *found* poem. Although it may at first glance appear to be identical to the original material, in actuality, making the text into the form of a poem creates new meanings. In the 1960s, found poetry came to public attention in the United States with the publication of two anthologies, *Pioneers of Modern Poetry* (Peters and Hitchcock, 1967) and *Losers and Weepers: An Anthology of Found Poems* (Hitchcock, 1969). Considered by many at the time a sub-genre of poetry, found poetry "found" its place in the experimental work of some noted poets who considered found material useful for the creation of a poem. (An example is Charles Reznikoff's *Testimony* based on courtroom trials (Reznikoff, 1965).

In sum, if poetry is a universe, then found poetry exists at the edge of that universe. And that is exactly why found poetry is so instructive: if students can see the poetry in found poetry, then they will certainly be able to see the poetry in the universe of science poetry. In this sense, found poetry offers a highly instructive tool for developing students' poetic eyes and defining more precisely, *what is poetry.* [3]

Reading the Found Poem, "Parents," by Julius Lester

Begin by distributing to students, without comment, the poem "Parents" by the poet, Julius Lester. Read the poem aloud to students, or, if you prefer, have students read the poem silently to themselves.

Parents

New York Times, February 7, 1968

Linda failed to return home from a dance Friday night.
On Saturday
she admitted she had spent the night
with an Air Force Lieutenant.

The Aults decided on a punishment
that would "wake Linda up."
They ordered her

to shoot the dog
she had owned about two years.

On Sunday,
The Aults and
Linda
took the dog into the desert
near their home.
They
had the girl
dig a shallow grave.
Then
Mrs. Ault
grasped the dog between her hands and
Mr. Ault
gave
his daughter
a .22 caliber pistol
and told her
to shoot the dog.

Instead,
the girl
put the pistol
to her right temple
and shot herself.

The police said
there were no charges
that could be filed
against the parents
except possibly
cruelty
to animals.

– Julius Lester (1969: 3–4)

The reading of the poem, "Parents," elicits immediate, unsolicited responses. Most students are genuinely shocked, some even outraged: "How could the parents do such a thing?" Allow your students to air their emotional reactions and opinions. In my experience teaching "Parents," lively debates ensue as some students react with disbelief while others conjecture, "It could have happened." After encouraging the airing of views, ask students: "Is there a way to tell if this event actually happened?" Often a perceptive student will point to the citation at the beginning of the poem. Some students may suggest that the poem was published in the *New York Times*. Raise the question: "How often are poems published in newspapers?" At this point of heightened curiosity, announce that you have a copy of the actual news article.

Reading the News Article

Distribute the news article from the *New York Times,* February 6, 1968.

Then, for comparison, instruct students to place the news article next to the poem, "Parents," on their desks. Read the news article aloud, asking students to follow along. When you get to the parents' account in the article, tell students to look back at the poem as you continue to read.

Coed Kills Herself
To Spare Pet Dog
Doomed by Father

Phoenix, Ariz. Feb. 6 (AP) – Linda Marie Ault killed herself, policemen said today, rather than make her dog Beauty pay for her night with a married man.

"I killed her. I killed her. Its just like I killed her myself," a detective quoted her grief-stricken father as saying.

"I handed her the gun. I didn't think she would do anything like that."

The 21-year old Arizona State University coed died in a hospital yesterday of a gunshot wound in the head.

The police quoted her parents, Mr. and Mrs. Joseph Ault, as giving this account:

Linda failed to return home from a dance in Tempe Friday night. On Saturday she admitted she had spent the night with an Air Force lieutenant.

The Aults decided on a punishment that would "wake Linda up." They ordered her to shoot the dog she had owned about two years.

On Sunday, the Aults and Linda took the dog into the desert near their home. They had the girl dig a shallow grave. Then Mrs. Ault grasped the dog between her hands, and Mr. Ault gave his daughter a .22 caliber pistol and told her to shoot the dog.

Instead, the girl put the pistol to her right temple and shot herself.

The police said there were no charges that could be filed against the parents except possibly cruelty to animals.

After reading the news article, once again, spontaneous responses typically abound. Encourage students to air and share their reactions. My English class students quickly observe that the poem is identical to the parents' account. Responses include: "Hey, its exactly the same!" "The poet copied the news article." "Isn't this plagiarism?" "This can't be a poem. It's just a story."

Comparing and Contrasting the Poem and the News Article

Now lead a discussion comparing and contrasting the poem with the news article. Ask your students:

- *What did you learn from the news article that you didn't know before?*
- *What facts did Lester leave out of the news article?*
- *Did the poet's omissions change your feelings or opinions? Why do you think he left them out?*

Students will identify four essential new facts: (1) The Air Force lieutenant was married; (2) The parents were "grief stricken" and remorseful; (3) Linda was 21 years old; and (4) The dog's name was Beauty. Most of my English students are surprised Linda was twenty-one. In the poem, they picture her much younger. Many admit they some sympathy for Linda when they discover in the news article that she is an adult. They question her maturity and mental stability, wondering how a twenty-one year old could submit to the tyranny of such parents.

Lead a discussion comparing and contrasting the aim of a reporter with the aim of a poet. Ask students: "What is the aim of a news reporter? What is the aim of a poet?" High school students are taught that a reporter's task is to be objective in reporting the news, to show both sides and report the facts, whereas a poet's task is quite different, to be subjective in communicating the poet's personal feelings, experience, and vision. Emphasize to your students that news reporters and poets use language differently: the former to communicate *information*, the latter to communicate *experience*.

Explicating the Poem "Parents"

Now turn to a careful explication of how the poem communicates in contrast to the news article. Focus attention on the title. Ask students to recall how they first engaged with the poem when they did not know anything about its contents. As you explicate the poem, point out to students how the title engages; all they know is that the poet is saying something about "parents," and they are free to imagine their own parents and their own feelings about parents in general. Then show students how they next read what Linda did and what she admitted. Continue explicating the poem, emphasizing the words that Lester placed on lines by themselves. Show students how the accusatory cadence builds suspense culminating in the climatic word, *Instead*. When they get to this turning point in the poem, ask them: "Instead, what?" " What did you think at this moment in the poem?"

Most of my students admit they thought that Linda would or should have shot her parents. They are surprised that others in the class were led to the same private thought. I stress how the poem enabled them to "be in Linda's shoes," to experience the moment with all its choices and inexplicable emotions. I suggest that the poem, unlike the news article, engaged them to participate imaginatively in the event. In doing so, Lester skillfully leads them to place blame on the parents.

Now, call your students' attention to the end of the poem, asking them to interpret the meaning of the lines, *there were no charges / that could be filed / against the parents / except possibly / cruelty to animals*. Ask them: What kind of cruelty exists? Who are the animals? My English students quickly recognize the irony. Multiple meanings resonate for them. Ask your students for a literal or primary meaning first; they will undoubtedly identify *animals* as referring to the actual dog, Beauty. Then lead your students in a discussion to discover figurative and symbolic meanings: Linda is treated as an animal; the parents in their cruelty behave as animals; both the parents and society in its lesser charges are the real "animals." Sometimes students even note the symbolic significance of the dog's name. Yes, "Beauty" was killed on that fateful day.

Finally, instruct students to look back at the news article to consider how it communicates in contrast to the poem. Ask: "Was the news article as evocative, empathetic, and engaging for you as the poem?" Encourage a lively debate. Focus attention on the headline and ask students to compare this to the title of the poem. Students will easily see how the headline tells all, negating the suspense created in the poem. Show them how they know from the outset that Linda killed herself. Ask them: "How many of you finish reading a news article?" As students readily acknowledge, most readers want their information upfront. Together, note the journalistic function of the five W's (who, what, where, when, why) in the opening paragraph. For most students the poem creates far greater emotion and engagement.

Defining a Poetic: Capturing that Rare Bird for Your Students

Students are now prepared to define *what is poetry*, developing a poetic criteria that will distinguish poetic language from informational and practical language. Tell students that many authorities consider found poetry to be a low form of poetry, a sub-poetry, since its words are not original and its text is primarily expository, informational prose. Tell students to think back to their first reading of the poem. Ask: "Did the poem seem un-poetic to you, and if so, why?" Students usually acknowledge that the poem, "Parents," lacks what they have previously assumed poetry must incorporate: rhyme, meter, stanza form, sound devices or musicality, and figurative language. They note the poem's narrative impulse and that it sounds like a story or report. Suggest to students that they test "Parents" against a poetic offered by David Swanger in *The*

Poem as Process (Swanger, 1974: 57–59). Together, test Lester's found poem against the following criteria:

- *Is the poem evocative? Does it evoke emotion in you?*
- *Is the poem empathetic? Does it engage you to imaginatively participate?*
- *Is the poem experiential? Does it communicate as its primary function experience, real or imagined?*
- *Is the language excited? Fresh and original?*
- *Is the language precise? Is it difficult to translate into other languages?*
- *Is the language concise? No unnecessary words?*
- *Is there meaning making? Does it move from literal meaning to something more – figurative, metaphoric, or symbolic meaning?*

My English students generally agree that "Parents" is evocative and empathetic for them – it shocked them and made them feel compassion for Linda. They also see how the poem involves the subject's real experience, the poet's emotional experience, and their own personal engagement. They note that the poem is concise because the poet generally does not add words to a found poem, and therefore each word in the poem is essential. Most importantly, they confirm that there is meaning-making in the poem, especially at the end. Although students recognize poetic elements in "Parents," they also see non-poetic elements as well: the lack of excited language ("it's just newspaper reportage") and the ease of translation – most words denote a single meaning. The large majority of my students conclude that "Parents" is a poem, but not a highly poetic one. I confirm their conclusion, suggesting they view poetry and poetic language on a continuum, from somewhat poetic to highly poetic. Understanding the concept of the continuum will help students define and appreciate more readily the science poetry to come.

What is Poetry? Applying the Poetry Litmus Test

Although poetry defies simple definition, complex and poetic definitions abound. In fact, there is probably not a poet past or present who has not written a poem on the subject of poetry. As teachers of poetry, it is important to disabuse students of certain misconceptions and confusions about poetry and poetic language. Here I rely on the standard bearer, Laurence Perrine, for guidelines from *Sound and Sense: An Introduction to Poetry* (Perrine, 1982: 8–10). I read from Perrine, and then I add my own reflections and commentary:

- *Between poetry and other forms of imaginative literature there is no sharp distinction* (Perrine, 1982: 9). You cannot define a poem by its form alone. The prose of Annie Dillard for example, is far more poetic than the cliché rhyme, "Roses are red / violets are blue." Serious poetry may be written in prose form; such poems are called "prose" poems.
- *Poetry is a multidimensional language. Poetry adds to the intellectual dimension, a sensuous dimension, an emotional dimension, and an imaginative dimension* (Perrine, 1982: 10).

I often suggest to my students that the way poetry engages us may be closer to painting or music than to other forms of literature. I want students to think of poetry as a dynamic art form, one they can go back to time and time again for new meanings and insights. I ask them: "How many times do you listen to a favorite piece of music? Is your response always the same?" I encourage them to revisit poems as they revisit their favorite works of art.

Given the understanding that poetry is a form of literary language, and that there is no sharp distinction between poetry and other forms of literature, how are students going to be able to discern what is a poem? Hopefully, the found poetry exercise will lead the way, but for the sake of simplicity, I teach students to apply the What-is-Poetry Litmus Test.

What-is-Poetry Litmus Test
1. Does the poem have a literal base or primary meaning?
2. Does the poem move from its literal base or primary meaning to meaning something more?
3. Is there meaning making in the poem; that is, does the poem move from the literal to the figurative, metaphoric, or symbolic?

Answer: If the language is purely literal, it is not a poem.

PART THREE: RESPONDING TO NON-LITERARY TEXTS AND SCIENCE TEXTBOOKS

ACTIVITY #4: WRITING A FOUND SCIENCE POEM

Students are now prepared to write their own found science poems. Before distributing the instructions, ask students to consider the paradoxical nature of the discovery process itself. Ask students: "How many of you have had trouble finding something only to suddenly or finally find it when you stop looking for it?" My students usually smile and nod in recognition to this question. Taking the paradox you-won't-find-it-if-you-are-looking-for-it into consideration, distribute the long-range assignment, giving students an extended amount of time to complete the task. Emphasize to them that their purpose is to forever keep their new poetic eyes open.

Long Range Assignment: Writing a Found Science Poem

Search newspapers (science section of the *New York Times*), scientific magazines and journals (*Nature, National Geographic, or Scientific American*), science textbooks, science manuals, and any non-literary texts for hidden poetic potential. Lift and isolate at least three consecutive lines or more from the text and arrange the lines to expose new meanings. Keep the words in the same order. Do not add words to change the original material. You may add a title, space breaks, or line breaks. Search for ironies, puns, and incongruities and bring them "to light." After you have written your poem, be sure to note the original source either at the beginning or end of your poem. This citation indicates that it is a found poem, not original material. Have fun finding science poetry in all the "wrong" places!

Although the objective of Activity #4 centers primarily on process (practice using the poetic eye) rather than product (producing a truly original poem), you may be pleasantly surprised, as I have been, by some of your students' enlightened textbook discoveries. If at all possible, students should get started with their search in the classroom setting. Distribute a variety of scientific texts and instruct students to search for found science poems. For more able students, this step can be done as a long range assignment. For students needing guided writing, allow time in class to begin finding and writing a science found poem. Consider using a collaborative writing strategy. Students generally enjoy discovering found poems with partners or in small groups. On the other hand, the long-range assignment affords students the opportunity to experience the surprise of the unexpected found science poem, as Colin Hostetter discovered while reading his chemistry textbook.

Model Student Response

A Found Science Poem

Colin Hostetter, student, explains his found science poem discovery this way:

I happened to have a chemistry test on Thermodynamics the same day that the science poetry writing assignment was due in A.P English Language and Composition class. While studying for my chemistry test, I came upon these couple of sentences, and they seemed rather poetic, so I thought I'd turn them into a found science poem.

The Activities of a Bricklayer
from *General Chemistry: Principles and Structure*
(Brady, 1990: 471)

The second law of thermodynamics
deals with the criteria
for spontaneity,
and it applies to changes of all kinds.

One statement
of the second law
is that
in any spontaneous change,
there is
always
an increase
in the entropy of the universe.
This has very profound meaning
not only in chemistry
but also
in the way our world works.

Whenever we see something happening,
we know
that the
entropy
of the world
is
increasing.

Even if some change has been accompanied
by a lowering of the entropy,
such as the creation
of a brick wall
from a pile of bricks,
we can be sure
that something else has occurred
that has produced an even larger entropy increase,
such as
the activities
of
a bricklayer.

                                    – *Colin Hostetter*, student

Colin's science found poem is a remarkable result inspired by his reading of the model found poem, "Parents." Colin follows structural and rhetorical clues demonstrated by Julius Lester:

long lines for the rush of ideas, single words to slow the pace of the poem allowing for engagement and imaginative thinking, all leading to a similarly climatic and thought provoking ending, *the activities of the bricklayer*. Placing *we know* on a line by itself raises a sense of wonder: What do we really know? And paradox: *in any spontaneous change / there is / always / an increase / in the entropy of the universe*. Colin's poem moves from the abstract enormity of the universe with its *second law*, and *profound meaning*, to the singular, very concrete (no pun intended!), human image of a *bricklayer* who somehow produces an *even larger entropy increase*. For me irony rings. I am left in awe, wondering how a bricklayer could have such a profound effect.

However, what impresses me most about Colin's poem has nothing to do with his poetic prowess and skill, and much more to do with how the process of writing a science found poem frees Colin to express his personal opinions and feelings. Once again, in Colin's words:

Colin's Commentary

In context, the lines [of my found poem] seem somewhat clinical and are obviously just a convenient explanation of the concept of entropy. But taken alone and transcribed into poetic form, they become more of a pessimistic statement about the way our world works. This suggests that everything falls apart, regardless of whatever great or small efforts we as humans make to keep it together; our efforts to slow entropy only speed it up. The second law of thermodynamics really is one of the most depressing things I've ever read.

As a teacher, I wonder if the chemistry test Colin took that day revealed in any way the depth of his understanding as well as the passion of his emotions. Clearly, the process of writing a science found poem enables students not only to express their knowledge of science, but their passion, feelings, and opinions as well. In this sense, it encourages a deeper engagement with the subject matter of science.

THE VALUE OF TEACHING FOUND POETRY: DEVELOPING THE POETIC EYE

Once students understand what found poetry is, once they have developed their poetic eyes, found poetry writing becomes a natural response to the reading of any textbook material. And that kind of awareness – the ability to see or read through multiple lenses – is precisely the value of found poetry and its utility as a teaching tool. Whether in science or English class, whenever you assign textbook reading, the opportunity for students, seeing through the eyes of poetry, to "find" poetry in other texts presents itself without altering your required reading curriculum. As a consequence, the process of writing a found poem will enhance your curriculum by facilitating close reading, reading comprehension, study skills, and creativity. Consider for a moment how the processes of (1) reading more slowly through multiple eyes; (2) lifting a selected text (a research and note taking process); (3) typing up the text to consider the meaning of the language (a study skill); and then, eventually, (4) writing a science-based poem (a writing skill) may support and facilitate the understanding of your science or English curriculum. Clearly, found poetry is a creative, practical, and instructive tool to help your students find not only poetry, but the universe of science poetry as well.

Notes

1. This poetry awareness poll was originally developed for English class instruction by the author in "Poetry to Engage the Person" (Gorrell, 1990: 36–37), a unit lesson plan for teachers of English. The original poetry awareness poll has been adapted for this book to include science poetry for science poetry teaching.

2. This introductory poetry lesson was originally developed for English class instruction by the author in "Let Found Poetry Help Your Students Find Poetry" (Gorrell, 1989: 30–34). For this book, the lesson has been adapted for inclusion of science poetry instruction.

3. Several noted poets and poetry writing teachers in the last several decades have adopted the strategy of found poetry as a useful tool to introduce poetry writing to high school students. For example, see poets Stephen Dunning and William Stafford's opening chapter, "Found and Headline Poems," in *Getting the Knack: 20 Poetry Writing Exercises* (Dunning and Stafford, 1992).

3 What is Science?

Developing the Scientific Eye

Science is a state of mind. It is a way of viewing the world, of facing reality square on but taking nothing on its face. It is about attacking a problem with the most manicured claws and tearing it down into sensible, edible pieces.

– Natalie Angier
The Canon: A Whirligig Tour of the Beautiful Basics of Science
(Angier, 2007: 19)

The ideal scientist thinks like a poet, and works like a bookkeeper, and I suppose that if gifted with a full quiver, he also writes like a journalist.

– Edward O. Wilson
Consilience: The Unity of Knowledge
(Wilson, 1998: 57)

OVERVIEW: FOUNDATION LESSON THREE

To answer the question, *What is science?*, Chapter 3 begins with Part One, a series of introductory reflections – etymological, scientific, personal, historical, and pedagogical – that bear on the understanding and teaching of science and the science–poetry connection. These reflections offer for the science and English teacher the scientific background and pedagogy necessary for more effective teaching of science poetry and the student activities that follow in Part Two.

Keeping these introductory reflections in mind, the aim of Foundation Lesson Three is to prepare students to enter the universe of science poetry. In order to do so, students must find new eyes; that is, not only to see the world through the eyes of poetry, but to see the world, <u>simultaneously</u>, *through the eyes of science* as well. This dual seeing is essential if students are to appreciate the fusion of science and poetry in the form of the science poem. In this regard, the ultimate aim of Foundation Lesson Three is to:

- *Introduce students to the universe of science;*
- *Raise their awareness of their own scientific literacy;*
- *Explore their attitudes toward science;*
- *Develop their scientific eyes; and*
- *Define what science is.*

To this end, Part Two offers three student activities. Activity #1, a science awareness poll, raises students' awareness and helps evaluate students' scientific literacy. This activity parallels the poetry awareness poll in Chapter 2. Activity #2, freewriting science memories, further explores student attitudes and experiences with science in and out of the classroom setting. Activity #3, Robert Graves' poem, "In Broken Images," engages students to enter, poetically speaking, a discussion between two voices regarding contrasting views of science and the scientific method.

Foundation Lesson Three at a Glance

<u>Part One</u>: **A Series of Reflections**

<u>Part Two</u>: **Student Activities to Develop the Scientific Eye**
Activity #1 Science Awareness Poll: Evaluating Scientific Literacy
Activity #2 Teacher and Student Science Memories: Freewriting
Activity #3 Entering the Scientific Method: "In Broken Images"

Materials Needed

Science Awareness Poll (provided)
Poem "In Broken Images" by Robert Graves (provided)
Poem "When I Heard the Learn'd Astronomer" by Walt Whitman
(available online)

SUGGESTIONS FOR USING THIS LESSON

Part One, the introductory reflections, provides both science and English teachers with the scientific background and pedagogy necessary for effective teaching of the activities in Part Two as well as the science poetry writing lessons to follow in subsequent chapters. My science partner and I encourage both science and English teachers to consider creative uses of these reflections, connecting them to aspects of their required science and English curricula. Science teachers in particular will find the opening reflections on the history of science and the scientific method useful to inform students and to dispel misconceptions about science.

Part Two offers three foundation activities, all basic and introductory in nature, that are highly accessible, engaging, and appropriate for science and English students of all levels and abilities. My science partner and I have successfully used these activities and writing prompts with our Science Academy English students, as well as with the more advanced Research Science and AP English Language and Composition students. Science teachers will find Activity #1, the science awareness poll, a valuable tool for assessing students' scientific literacy. Both science and English teachers will find it informative to have students compare and contrast the results of the science awareness poll in this chapter with the poetry awareness poll in Chapter 2. Such comparisons will most likely raise students' awareness of the necessity to further their literacy in both disciplines.

Both science and English teachers should consider Activity #2, freewriting science memories, as an ideal discussion starter for any science poetry unit or science course. This activity encourages students to explore in writing their attitudes and experiences concerning learning science in and out of the classroom. Sharing such experiences affords them the rare opportunity to exchange views, clarify misconceptions, and dispel myths regarding science. Most importantly, this activity also encourages teachers, particularly science teachers, to share their memories. Students will benefit immeasurably when their science teachers give context to the origins of their scientific passions. Both science and English teachers will find "In Broken Images" a thought provoking and effective way to engage discussion regarding contrasting views of the scientific method, and how both scientists and poets wrestle with the unknown and ambiguity. In addition, Graves' poem serves as an ideal segue to Chapter 4, "What is Science Poetry?"

Suggested Time Allocations

Time allocations for each activity will vary depending upon the level of students and length of follow-up discussion. Recommended guidelines:

<u>Part Two</u>: Foundation Lesson Three
      Activity #1 (25 minutes)
      Activity #2 (20 minutes)
      Activity #3 (15 minutes)

PART ONE: A SERIES OF REFLECTIONS

ETYMOLOGICAL REFLECTIONS

This book adopts a broad view of science, one defined by Kurt Brown in *Verse and Universe* as "the pure study of the universe and all it contains for the sake of knowledge and understanding alone, keeping in mind the Latin root of the word scire, to know" (Brown, 1998: xiii). Brown includes in his definition the physical sciences – physics, astronomy, chemistry, and geology – and the life sciences, which include biology, botany, zoology, and physiology, among others (Brown, 1998: xiii). John Burnside adds to this definition a further etymological distinction: "The Latin word scientia suggests …knowledge, yes, but the heuristic, questing, sometimes intuitive knowledge by which we come to an understanding of – and with – the world, and of our place in it" (Burnside, 2006: 94). Edward O. Wilson, I believe, would agree. He explains: "Original discovery is everything. Scientists as a rule do not discover in order to know but rather, as the philosopher Alfred North Whitehead observed, they know in order to discover" (Wilson, 1998: 56).

Taken together, these etymological views embrace a science that is at once knowing in the "pure" objective sense and knowing in the questing and intuitive sense; the former a more scientific type of knowing while the latter a more poetic type of knowing. Such consilient views of science find a comfortable place in science poetry that fuses, by this book's working definition, two ways of knowing: *knowing about things* (using quantitative data) and *knowing things* (using qualitative data). In the view of Wilson, "Scientific research is an art form in this sense: It does not matter how you make a discovery, only that your claim is true and convincingly validated" (Wilson, 1998: 57).

SCIENTIFIC REFLECTIONS: WHAT IS SCIENCE?

If there is a consensus in the scientific community concerning the question, it is that science is <u>not</u> a body of facts. Science may have its etymological roots in the Latin word, *scire*, to know, but according to Carl Sagan, science is much more a "way of knowing" than a "body of knowledge" (Holub, 2001: 53). Unfortunately for many high school students, science is often taught as a body of knowledge or facts. Neil Shubin, paleontologist, recalls his high school science experience. Science was a "body of facts and laws you had to memorize. The Krebs cycle, Linnaean classifications. Not only does this approach whip the joy of doing science right out of most people, but it gives a distorted view of what science is" (Angier, 2007: 19).

Yet the question still remains: If science is not a body of facts, then what is it? I asked just this question to Steven Handel, botanist. He responded without hesitation to a view widely accepted in the scientific community:

Science is based on observable phenomena that anyone can experience as opposed to faith or opinion that is personal and not rooted in observable phenomena. The power of science is the community of scientists who use this approach and only then is it a fact. Scientific truth depends upon the scientific community accepting it (Interview with Steven Handel; Gorrell, 2007).

Michael Duff, theoretical physicist, agrees that science is not a "collection of rigid dogmas," and what we call "scientific truth is constantly being revised, challenged, and refined" (Angier, 2007: 20). He emphasizes that for scientists, there are always more questions than answers: "As a scientist, you know that any new discovery you're lucky enough to uncover will raise more questions than you started with, and that you must always question what you thought was correct and remind yourself how little you know…. Science is a very humble and humbling activity" (Angier, 2007: 20).

In sum, Edward O. Wilson defines science as "the organized enterprise that gathers knowledge about the world and condenses that knowledge into testable laws and principles (Wilson, 1998: 53). To further clarify, he identifies five distinguishing or diagnostic features of science: *repeatability*, *economy*, *elegance*, *mensuration*, *heuristics*, and *consilience*. According to Wilson, these diagnostic features distinguish science from pseudoscience (p. 53). For our purposes, science, like poetry, is a way of thinking, knowing, and experiencing. As Neil Shubin, paleontologist affirms, it is first and foremost a "dynamic process of discovery…as alive as life itself" (Angier, 2007: 19).

PERSONAL REFLECTIONS: THE SCIENCE OF MY FATHER

When I was in third grade in the early 1950s, my teacher, Miss Gillen, told us that for "show and tell" we would have to stand up and say what our fathers did for a living. (I think this was somehow Miss Gillen's idea of career education). I for one was filled with trepidation. I asked my mother, "What does daddy do?" My mother replied, "He's a scientist."

"What's that?" I asked her again. My mother paused for a moment, and then said, "Well, just say he's an engineer." That thought filled me with even greater trepidation.

"The kids might think he drove a train," I said, and I knew he didn't do that. But what he did exactly, I didn't know.

My father's science was always shrouded in mystery. In fact, his work was just that – top secret and classified. He served most of his professional life as Chief Engineer of the United States Munitions Command at Picatinny Arsenal in Dover, New Jersey. On the morning of May 25, 1953, in Frenchman Flat, Nevada, an artillery crew fired its gun, and a streamlined shell went hurtling over seven miles of desert to explode in a great mushroom cloud 500 feet over its target. That explosion marked the world's first successful atomic artillery shell. Its designer and executor was my father, Robert M. Schwartz, known at that time as the architect of the atomic shell.

As the story is recorded in the November 21, 1953 issue of *The Saturday Evening Post,* my father's achievement actually occurred four years earlier, in 1949, when Colonel Del Campo from the United States Army's munitions command summoned my father, all of 29 years age, to the Pentagon. After intensive security checks, he was given his task – to design an atomic artillery shell for field ground use. His challenge? To squeeze fissionable matter into a shell 11 inches in diameter so that it would withstand the blast of its propellant charge – about 4,000 times as much force as atomic bombs have to take – and the shell's spinning force of more than 6,000 revolutions per minute. Remarkably, my father and his selected team successfully completed the design on paper two weeks ahead of schedule. For his achievement he was awarded the Army's Exceptional Civilian Service medal, and years later, he was inducted into the Military Hall of Fame in Aberdeen, Maryland.[1]

Although the firing of that atomic shell occurred most likely six months before my "show and tell" moment (how was I to tell my classmates about that?), I had no knowledge of the event. My father never talked about his work. To this day, I have no memory of what I actually did say to my classmates at that "show and tell," but I doubt I said, "my father is a scientist," since I never visited Picatinny Arsenal, nor did I ever actually see him doing "science" in his place of work. In retrospect, I can certainly appreciate my mother's dilemma when I asked her, "What does daddy do?" The closest I ever came to knowing the science of my father remains one indelible memory I hold dear: my father, sitting at his desk at home, pipe in one hand, and slide rule in the other, studying something intently on paper.

That was the science of my father. I loved that slide rule and my father often let me play with it. It was about a foot long and approximately three inches wide with glossy white sliding bars engraved with blue numbers and occasional red symbols. I would slide the bars trying to fathom the meaning of the "game." As I grew older, I tried to imagine using it when I did science, but somehow, that slide rule was never required in my high school math and science courses. Along with the slide, my father's science was inextricably tied to his favorite word – *methodical*, which he repeated in various contexts with reference to my mother, my sisters, and myself. For example, my father was *methodical*; we at times were not, and he preached: everything had to be done *methodically*. I actually loved the sound of the word, which preceded its meaning; in fact, it was one of those long words I secretly cherished as a young child – a part of my father and his mysterious science.

Upon reflection, I now realize that I grew up in a home of two cultures. My father, the scientist – silent, methodical, and remote, and my mother – the passionate, gregarious gardener, cook, and lover of nature – who introduced me to the natural world, poetry, and the arts. Although my mother taught me the names of the flowers and the leaves on the trees (which we would iron between two pieces of waxed paper and display in our windows), I never considered her world of nature to be science. In my home, literary archetypes prevailed: my father in the realm of the heavens and reason, my mother of the earth, passion, and intuition. As I was writing this book, my mother and father celebrated 68 years of marriage. I think of the longevity of their marriage less as an affirmation that, scientifically and poetically, "opposites attract" and more as an affirmation of the necessity for different "natures" to complement each other. My mother and father each needed the other for completion; together, in their marriage, they somehow created a greater, more meaningful whole, one that I believe they recognized and cherished.

In this regard, the science of my father, so shrouded in mystery, becomes today for me a source of insight. I see the fusion of both worlds – the worlds of science, the arts, and poetry – as a natural consequence of their complementary natures. And so I relish at once the meaning of difference – and there are differences between science and poetry – as well as the meaning of fusion – the similarities that provide a unified, connected vision of the universe.

REDUCTIONIST REFLECTIONS: THE SCIENTIFIC MINDSET

Although my father was a civil engineer by degree and training, he was a scientist because he had a scientific mindset: he thought scientifically and he tackled problems scientifically. In other words, he was imbued with the reductionist mindset. To quote Edward O. Wilson: "The cutting edge of science is reductionism, the breaking apart of nature into its natural constituents...the search strategy employed to find points of entry into otherwise impenetrably complex systems" (Wilson, 1998: 54). Wilson describes reductionism in terms of series of questions that might appear in a user's manual.

> *Let your mind travel around the system. Pose an interesting question about it. Break the question down and visualize the elements... Think out alternative conceivable answers. Phrase them so that a reasonable amount of evidence makes a clear-cut choice possible.... Design the experiment so that no matter what the result, the answer to the question will be convincing. Use the result to press on to new questions, new systems.* (Wilson, 1998: 54)

When I read Wilson's description of how reductionism works, I think of my father, and how he solved the problem, so complex, of squeezing fissionable matter into a shell 11 inches in diameter. Although the answer to the atomic shell remained top secret at the time, my father explained his design solution in the *City College (NY) Alumnus* magazine by asking a question and then drawing an analogy:

> *If you're going to protect your watch against a two-ton hammer blow, how would you go about it? I proposed letting all the intricate parts mold into one glob of steel to withstand the force of the hammer blow and then free themselves to function after the blow.* (Schwartz, 1954: 4)

It sounded simple in theory. But it did not appear so simple to the Pentagon officials. After months of consideration, Colonel Del

Campo finally gave the go-ahead to my father to hand pick a crew to build and test the atomic shell.

According to Wilson, for "practicing scientists whose business is to make verifiable discoveries (Wilson, 1998: 59), "dissection and analysis prevail, but they are not all that scientists do. Wilson adds that "synthesis and integration, tempered by philosophical reflection on significance and value" are also "crucial" (p. 54).

For me, my father exemplifies reductionism. He could break down, dissect, and analyze any problem. But he also had to build the atomic shell, and that took synthesis and integration of the parts to create a whole. Ultimately, science is, as Steven Handel affirms, "a very creative discipline," filled most certainly with more questions than answers (Interview with Steven Handel; Gorrell, 2007).

HISTORICAL REFLECTIONS: THE THREE PARADIGMS OF SCIENCE

In his essay, "Poetry and Science: The Science of Poetry / The Poetry of Science," Miroslav Holub, Czech scientist and poet, asserts that *science* is best understood in terms of a slow transition from three paradigms: the First Science, the Second Science, and the Third Science (Holub, 2001: 49).[2] For our purposes, these paradigms clarify historical developments in scientific methods and philosophy essential for understanding both science poetry and the science–poetry connection.

According to Holub, the First Science paradigm, introduced by the ancient Greeks, was essentially more philosophical than scientific: "The method consisted of forming axioms from which certain theorems could be deduced by the application of logical systems that today would be regarded as 'philosophical' rather than 'scientific'" (Holub, 2001: 49). For example, in about 60 B.C. the Roman poet Lucretius wrote *De Rerum Natura,* an epic poem describing nature as viewed in Lucretius' time. This poem included "atomic theory, meteorology, astronomy, the origin of life, and the mechanics of perception" (Garfield, 1983: 223). Gradually during the Renaissance, according to Holub, the First Science was replaced by the Second. He explains the development of the Second Science as a critical time defined by measurement, the tools of measurement, and the method and mindset of reductionism:

> *[The Second Science] was based on systematized observation with the naked eye or with tools developed at the time. It invented the interrogation of nature through experiments, which in turn were based on assumptions derived from direct observations, on entities conveyed by observation, on entities very similar to or identical to the data of everyday sensual experience.* (Holub, 2001: 49)

The Second Science paradigm is very much the science that high school students learn and know today. It "resulted in an enormous wealth of classifications, descriptions, and notions of objects and elementary forces" (p. 49). According to Holub, this paradigm is metaphorically represented by "the reality of scientific libraries bulging with wisdom" and "scientific laboratories where uninvolved observers ask their questions and manipulate disparate objects, dissect them and rearrange them in chains of facts and abstractions" (p. 49). Holub credits the Second Science for enriching our vocabulary with an "enormous wealth of terms and denotations attributed to natural objects and technological processes" (p. 50). He also credits this burgeoning scientific vocabulary for having a "marked positive effect on the literary mind," (p. 50) enabling the use of concrete, specific terminology rather than broad, general descriptors.

As a result, by mid-19th century, the term *science* came to be used in a narrow sense to refer just to the *physical* or *natural sciences*; compilers of the *Oxford English Dictionary*, setting to work in the late 19th century, cite *science* as "expressing physical and experimental science, to the exclusion of the theological and metaphysical" (Collini, 2007: xi–xii). In addition, Stefan Collini points out that the beginning of the 19th century was also a time of increasing "anxiety that some such fissure in types of knowledge might be opening up" (Collini, 2007: x). He argues that this anxiety related at first to the worry that "calculation and measurement generally might be displacing cultivation and compassion" (p. xi). Such a view helped to foster the cultural divide decried by C. P. Snow in his "Two Cultures" essay.

Eventually, the Second Science came into conflict with art. Roald Hoffmann notes that

> ...in Pope's day it was not unusual for a 'natural philosopher' to be both a poet and a chemist. Trying to understand the world around and within us requires all the resources of art and science. But in the beginning of the 19th century things changed. Small wonder – it was getting awfully dark, the smog and stink of the industrial revolution coming down over the Midlands and the Ruhr, and there were all these distracting wild noises, romanticism beating its chest. (Hoffman, 2002: 138)

Although the influence and practice of the Second Science remains pervasive in our schools and culture, Holub argues that in the 20th century, the Second Science "has been broken up and is vanishing bit by bit" in the face of a new paradigm, that of Goodall's Third Science "struggling with the 'fluent' nature of things" (Holub, 2001: 51). It is here, in the Third Science, that art, poetry, and science can once again find common ground. According to Holub, "the first step was the development of physics where the material world was found to consist of entities basically different from anything we can experience with our senses," in particular, quantum mechanics, relativity, and "the revolutionary idea that chance and indeterminacy are among the fundamental character- istics of reality" (Holub: 2001: 51–52). In this context, Holub notes the Heisenberg principle: "Even in science the object of research is no longer nature itself, but man's investigation of nature" (p. 52). Heisenberg's principle, recognizing the involvement of the observer in the observed, challenges earlier views of an objective reality. By the end of the 20th century, Wilson in *Consilience* poses and answers the question that confirms the movement from the Second to the Third Science:

Can we devise a litmus test for scientific statements and with it eventually attain the grail of objective truth? Current opinion holds that we cannot and never will. Scientists and philosophers have largely abandoned the search for absolute objectivity and are content to ply their trade elsewhere. (Wilson, 1998: 60)

REFLECTIONS ON THE THIRD SCIENCE AND THE SCIENCE–POETRY CONNECTION

Without question, authorities agree that science and poetry find common ground in the Third Science paradigm of the 20th century, more specifically, the movement from classical to post-classical physics. Stefan Collini notes how physics had long been seen as the "hardest of the 'hard sciences,' a kind of gold standard against which weaker or debased forms of science could be measured" (Collini, 2007: xlvii). Nevertheless, he argues that the "new physics," in particular quantum physics and chaos theory, have modified this model, installing "unpredictability" and "open-endedness" in its findings about the nature of matter and the origins of the universe (p. xlvii).

Most importantly for the purposes of the science-poetry connection, Collini recognizes the critical role of imagination, metaphor, and analogy:

The role of imagination, of metaphor and analogy, of category-transforming speculation and off-beat intuitions has come to the fore much more (some would argue that these had always had their place in the actual processes of scientific discovery, whatever the prevailing account of 'scientific method'). As a result, more now tends to be heard about similarity rather than the difference of mental operations across the science/humanities divide. (p. xlviii)

Roald Hoffmann also recognizes the critical influence of the Third Science on the science–poetry connection. In this regard, his observation that "the language of science is a language under stress" is particularly relevant (Hoffman, 1988: 10). Hoffmann explains how "words are being made to describe things that seem indescribable in words – equations, chemical structures and so forth (p. 10)." He points out the paradox: "words don't, cannot mean all that they stand for, yet they are all we have to describe experience. By being a natural language under tension, the language of science is inherently poetic. There is metaphor aplenty in science" (p. 10).

Given Hoffmann's argument that the language of science is "inherently poetic," it comes as no surprise that the poetry of contemporary poets has been heavily influenced by the advances of the Third Science. Adalaide Morris, in "The Act of the Mind: Thought Experiments in the Poetry of Jorie Graham and Leslie Scalapino," demonstrates how three scientific theories – catastrophe, chaos, and complexity – situated in the "borderland" between "causality and chance, order and chaos, determinacy and indeterminacy," have shaped the experimental poetry of Jorie Graham and Leslie Scalapino (Morris, 2006: 157). Morris shows how the poetry of Graham is in itself a thought experiment not unlike the early thought experiments of Einstein. Similarly, Daniel Tobin in an essay, "A. R. Ammons and the Poetics of Chaos," demonstrates how Ammons' poetry is a study in chaos theory and the field concept–"the notion that things are interconnected in a kind of 'cosmic web' of energy patterns. Reality is a dance, an all encompassing motion that ultimately dismisses the notion of a purely objective observer" (Tobin, 2001: 130; see Chapter 10 for Ammons' poem "Cascadilla Falls").

Clearly, the more old paradigms fade and new ones prevail in science, the more scientists need visualization, thought experiments, and metaphoric seeing to make the unknown, known – in other words, the more scientists need poetry, and, in particular, science poetry.

REFLECTIONS ON THE SCIENTIFIC METHOD: STRONG INFERENCE

Any attempt to define science must include a discussion of the scientific method whereby scientific discoveries proceeded "by a combination of rigorous deduction and controlled inferences from empirical observation" (Collini, 2007: xlviii). Although Wilson (1998: 58) in *Consilience* asserts, "There is no fixed way to make and establish a scientific discovery," he later qualifies his assertion: "It is occasionally possible to encapsule a method of science as a recipe. The most satisfying is that based on multiple competing hypotheses, also known as strong inference" (p. 59).

In 1963, John R. Platt, professor of biophysics and physics at the University of Chicago, delivered a ground-breaking address to the American Chemical Society originally entitled, "The New Baconians," and later published as "Strong Inference" (Platt, 1963). Attributing the rapid advances in molecular biology to "inductive inference," Platt (1963: 347) called upon his fellow scientists to adopt the method, what he named "strong inference" because of its particularly rapid and effective results." Platt outlined the steps of strong inference, "familiar to every college student" and "practiced, on and off, by every scientist":

- *Devising alternative hypotheses.*
- *Devising a crucial experiment (or several of them) with alternative possible outcomes, each of which will, as nearly as possible, exclude one or more of the hypotheses.*
- *Carrying out the experiment so as to get a clean result.*
- *Recycling the procedure, making sub-hypotheses or sequential hypotheses.* (Platt, 1963: 347)

The essence of Platt's advocacy centered on persuading scientists to adopt a "strong inference attitude," one that would replicate the rapid advances of both molecular biology and what he called, "high energy physics" (pp. 348–349). Citing Karl Popper that "there is no such thing as proof in science–because some later alternative explanation may be as good or better," Platt concurred that "science advances only by disproofs" (p. 350). Therefore, to assure that scientists do not become too attached to one single hypothesis, Platt called for "multiple working hypotheses," and "sharp exclusions" at every step of research to guard against the problem of the "Ruling Theory" (p. 350).

In addition, Platt urged his colleagues to adopt as a scientific method what he called, "The Question" of disproof: "'But sir, what hypothesis does your experiment disprove?'" This question remains the test or touchstone of strong inference – whether there is or is not a testable scientific step forward in any given experiment or inquiry (p. 352). Perhaps, in this sense, a strong inference attitude and "The Question" that reflects that attitude offer a useful litmus test for answering the question: *what is science*?

"The Question" or Scientific Litmus Test

What hypothesis does my experiment disprove?
<u>Or</u>
What hypothesis does your experiment disprove?

(Platt, 1963: 352)

For our purposes, Platt posed a critical question: *How can we learn the method and teach it*? His answer remains highly relevant for science and English teachers alike. He argues that scientists must be "explicit and formal and regular about it," devoting "a half hour or an hour to analytical thinking every day, writing out the logical tree and the alternatives and crucial experiments explicitly in a permanent notebook" (p. 352). To illustrate, he references Faraday's famous diary and Fermi's notebook methods. He describes "the man with the notebook, the man with the alternative hypotheses and crucial experiments" as the man who knows how to problem-solve and answer the "The Question" of disproof.

STRONG INFERENCE ATTITUDE AND THE POETIC MINDSET

Platt's advocacy for adoption of a "strong inference attitude" on the part of scientists may very well find common ground with poets and poetry writing which requires an attitude of openness and receptivity to ambiguity; multiple perspectives; and ways of seeing, knowing, and experiencing the unknown. In fact, the art of poetry writing may be regarded as the exploration of such multiplicities, complexities, and "alternative hypotheses," a crucial experiment, to adopt Platt's terminology, whereby the poet engages more with a "problem"– writing an authentic poem – rather than a "method," writing a formulaic poem. In the process, the poet discovers and makes multiple or "alternative" meanings. Encouraging students in both science and English classes to adopt a strong inference attitude may go a long way in fostering scientific, poetic, and most importantly, vital writing skills.

REFLECTIONS ON THE ANTI-SCIENCE MINDSET: WALT WHITMAN'S "WHEN I HEARD THE LEARN'D ASTRONOMER"

If there is one highly referenced poem that seems to exemplify the anti-science mindset prevalent in poetry circles since the time of the Industrial Revolution and Romanticism, it is Walt Whitman's "When I Heard the Learn'd Astronomer." Whitman's poem begins with the speaker/poet listening to a technical, scientific lecture dominated by *proofs*, *figures, columns, charts* and *diagrams*, to *add, divide, and measure them*. The speaker's reaction: *How soon unaccountable I became tired and sick / Till rising and gliding out I wander'd off by myself / In the mystical moist night-air, and from time to time / Look'd up in perfect silence at the stars* (Whitman, 1982: 409–410). Viewed by many authorities as confirming the schism between science and the arts – the former associated with analysis, dissection, and objective reality – the latter with sensory experience, synthesis, and subjective reality – Whitman's poem, upon closer examination, offers a more science-affirming mindset. Here, it is important to consider C. P. Snow's mid-century thesis that scientists and nonscientists need to try to understand each other's language. In this regard, we might note that the speaker, or poet, is at least there, in the science lecture, listening, the first step in effective communication. Although the speaker/poet leaves the lecture, we need not assume that some knowledge or even some sympathy has not been gained by the listener, however passive.

This thesis may not seem so far-fetched when we consider Whitman's biography and his fascination with science and scientific knowledge. Jonah Lehrer opens his chasm-bridging work, *Proust was a Neuroscientist*, with discussion of how the poetry of Walt Whitman anticipated the discoveries of neuroscience, presaging advances in the brain-body connection: "Long before C. P. Snow mourned the sad separation of our two cultures, Whitman was busy studying brain anatomy textbooks and watching gruesome surgeries" (Lehrer, 2007: xi). Whitman's fusion of body and soul on the very first page of *Leaves of Grass*, *Of physiology from top to toe I sing*, was rooted in his first-hand experience as a wound dresser in Union hospitals during the Civil War (Lehrer, 2007: 15). For three years he dressed the flesh of amputees and observed the phenomena of phantom or "ghostly limbs" which he transmuted into poetry (Lehrer, 2007: 11–12). Lehrer demonstrates how "modern neuroscience is now discovering the anatomy underlying Whitman's poetry. It has taken his hypothesis – the idea that feelings begin in the flesh – and found the exact nerves and brain regions that make it true" (Lehrer, 2007: 19).

Viewing Whitman as a more science-friendly poet than previously acknowledged is not just an academic argument. For the anti-science mindset prevails today among many of our poetry-loving students, and even, perhaps, teachers. In fact, in teaching science poetry in high school English classes, I received several science-subject poems reflecting anti-science attitudes. These attitudes, ingrained by a predominance of the Second Science reductionist paradigm, protest too much emphasis on analysis, dissection, and *microscopic* seeing, to the exclusion of appreciation through wonder, awe, and feeling. One such example, written by Theresa Gold, a student, illustrates this mindset. In "Look Up," Theresa addresses with disdain the scientist "lost" in the world of the *microscope*. Here the microscope is not an instrument of vision and discovery, but rather a symbol of myopia and lack of feeling on the part of the scientist/subject.

Look Up

Place the slide into view
Turn the knobs, adjust the screws
Lenses to refract the light
Forcing the unseen into sight.

Tiny worlds that you reveal
Unlocking mysteries with such zeal
Organisms previously unknown
Spawned in a Petri dish of your very own.

Lost in your world of the microscopic
Never seeing beyond the magnified optics
Trapped in a prison of your mind
A slave to thought, you remain confined.

So place your samples in a vial
Store the world up on a shelf
Perhaps you should turn the scope on yourself.

—Theresa Gold, student

SCIENCE POETRY WRITING AS A CORRECTIVE TO THE ANTI-SCIENCE MINDSET

For pedagogical purposes, science poetry writing has a critical role to play as a corrective for such dichotomous attitudes and misconceptions. An alternate way of reading Whitman's poem might be to confirm to students the need for poets to listen to the language of science. In fact, Alison Hawthorne Deming suggests just that, describing in "Science and Poetry" how the language of science does not repel her, but rather "attracts" her. Deming states she is "wooed" by "the beautiful particularity and musicality of the vocabulary [of science]. I am wooed by words such as *hemolymph, zeolite, cryptogram, sclera*...and I long to save them from the tedious syntax in which most science writing imprisons them" (Deming, 2001: 185). As English and science teachers, we too need to "woo" our students to the beauty of the language and wonder of science. In this regard, science poetry writing may play a critical role as a corrective to the anti-science mindset.

FINAL REFLECTIONS: ON THE COMPLEMENTARY NATURE OF SCIENCE AND POETRY

Writing three years before C. P. Snow delivered his controversial Rede lecture on "The Two Cultures," Laurence Perrine, in *Sound and Sense,* suggested: "The two approaches to experience – the scientific and the literary – may be said to complement each other" (Perrine, 1982: 5). Perrine used for illustration a specific bird, the eagle. To this end, he juxtaposed scientific understanding about the eagle from a book of natural history with literary understanding of the eagle from a poem by Alfred Lord Tennyson, "The Eagle" (Perrine, 1956: 4–5). Perrine explained that the two approaches to experience and knowing support two very different approaches to the use of language. The scientific approach uses language to communicate "information," or "knowing *about* things"; the poetic approach uses language to communicate "experience", or "knowing things" (p. 4).

Although Perrine delineated this fundamental difference between science and poetry in terms of ways of knowing and uses of language, he was not drawing a line in the sand. Quite to the contrary, his view that the two approaches "complement" each other remains most instructive for our purposes. It is the key to understanding and appreciating the science–poetry connection.

PART TWO: STUDENT ACTIVITIES TO DEVELOP THE SCIENTIFIC EYE

ACTIVITY #1: SCIENCE AWARENESS POLL

Taking the Poll

Distribute the following poll to your students. Have them answer the questions individually on a separate piece of paper. If you prefer, you can orally dictate each question, waiting for written responses, and then proceed to the next question. If your students struggle to find answers, feel free to ask guiding and clarifying questions. Try to reserve discussion of specific answers, comments, and responses until all students have completed the poll.

Science Awareness Poll

1. Name five deceased American or world-renowned scientists. Identify their branch of science and their contribution to that branch of science.
2. Name five living American or world-renowned scientists. Identify their branch of science and their contribution to that branch of science.
3. Identify the steps of the scientific method.
4. Identify five different branches of science.
5. Define each of the five branches of science you identified in #4.
5. Can you recall a major scientific event? Identify the event. Can you remember when this event occurred? If so write the date and time frame.

7. Have you conducted science experiments in school? If so, identify the first time you remember conducting an experiment. Describe the experiment and the reason why you were running the experiment.

8. Have you ever conducted a science experiment at home? If so, identify the experiment. Describe what you did and why you were running the experiment.

9. Have you ever shared the findings of your experiment with someone? If so, explain.

10. Have you ever thought of yourself as a scientist? Why or why not?

11. When asked to think about a scientist, what characteristics come to mind?

12. Have you ever received a gift related to science? If so, what was it, and when did you receive it?

13. Have you ever given a gift related to science? If so, what was it and why did you give it?

14. Have you ever been to a science museum? If so, name the museum(s).

15. Have you ever witnessed science for yourself, *live and in action* outside of the classroom? If so, name one such event and describe it.

16. If you wanted to witness science for yourself, *live and in action* outside of school would you know where to go? If so, where would you go?

17. Do you have a favorite branch of science? If so, why is it your favorite?

18. Do you have a favorite scientist? If so, who is your favorite scientist? Why?

19. How do you feel about science? Explain your attitude.

20. What do you think science is? Comment on your definition.

21. What do you think science poetry is? Comment on your definition.

Discussing Science Awareness Poll Results

When students are finished taking the poll, discuss, in numerical order, the answers to each question. Use student responses to questions #1 and #2 to inform students about noted scientists and scientific discoveries relevant to their selected branches of science. Use student responses to questions #3, 4, and 5 to review the scientific method and major branches of science. Use questions #10 and 11 to air views and dispel myths and stereotypes about scientists. Encourage students to share their attitudes and experiences regarding science and scientists. If you are a science teacher, take the opportunity to familiarize your students with the most noted scientists and scientific discoveries in your particular branch of science. Last, use responses to question #20 to open the topic of *what is science* and *what is science poetry*. After exchanging view, tell students Activity #3 will introduce them to seeing and responding as scientists and poets.

Evaluating Students' Scientific Literacy

To the surprise of both my science partner and myself, the science awareness poll invariably uncovers the lack of general knowledge many high school science students have regarding all branches of science. Given that Morristown High School's students are required to take three years of laboratory science to graduate, we expected to see far greater scientific literacy than poetic literacy on the part of our science students. The results of the science awareness poll proved otherwise. Capable, above-average as well as superior science students in Erin's Research Science and Honors Biology classes faired no better than comparable students in my English classes when it came to general knowledge of their respective disciplines of study.

Science students were unable to recall noted scientists, dead or alive, or to identify their contributions to science. Only when Erin prompted her students to think of each branch of science could they begin to recall noted scientists and their contributions. Students in both classes universally identified Albert Einstein as their number one response. Other scientists commonly mentioned included: Alexander Graham Bell, Watson Crick, George Washington Carver, Charles Darwin, Thomas Edison, Henry Ford, Sir Isaac Newton, and Galileo. None of Erin's students mentioned any living scientists or women scientists. Although students could readily identify the steps in the scientific method (they are taught this in order to write laboratory reports), they were unable to identify or define the five branches of science without prompting. In recalling a "major scientific event," most students noted volcano eruptions, hurricanes, earthquakes, and other natural disasters. They did not think historically of great moments of scientific discovery or experimentation. Regarding conducting experiments in school or at home, most students recalled self-discovery experiments and experiences in their elementary and middle school years. Few recalled any experiments or laboratory reports conducted in high school. Ironically, this was also the case with English students' recall of poetry and poetry writing experiences. Many students did recall conducting science experiments at home with science kits given to them by their parents. Most of these experiments were environmental or electrical in nature, the most common being the growing of plants or crystals.

When asked if they had ever thought of themselves as scientists, the large majority said "no." On the other hand, when asked "to think about a scientist," Erin's students quickly responded with several positive character traits: dedication, patience, passion, and "hard work." Interestingly enough, they did not identify any negative or gender stereotypes. Student responses to questions #12–16 indicated a general lack of familiarity and experience with science outside the classroom. Students generally responded that they would go to a museum to find out about science, not considering all of the possible laboratories, corporations, natural environments, and media resources available for first-hand observation of science in action. Few students had a favorite branch of science or a favorite scientist. Most responded to the attitudinal question, "How do you feel about science?" with an open-minded neutrality and an immediate recognition of the simple fact: "It's hard work." In responding to the question, "What do you think science is?" students in both of Erin's classes answered with similar definitions: "Trying to find answers to questions about what everything is, and to question everything around you."

Perhaps one of the most significant and revealing results of the science awareness poll came from its affect on the student responders themselves. They took the "test" very seriously and were openly embarrassed about their lack of scientific literacy. Erin was particularly surprised to see how embarrassed her students felt. They clearly thought they "should know it," and of course, with prompting from Erin, they were readily able to recall more facts and information than on their own. Although their scientific literacy was no more lacking than comparable English class students' poetic literacy, my students in English classes commonly reacted with humor and laughter rather than embarrassment at their lack of knowledge. This observation alone speaks volumes about how students regard the nature of the two cultures and disciplines.

In evaluating the results of the science awareness poll with your students, lead them in a discussion considering the following questions:

- *What does the science awareness poll reveal to you about your knowledge of science?*
- *What does the science awareness poll reveal to you about your experience with science?*
- *What does the science awareness poll reveal to you about your attitudes toward science?*
- *What does the science awareness poll reveal to you about science education?*

ACTIVITY #2: TEACHER AND STUDENT SCIENCE MEMORIES

Freewriting

To further explore attitudes and feelings about science, consider having students freewrite their science memories. To inspire them to do so, you might consider writing your own memories with your students, and then sharing those memories together in a reading circle. Or, if you prefer, read to your students my personal reflections, *The Science of My Father*, in Part One of this chapter. If students keep a laboratory notebook or journal, have them record their personal reflections in their notebooks or journals. In concert with the science awareness poll, this writing activity serves as an ideal first day or opening activity for any science poetry unit or science course.

Writing Prompt: Science Memories

Freewrite for 20 minutes your memories, feelings, and attitudes toward science. When did you first learn about science? When do you remember first engaging with science? Who or what were your teachers? How did your parents and teachers influence attitudes about science? What role did school play? After you finish writing, reflect upon the meaning of your memories to your developing attitudes and experiences.

ACTIVITY #3: ENTERING THE SCIENTIFIC METHOD

"In Broken Images" by Robert Graves

When I asked Steven Handel, professor of botany, to define the scientific method, he shared with me not only Platt's "Strong Inference" essay but also Robert Graves' poem, "In Broken Images," adding: "I have always felt this poem is a crystalline expression of the scientific method. I give it to all my graduate students. I think it is a masterpiece" (Interview with Steven Handel; Gorrell, 2007). Graves' poem, written in six couplets, captures the paradoxical, and, as Steven Handel put it, "messy" nature of the scientific method. For interested teachers, Activity #2 offers a creative approach to teaching the scientific method. In his poem, Graves juxtaposes two subjects, *He* (scientist-subject #1), and the speaker, *I* (scientist-subject #2), representing two different approaches to scientific discovery and investigation. For a dramatic reading, assign two students in your class to read the voices of scientist-subject #1(*He*) and scientist-subject #2 (*I*), respectively.

In Broken Images

He is quick, thinking in clear images;
I am slow, thinking in broken images.

He becomes dull, trusting to his clear images;
I become sharp, mistrusting my broken images.

Trusting his images, he assumes their relevance;
Mistrusting my images, I question their relevance.

Assuming their relevance, he assumes the fact,
Questioning their relevance, I question the fact.

When the fact fails him, he questions his senses;
When the fact fails me, I approve my senses.

He continues quick and dull in his clear images;
I continue slow and sharp in my broken images.

He in a new confusion of his understanding;
I in a new understanding of my confusion.

                              –*Robert Graves* (Graves, 2003: 296)

After the oral reading of the poem, open discussion as to the different points of view each voice represents concerning the scientific method. Clearly, Graves' thought provoking poem supports Platt's "strong inference attitude," with its acceptance of multiple or alternative hypotheses – *I am slow, thinking in broken images* – and its acceptance of ambiguity – *I in a new understanding of my confusi*on. Steven Handel gives his graduate students this poem to foster the habits of the mind he deems essential for framing effective scientific experiments and investigations (Gorrell, 2007). Whether you are a science or English teacher, emphasize to your students the commonalities between science and poetry this poem suggests:

- *Appreciation of ambiguity*
- *Appreciation of paradox*
- *Approving sensory experience*
- *Appreciation of the slow and methodical*
- *Appreciation of the "broken" or dissection of images or reality*
- *Appreciation that things are not what they seem*

In so doing, you will be helping your students make connections between the world of science and the world of poetry so vital for the science poetry writing to come in Chapter 4.

THE VALUE OF DEVELOPING THE SCIENTIFIC EYE

Once students understand what is science, once they have developed their scientific eyes, responding to literature, nature, and science in the form of the science poem affords them the opportunity to engage in a wide range of evocative, empathetic as well as critical and creative discoveries. For English students in literature classes, this scientific awareness offers a broader context for interpreting literature, breaks interdisciplinary stereotypes, and challenges critical reading and reasoning skills. For science students, the awareness of what is science based on the information and activities in this chapter offers a broader context for engaging with science, breaks interdisciplinary stereotypes, and challenges critical reasoning and creative thinking skills. Whether you are a science or English teacher, developing your students' scientific eyes will prepare them for the tsunami of possibility that is science poetry writing.

Notes

1. The information about my father and the atomic artillery shell originate with my mother, Lillian Schwartz, and an article by Edwin Diehl in *The Saturday Evening Post* (November 21, 1953) and *The City College Alumnus*, April 1954. The atomic artillery shell was never deployed in war, but it was considered at the time by Arthur Radford, chair of the Joint Chiefs of Staff, to be "a milestone in the history of atomic weapons," playing a critical, strategic role at the time in terms of the balance of power.
2. Holub (2001) credits the following authorities and works for the three paradigm thesis: Thomas C. Kuhn, *The Structure of Scientific Revolutions* (Kuhn, 1962); M. C. Goodall, *Science and the Politician* (Goodall, 1965); and Conrad H. Waddington, *Behind Appearance* (Waddington, 1970).

4   What is Science Poetry?

A "Tsunami" of Possibility

Neither science nor the arts can be complete without combining their separate strengths. Science needs the intuition and metaphorical power of the arts, and the arts need the fresh blood of science.

> – Edward O. Wilson, *Consilience, The Unity of Knowledge*
> (Wilson, 1998: 211)

I have no problem doing (or trying to do) both science and poetry. Both emerge from my attempt to understand the universe around me, from my personal affection for communicating, teaching what I've learned, and from my infatuation with language – the English language…. I love words.

> – Roald Hoffmann, "How I Work as Poet and Scientist"
> (Hoffmann, 1988: 10)

OVERVIEW: FOUNDATION LESSON FOUR

The aim of Foundation Lesson Four is to introduce students to the "tsunami" of possibility that is the universe of science poetry writing. Once students understand *what is poetry* and *what is science*, they are ready to fuse the two together to create their first science poems. For this purpose, Chapter 4 centers upon a short, accessible science poem, "Tsunami," by Nobel prize-winning chemist, Roald Hoffmann. Hoffmann's poem not only models for science and English students all of the essential elements of our working definition, but it inspires and prompts skillful, startling, and, for many students, personally relevant science poems as well. In this regard, the ultimate aim of Foundation Lesson Four is to:

- *Define science poetry;*
- *Present an inspirational science poetry model; and*
- *Engage students to write their first science poems.*

Foundation Lesson Four consists of four parts. Part One offers Activity #1, a lesson of definition based on the science poem, "Tsunami" by Roald Hoffmann, followed by first science poems written by students in AP English Language and Composition classes. These tsunami-inspired responses model the rhetorical progression common to Hoffmann's science poetry: movement from scientific description to personal reflection. Part One ends with a handout summarizing how to write any science poem. Part Two offers for interested teachers an extension activity, "Tsunami Song," a poem by Stanley Moss. In this extension activity, students compare and contrast the science poem, "Tsunami," with the lyrical poem, "Tsunami Song," furthering their understanding and appreciation of science poetry. Part Three offers a discussion of "The Issue of Science Poetry and Accessibility" and Part Four offers a discussion of "Related Scholarship and Pedagogy: Poetry and the Physical Sciences."

Foundation Lesson Four at a Glance

<u>**Part One**</u>: **What is Science Poetry?**
Activity #1 A Lesson in Definition: "Tsunami."
Model Student Responses:
"The Second Law of Thermodynamics" by Alex Davis
"Sandcastle of Stars" by Anne Schwartz
"Beyond Configuration" by David Pitt
"A Love Song" by Ben Levenson

<u>**Part Two**</u>: **Furthering Understanding and Appreciation**
Extension Activity: "Tsunami Song" by Stanley Moss

<u>**Part Three**</u>: **The Issue of Science Poetry and Accessibility**

<u>**Part Four**</u>: **Related Scholarship and Pedagogy**
Poetry and the Physical Sciences

Students begin by explicating the poem, "Tsunami," by Roald Hoffmann. Then they test our working definition of science poetry, applying that definition to "Tsunami." Next they analyze Hoffmann's poetic techniques and rhetorical progression, exploring the question: How does a poem move? So informed and inspired, students respond with their own science poems modeled after "Tsunami." At the conclusion of Foundation Lesson Four, students share their first science poems and their attitudes and opinions about writing science poetry.

Materials Needed

Science Poem "Tsunami," by Roald Hoffmann (provided)
Lyrical Poem "Tsunami Song," by Stanley Moss (provided)

SUGGESTIONS FOR USING THIS LESSON

Foundation Lesson Four serves as the signature lesson in this book, defining science poetry and inspiring students of all levels to write their first science poems. Both science and English teachers will want to teach this lesson to launch any science poetry unit of study.

English and creative writing teachers will find the poetry writing strategies both instructive and inspirational. Students model the concept of poetic movement or "leaping" poetry to produce highly original and informative science poems. English teachers will find the universal rhetorical progression demonstrated in Hoffmann's poem relevant for literary analysis of other texts. In addition, English teachers in particular will find the extension activity an effective and challenging method of instruction for teaching the literary analysis and the comparative essay. Science teachers will find Hoffmann's subject, tsunamis and solitons, relevant to the understanding of aspects of physics and advanced mathematics. A reading of "Tsunami" might well provide an engaging and creative introduction to a lesson in wave theory.

Suggested Time Allocations

Time allocations for Activity #1 will vary depending upon students' level and the length of follow-up discussion. Allow time for students to begin drafting their first science poems in class following explication and analysis of "Tsunami." It is preferable to complete Activity #1 in one class period or block.

Part One, Activity #1 (60–80 minutes)
Part Two, Extension Activity (30 minutes)

PART ONE: WHAT IS SCIENCE POETRY?

ACTIVITY #1: A LESSON IN DEFINITION – "TSUNAMI" BY ROALD HOFFMANN

Presenting Our Working Definition of Science Poetry

Begin by presenting our working definition of science poetry. The criteria are clear, simple, and readily understood by upper level high school students.[1]

Science Poetry: Our Working Definition

Any poetry inspired and informed by scientific facts, phenomena, principles, theories, questions, observations, and experience may be considered **science poetry** if it includes all or most of the following elements:

- *Utilizes both quantitative and qualitative data in a poem;*
- *Utilizes scientific facts, information, or experience to prompt or begin a poem;*
- *Utilizes science, scientific theories, or phenomena as allusion in a poem;*
- *Utilizes science, scientific theories, or phenomena as metaphor in a poem;*
- *Utilizes science, scientific theories, or phenomena as imagery in a poem;*
- *Utilizes specific scientific and technical vocabulary in a poem;*
- *Utilizes science as the subject or theme of a poem.*

Reading the Model Science Poem: "Tsunami" by Roald Hoffmann

After going over the points in the above definition, then distribute or project for illustration Roald Hoffmann's science poem, "Tsunami."

Tsunami
> *for Maria Matos*

A soliton is
a singularity
of wave
motion, an edge
traveling just

that way. We saw
one, once
filmed moving heed-
lessly cross
a platinum surface.
Solitons pass
through
each
other
unperturbed.

You are a wave.
Not standing, nor
traveling, satisfying
no equation.
You are a wave
which will not be (Fourier)
analyzed.
You are a wave; in
your eyes I sink
willingly.

Not solitons,
we can't pass through
unaltered.

– Roald Hoffmann (Hoffman, 2002: 3)

Explicating the Model Science Poem

Encourage students to see first through the *eyes of science* by
asking them:

- *What science do you see in the poem?*
- *What science do you need to know to understand the poem?*
- *What are the scientific allusions, concepts, or vocabulary in the poem?*

Without giving my English students prior information or knowledge, most identify *soliton*, *tsunami*, and *Fourier*. They also readily notice that Hoffmann begins his poem by presenting, quite literally, a definition of a soliton. At this point, offering further scientific explanation of solitons or wave theory is not essential for poetic understanding.[2] Instead, suggest to your students that poets want readers to engage immediately with their poems, and in that spirit, they should go where the poem leads them. After spending time on the three points above, explicate stanza one with your students. Lead them to see the language as literal and definitional: *We saw / one, once / filmed moving heed- / lessly cross / a platinum surface.* Ask your students: "What do you think is the significance of *once*? Students generally speculate that perhaps solitons are rare and difficult to see, or perhaps the speaker saw a soliton only one time with this other person, identified only as *we*.

Stanza one of the poem ends literally with a statement of scientific fact: *Solitons pass / through / each / other / unperturbed.* At this point, my English students see "Tsunami" as a science poem that begins by directly stating, describing, or defining a scientific phenomenon. Yet the question remains: Is there any poetry in the poem? Guide your students to recognize ambiguity by asking: Who is Maria Matos? And where are the subjects? Explicate further: *We saw / one, once*, but where? Direct students to find the clue: *filmed moving heed- / lessly cross / a platinum surface*. Not knowing advanced science or wave theory, students may be puzzled at this ambiguity, but certainly they conclude that this particular soliton was seen on film and not in nature.[3]

In stanza two, the speaker "leaps," by striking a metaphor, from the world of science to the very human world of poetry: *You are a wave*. Now "Tsunami" becomes a poem of address. Point out to students how the speaker repeats this metaphor three times in stanza two. Most of my English class students assume the speaker is addressing Maria Matos, since the poem is dedicated to her. I suggest that the poem turns on the word, *you*, and I ask students for further interpretation. Although most of my students see *you* as a person, several entertain the possibility that the poet could be addressing a soliton, which is a wave on the *micro* level, or a tsunami, which is a catastrophic wave on the *macro* level. Perhaps, one of my students speculates, the poet is describing an aberrational or renegade soliton – *Not standing, nor / traveling, satisfying / no equation* – a personified one that does not want to "satisfy" an equation under Fourier's analysis. Or, perhaps, another student speculates, this wave is so fascinating to the speaker that he wants to connect with it or understand it not only on a scientific level, but on a more personal, human, and emotional level as well. Lead your students in a similar discussion of possible interpretations of the ambiguous *you*. At this point, I usually note that Fourier was a wave theorist, and that wave theory poses some of the most complex equations in higher mathematics.[4] Hoffmann certainly would know these equations. I speculate that perhaps he did not want to see the soliton exclusively through the eyes of laboratory science, but rather through the eyes of poetry.

"Tsunami" climaxes in the last three lines of stanza two: *You are a wave; in / your eyes I sink / willingly*. These evocative lines lead my students to the human connection. The overwhelming majority sees the poem as a love poem (so much so that several wrote their own love poems in response). To them, the suggestive images of *wave*, *eyes*, and *sink* connote romance. I suggest to my students to consider other types of love: perhaps Maria Matos is Hoffmann's friend or colleague? I tell students that although they may never know definitively Maria Matos' identity, "Tsunami" remains a poem of love, whether that love is the *eros* of romance, the *philia* of collegial friendship, or the *passion* of a scientist in love with his subject.

Now direct your students to explicate stanza three of the poem, a deceptively simple statement, one that challenges students to see simultaneously through the eyes of science and the eyes of poetry: *Not solitons, / we can't pass through / unaltered*. Stanza three incorporates the fusion of science and poetry that is the hallmark of the art form. Thinking structurally,

- *Stanza one represents the world of science;*
- *Stanza two represents the world of poetry; and*
- *Stanza three fuses the two, creating the world of science poetry.*

In this context, ask your students to consider the meaning of the title: "How does this *singularity of wave / motion* connect to your understanding of tsunamis? A "wave" of understanding rises in the classroom when I ask this question. My students see the interplay of many levels of "waves" at once: the singularity of the soliton, the catastrophic wave of the tsunami, and the human waves of emotion that love or friendship evokes. I ask rhetorically: "Has love or friendship ever been a 'tsunami' for you?" Most high school students can readily relate to this image of tsunami, agreeing that humans, not being solitons, *can't pass through / unaltered*.

After explication, lead a discussion guiding your students to see the nature of science poetry. Tell them that "Tsunami" is not a poem about science or about scientific phenomenon, but rather a poem using science as a metaphor to express human emotions and human nature. Suggest to them that we, as humans, cannot escape our connectedness; we cannot pass through "unaltered." I often extend the metaphor by mentioning that "Tsunami" is the opening poem in *Soliton*, Hoffmann's fourth book of poetry. I ask: Could Hoffmann be suggesting that readers of science poetry *can't pass through / unaltered* as well? I certainly think so, as the results of the student poetic responses that follow will confirm.

Testing our Working Definition of Science Poetry

Before turning to the science poetry writing phase of Activity #1 (the second half of your class period), ask your students to apply, point by point, our working definition of science poetry to Hoffmann's poem. Does Hoffmann's poem meet the criteria? Here are some student observations confirming "Tsunami" is a science poem.

- "Tsunami" is clearly a poem informed by scientific facts, phenomena, and first-hand observation.
- "Tsunami" is clearly a science subject-based poem, utilizing scientific vocabulary, concepts, and knowledge. The poem appears to be <u>about</u> science at first, but then "leaps," by striking a metaphor, to say something more.
- "Tsunami" uses a scientific definition as a starting point as well as scientific allusions: Fourier and wave theory.
- "Tsunami" uses science as metaphor to say something else about self, the world, and human nature and emotions.
- Although "Tsunami" does not use stated quantitative data (numbers or mathematics), it does use qualitative data to describe a scientific phenomenon and observation. (Interestingly enough, for those possessing advanced scientific knowledge, "Tsunami" may suggest pertinent quantitative data, thereby bringing a quantitative under-standing to the poem.)

Pre-Writing

Upon conclusion of the defining phase of Activity #1, tell your students to look for a moment at "Tsunami" to see more precisely how Hoffmann wrote his science poem. Identify with your students Hoffmann's rhetorical process: how he begins with science, in this case, a scientific definition of a phenomenon, a soliton; how he describes his observation of a soliton, *We saw/ one once*, injecting his experience as a working scientist; and how he inserts a space, and then "leaps," by striking a metaphor, into the world of poetry. Define for your students the technique of "leaping" poetry as a tool of association, popularized by Robert Bly, to move a poem to another level of meaning: for example, the known to the unknown, the conscious to the subconscious, the particular to the universal, and the self to the larger world of humanity (Bly, 1972).[5] Finally, instruct your students to turn to the poem's ending where Hoffmann offers a final thought for reflection, one that resonates with irony: *Not solitons / we can't pass through / unaltered*. At this point, identify for your students the rhetorical progression of description and reflection, modeled by Hoffmann, and commonly utilized by poets and writers alike, as an inductive process, one that moves from the specific to the general.

Universal Rhetorical Progression

- **Describe** a scientific phenomenon, theory, principle, or experience presenting the quantitative facts and data with specific scientific details and vocabulary. Use science as a starting point.
- **Connect/Associate/Leap** from the scientific to the self or human dimension of experience. Use science as metaphor.
- **Reflect/Meditate** on the meaning or consequences of the phenomenon or experience.

Writing First Science Poems

Scientific poetry – a daunting task for me as a writer and reader – is, for me, even more paradoxical than traditional poetry. To boil down complex facts and formulas into simple truths and emotions is a skill that continually amazes me.

–Anne Schwartz, student poet

Reserve the remainder of your class period for the drafting of first science poems. Encourage your students to quickwrite or freewrite their ideas based on their general scientific knowledge. Do not require or demand scientific research at this point because you want students to write from their own knowledge, what they know and what matters to them. Showing students that they can write a science poem from their own scientific and poetic reserves will empower and motivate them to produce personally relevant and inspired work.

Distribute or project the following science poetry writing prompt.

Science Poetry Writing Prompt

Like Roald Hoffmann in "Tsunami," begin a poem by defining a scientific fact, theory, phenomenon, or principle. Then "leap" by association or metaphor to another realm, dimension, or level; for example, from the scientific to the human, or the scientific to the self, or the scientific to the poetic. You may also think of this as moving from *quantitative* data and language to more *qualitative* data and language. Try using as much specific, quantitative data or scientific vocabulary as you can recall from your general knowledge of science. In addition, try using *science as a metaphor* in your poem to say something more. Create a title for your poem, like "Tsunami," that resonates for you with multiple meanings. For your final draft, take the opportunity to research or confirm relevant scientific facts.

Give students 15 minutes to draft. Then ask for volunteers to share their works in progress. Take the opportunity to identify the fusion of science in the poems with poetry. Encourage students to consider, in writing their final drafts, a balance of scientific fact with movement to poetic levels. In addition, suggest to students that they take the time to fact-check the accuracy of the science before submitting their final poems.

Model Student Responses: First Science Poems

The following student science poetry responses were written in Ms. Furphey's AP English Language and Composition class as part of a larger science poetry-writing unit. Students engaged with Hoffmann's model science poem, "Tsunami," but they were given no additional scientific information or instruction. As advanced students taking upper level science and mathematics classes, Ms. Furphey and I expected them to draw on their scientific knowledge or to carry out research as needed to find pertinent scientific information.

"The Second Law of Thermodynamics" by Alex Davis

The Second Law of Thermodynamics

Everything is falling apart.

First the stars die, and light leaves the universe.

Then the galaxies disintegrate, and every unseen corpse of a
star is alone, until the atoms that compose it finally evaporate.

Black holes rule the blackness until they disappear, and the universe
reaches the state of perfection it has been chasing for eternity.

Sometime between the beginning of everything and the death of
the stars, something begins, and ends, and calls itself Alex.

– Alex Davis, student

When Alex shared his science poem in progress with the class,
there was a palpable sense of awe pervading the room. In a mere
ten minutes of writing time, Alex had somehow come face to face
with the eternal human struggle to find one's place within the
incomprehensible vastness of the universe. What better task for
science poetry? Drawing on his own scientific knowledge, Alex
begins with a statement of the 2nd Law of Thermodynamics –
Everything is falling apart – one that resonates poetically as well
as scientifically. He proceeds to describe this incomprehensible
"disintegration" both scientifically and poetically, using images
such as *corpse of a star*, and *black holes rule the blackness*. It is not
until the last two lines of his poem that Alex takes an intergalactic
leap, from the universe of science to the universe of self, from the
beginning of everything to the end, with the simple, transitional
word, *sometime*. Here *time* seems to reverberate for the universe
of science as well as for Alex and each and every single individual
who reads or listens to this poem. Alex has enabled us to somehow
connect ourselves with the abstractions of time, space, and our
place within this universe.

What began as an in-class practice exercise leaped quickly to
real poetry; that is, poetry that moves from the academic to the

authentic. Real poetry may be difficult to teach, but it is not difficult to notice, identify, and appreciate. You will know it when you see it by several features:

- *The poem is written in the students' natural voice;*
- *The poem is saying something that deeply matters to the student;*
- *The student values and owns the poem; and*
- *The poem reveals something true about that student.*

Alex's commentary on his poem confirms its authenticity:

Alex's commentary

Some people in class laughed when they heard the last line, as if it was a relief of tension. One girl commented, "I love how it starts so dark and ends on a lighter note." That's not how I see it at all. I see two sides to it. One is [my] Alex's insignificance in the face of eternity. I communicated this in part with "something begins, and ends," with nothing in between the beginning and the ending. The last line is like an engraving on a gravestone. Something lived and died and this is what it was called. There is nothing between the first date and the last date but a hyphen. The other side is a rejection of this anonymity. In the grand story of all the time and mass that exists, Alex must be mentioned. The last word is Alex; he is more important to this story than the death of light. I wouldn't call this a "lighter" note.

Neither would we as teachers. To the contrary, my science partner and I see Alex's poem as demonstrating the authenticity we want to foster in the writing of all our students.

At this point, it is important to note that many high school students at an advanced academic level have a personal scientific literacy particularly relevant to them, that is, a knowledge base consisting of what they know, what puzzles them, and what inspires them in the world of science. This personal scientific literacy incorporates what they can easily recall, what they have experienced first hand in the world of nature, and what they have learned or are learning in science classrooms and laboratories at the time of writing. In AP and Honors English classes, students readily tap their scientific literacy for poetry writing. They do so with consistent ease, producing on the spot highly creative and original poetry.

Science poetry writing, with its familiar use of definition, statement of fact, lack of rhyme, and prose-like structure, may be, for many non-poetry writing students, an ideal way to begin any poetry writing instruction. Such students readily draw on what they are learning in science classes at the moment, naturally transferring their knowledge from science class to English class. Case in point: several students wrote poems based on the 2nd Law of Thermodynamics (see Colin Hostetter's found poem, Chapter 2), a topic addressed in junior level (grade 11) chemistry classes. For the many hidden poets in our English classes, like Anne Schwartz, science poetry writing offers a *tsunami of possibility.*

"Sandcastle of Stars" by Anne Schwartz

Let's consider next Anne Schwartz's first science poem, "Sandcastle of Stars." Although she identifies herself as primarily an English or arts student, Anne had never before written poetry she would consider authentic. Nor was she confident in her own scientific knowledge. Anne explains her writing process as follows:

> *This was my first scientific poem. I was not supremely confident in my poetry skills – even less so in my scientific skills – so I decided to rely on a feeling of wonder, hoping that I could reinforce it with scientific fact and explain it with poetry. As the poem lengthened, I thought more about the statistic itself and made more connections between sand and stars and wishes. My poem is not very scientific or cleverly structured. It is more a scattering of ideas.*

Sandcastle of Stars

There are more stars in the sky
Than grains of sand on every beach.

Each
Grain
Of
Sand

Two hundred billion billion stars.
Two hundred billion billion
Glowing nuclear reactions of fusing hydrogen
Fiery orbs of heat and pressure
Wishes.

Imagine.
Imagine a plastic shovelful of stars
Imagine walking, leaving footprints
On a carpet of glowing gases
On a path of constellations and dreams

To scatter a fistful of sand across the night sky
To feel the stars
Hopes and dreams
Prayers whispered with clenched hands
No farther away than
The toes of your summer shoes.

– Anne Schwartz, student

I cannot read this poem without being overwhelmed by the intensity of the feeling and the concreteness of the experience in the face of the abstract enormity of the universe. Like Alex's response, Anne's "scattering of ideas" enables us to feel at once the *macro* level of the stars and the *micro* level of the grains of sand. As an English teacher, I make an automatic connection to Blake's "To See a World in a Grain of Sand," a poem which Anne was unfamiliar with, yet which could have inspired her own work. She was inspired instead by the science poem, "Tsunami," and we can clearly see Hoffmann's model in her work.

Anne begins her poem in couplet form with a statement of scientific fact she recalls from prior knowledge. Then in stanza two, she skillfully separates *Each / Grain / Of / Sand*, the words on separate lines as well, giving us pause and patience to picture the minute particularity of the sand below in contrast with the expansive grandeur of the stars above. In the next stanza, Anne reaches a mastery rarely seen in beginning poetry writing. In five succinct lines, Anne manages to move from quantitative data – *Two hundred billion, billion stars* – to scientific definition – *nuclear reactions of fusing hydrogen/fiery orbs of heat and pressure* – to the qualitative or emotional, *wishes*. In these lines the poem explodes with the powerful repetition of *Two hundred billion billion stars* and then leaps, quite unexpectedly, from the *Fiery orbs of heat and pressure* to the abrupt next line and the simple statement of equally "fiery" emotion, that of *Wishes*.

What is so unusual about this poem is how Anne takes what might be cliché, the association of wishes and stars, but, in the context of science poetry, creates something powerful, fresh, and new. Anne asks us to *Imagine / Imagine a plastic shovelful of stars / Imagine walking, leaving footprints / On a carpet of glowing gases*. She has now moved completely from science to the personal, the particular, and the present, with our *Hopes and dreams* and *prayers no farther away than / the toes* of our *summer shoes*. I particularly like how her poem ends with "looking down" at the image of our mundane toes, most likely in the sand, rather than at the celestial glory of other stars above. Yet the Anne skillfully brings the two together in a mystical exuberance: *To scatter a fistful of sand across the night sky / to feel the stars* is the prayer *whispered with clenched hands*. Although literally impossible, Anne's poem enables us to "feel" the stars. It is science poetry at its best, making the unknown known, the intangible tangible, the impossible possible.

The hand-written notes Anne submitted at the end of class (she did not choose to share them aloud in class) became her final draft. She merely typed up the poem and added a title. In our three-way conference, my science partner and I reveled in the poem's evocation but had no suggestions for edits or revision. For someone who had never written a mature poem before, Anne had demonstrated exceptional craft: economy of language, precise diction or word choice, concrete imagery, masterful line breaks, intentional repetition, rhythm, and musicality. But most importantly, she had discovered, quite unexpectedly, her own poetic voice. Yes, her poem was inspired by "Tsunami," and modeled its rhetorical progression, but Anne made her poem her own. Anne's poem speaks to the power of science poetry to launch not only our future Einsteins and Curies, but also our future Blakes and Dickinsons.

"Beyond Configuration" by David Pitt

"Beyond Configuration," written by David Pitt, exemplifies the science poem written by an exceptional science student possessing a wealth of scientific knowledge and interests. Although he identifies himself as a "renaissance student" (especially excelling in drama), David loves to wrestle with complex scientific ideas and philosophical issues. His first science poem, "Beyond Configuration," clearly models Hoffmann's "Tsunami." It was the first science poem that challenged my science partner and myself to ponder the multiple meanings of a scientific term, *azimuthal*, and the resulting poetic image, *azimuthal spin*, requiring a three-way conference to determine the ultimate sense of the poem. In doing so, David made revisions in his final draft, changing the title first from "Configuration" to "You," and then to "Beyond Configuration." These title changes reflect David's ability to bring to bear both scientific and poetic eyes which together enabled him to discover and uncover the meaning and mystery of his own work. For David, the greater the ambiguity, the greater the delight. David explains his poetic process this way:

> *Written in the style of Hoffman's "Tsunami," I am trying to capture in "Beyond Configuration" the perplexity of a scientific phenomenon (electron configuration) and also the perplexity of a human phenomenon (anxiety). Difference: Hoffman's metaphor in "Tsunami" examines the essential difference. I consider the essential similarity.*

Beyond Configuration

Electrons occupy
no single space
at any given
time.
Physics shows us
(we might say)
how these
two
associate
0.529 angstrom from the nucleus
simultaneously
as they orbit defined
regions
which we can almost
comprehend three-dimensionally.

You
whom I cannot define
Negative by nature.
Where are you
exactly?
(More
specifically than
in ubiquity)

You haunt my mind
you plague my conscience
swarming about my brain.
I recognize your patterns
almost
to the point
of graphing them.

Your azimuthal spin eludes me.
When I try to look
closer the rules change.

– David Pitt, student

When I first read David's poem entitled at the time "Configuration," I immediately headed for the dictionary to look up the meaning of the word, *azimuthal*. Webster's indicated three definitions of *azimuth*: (1) the horizontal arc expressed as the clockwise angle between a fixed point (such as true north) and the vertical plane through the object, the *azimuth of a star*; (2) a bearing, course or direction, *azimuthal*; (3) a great circle in the heavens which runs through both the zenith and the nadir, *azimuth circle*. I wondered: Was David's use of the term scientifically accurate, or was he using the term more poetically, as an image or metaphor? Stanza one seemed clear to me: a scientific description of electrons – the idea that *electrons occupy / no single space / at any given / time*. Paradoxically, electrons are everywhere and nowhere at the same time, orbiting *defined / regions / which we can almost / comprehend three-dimensionally*. Whether I knew the science or not, the poem still had to make sense as a poem. I then considered the title, "Configuration," and I still wondered. The title seemed to make sense for stanza one, the science part of the poem describing electron configuration, but I could not see the connection to configuration in stanza two of the poem, when the speaker addresses the ambiguous *You*.

Here the speaker leaps from science to another realm: *You / whom I cannot define / Negative by nature* seemed to me to refer to *either* the electron, certainly "negative by nature," or a person, equally "negative by nature." Could the speaker be striking a metaphor? Given the Hoffmann model, I considered the leap to the human level, the speaker addressing a girlfriend or love interest. This person "haunts" his mind, "plagues" his conscience, and "swarms" about his brain. He can recognize *patterns*, but when he looks closer, *the rules change*. Could "Configuration" be a love poem using the "azimuthal spin" of electrons as a metaphor for the vicissitudes of love that "elude" the poet?

In my first conference with David, he confirmed the ambiguity of the poem, indicating his intention to create several levels of meaning: *You* could be the electrons or *electron configuration*, or *You* could be a lost love, or the configuration of a lost love. But in actuality, David had something else in mind; he intended *You* to be the emotion of anxiety. Just when I thought I had finally understood this poem, I had to open my eyes to another way of seeing. I told David I certainly saw the speaker in the poem as addressing more than electrons, primarily because of the ending: *When I try to look / closer the rules change,* which seemed to me an attempt to understand the mystery of another person rather than the mystery of electron configuration (where the rules, I assume, don't change). I confessed that nothing in the poem led me to see *You* as addressing a particular emotion, anxiety. And yet, once David explained his intention, the poem made perfect sense. Like the "azimuthal spin" of the electrons, anxiety "haunts," "plagues," "swarms," in an incomprehensible three-dimensional reality, constantly "eluding" understanding; for whenever the speaker looks *closer the rules change* – a wonderful image for anxiety, but perhaps a stretch for most readers to see. I posed questions for David to consider:

- *Is your poem too ambiguous?*
- *Is your title the best one possible?*
- *How can you prepare readers to think, "anxiety"?*

With that thought in mind, David considered changing his title to "You." I suggested we might just need the eyes of science: enter my science partner.

At our three-way conference, David indicated to us that he wanted lots of meaning-making in his poem; he wanted to compel readers to think. My science partner explained her interpretation of the azimuthal spin. To her eye, the last two lines, *When I try to look / closer the rules change* suggested Heisenberg's Uncertainty Principle: in the process of observing a subject, you change its properties. David seemed pleased with our feedback, and he ultimately decided to change his title from "You" to "Beyond Configuration."

A Final Offering: "A Love Song" by Ben Levenson

Ben Levenson responds to "Tsunami" with an inspired example of the personally relevant science poem. Certainly, I expected from students the fusion of scientific fact or quantitative data with qualitative data, and then a possible leap to another realm, but I did not expect this in-class practice exercise to leap so quickly to the personally authentic love poem. Undoubtedly, I underestimated Hoffmann's model to empower students, especially teenage students, to speak about what matters to them, love. I also underestimated one other factor, the time of year, as a prime motivator for poetry writing. Quite coincidentally, this first science poetry-writing lesson in Ms. Furphey's AP English Language and Composition classes occurred on February 11, 2008, a few days before Valentine's Day.

A Love Song

1 year
365 days
8,760 hours
525,600 minutes
31,536,000 seconds
the earth travels 'round the sun
it retraces this familiar path again and again
the sun's gravity attracting and pulling, reeling it in
eventually, the earth and sun will collide and become one
that fateful moment when up becomes down and down becomes up
when that circular path happens no more
every second they are one

You are my sun
i wait for that moment

– Ben Levenson, student

Ben's Commentary

My girlfriend inspired me to write the poem "A Love Song." I wrote the poem the night before Valentine's Day, so naturally she was on my mind. When I wrote the poem I could not help but think of how our lives in some respects revolve around each other and this led me to the idea of the orbit of the earth around the sun. Also that day we had read Hoffman's "Tsunami," which inspired the structure and theme of the poem. I liked his use of science as a metaphor. In writing my poem I borrowed his technique of describing scientific and quantitative information and then abruptly shifting focus through parataxis. After writing the poem I gave the poem to her as a present for Valentine's Day, and she liked it a lot. Because she liked it, I am satisfied with the poem. Please note the lack of capitalization of the poem is important: the only word capitalized is "You."

Handout: Basic Steps for Writing Any Science Poem

Whether in English or science classes, or whether with an English teacher, science teacher, or a team of teachers, the basic steps for writing any science poem remain the same. Distribute these *Basic Steps for Writing Any Science Poem* to your students as a general guide to follow for science poetry writing.

Basic Steps for Writing Any Science Poem

The Science Part

1. Research or experience a phenomenon in science or nature that inspires you, causing a strong emotional reaction such as awe, wonder, reverence, or empathy. Study and research the science behind the phenomenon, its definition, history, and evolution.

Or,

2. Research or experience a scientific theory or principle that informs or perplexes you, causing you to wonder, question, imagine, or speculate.

3. Make a word bank of all of the appropriate scientific vocabulary and terms you would like to reference in your poem. Think of this as scientific facts, definitions, allusions, and quotes that you might use as well as specific *quantitative* data or numbers.

The Poetry Part

1. Choose a poetic stance: describing the subject, addressing the subject, taking on the persona of the subject, or stance blending.

2. Draft a poem using the universal rhetorical progression: begin by describing the science; then associate, connect, or "leap" to the poetry; finally reflect or meditate at the end of your poem.

Or,

3. Draft a poem using science as metaphor throughout the poem. Begin with the metaphor and then extend it throughout the entire poem.
4. Put a title on your poem that either clarifies meaning or adds an extra level or dimension of meaning.

PART TWO: FURTHERING UNDERSTANDING AND APPRECIATION

EXTENSION ACTIVITY: "TSUNAMI SONG" BY STANLEY MOSS

Comparing Science Poetry and Lyrical Poetry

For interested science and English teachers, this extension activity attempts to distinguish between science poetry, as defined by our working definition, and lyrical poetry as written by contemporary poets. If relevant to your course of study, compare with your students Roald Hoffmann's science poem, "Tsunami" (Hoffman, 2002), with Stanley Moss' lyrical poem, "Tsunami Song" (Moss, 2009). Both poems at first glance appear to be on a similar subject, the *tsunami*, but they produce qualitatively different poetic results. Hoffmann begins on the *micro* level, looks at a particular soliton, and then moves to a particular relationship. Moss begins with a particular relationship, father and daughter, and then moves to the catastrophe, the Indian Ocean tsunami, and then back to a particular relationship, this time a husband and wife. Suggest to your students how Moss' poem moves in wave-like motion from the particular to the universal and then back again. For comparative study, project or distribute "Tsunami Song."

Reading and Explicating the Poem, "Tsunami Song"

Tsunami Song

A father is teaching his daughter to swim
in the Indian Ocean,
near them a fisherman throws his net,
silver and pink fish leap out of reach,
the child, wearing water wings,
loves her accomplishment,
squeals and laughs.
The father is happy teaching his daughter
something useful that will give her joy
the rest of her life. He says, "Come to me."
When the great stone ocean falls from the sky,
for a second, the rest of her life,
the child thinks she is swimming–
then she is a pebble in the deep.
The father, reaching for his daughter,
disappears, a shard of blue glass.
Like a seagull the water wings fly
to the foot of the mountain.
Despite a broken wing
it tries to rise from the sand.

I walk along the North Atlantic
with my wife and two dogs.
A horseshoe crab writes in the sand
the sun disappears,
everything darkness with no one to see it,
the moon a skull in the sky.

– Stanley Moss (Moss, 2009: 49)

Begin by asking your students to describe what has happened
literally in the poem, and how the poem makes them feel, their
immediate reactions. The powerful simplicity of "Tsunami Song"

quickly engages students; they easily share their feelings and observations. Students readily picture the images of the father teaching his daughter to swim; they hear her *laughs* and *squeals*, and they openly identify with the loving relationship of the father and daughter and the apparent normalcy of the opening scene. Suddenly, *When the great stone ocean falls from the sky,* my students express overwhelming shock and empathy for the innocence and helplessness of the father and daughter. Several mention how the image of a *second* being the *rest of her life*, resonates for them as they picture her a *pebble* lost in the unfathomable *deep*, her father a *shard of blue glass* as he reaches for her. Although none of them have ever seen, firsthand, a tsunami, the poem enables them to imaginatively bear witness. Given the prevalence of so many natural disasters all too familiar to students in recent history, "Tsunami Song" does just what all great poetry should do: make the universal particular, and at the same time, the particular universal.

Ask your students to imagine the sounds of a tsunami, and then, what they hear at the end of Moss' first stanza. Students agree that they can hear the enormity of the symphony of the tsunami, *the tsunami's song*. At the same time, they can hear the particular notes, or cries, of the father, the daughter, and the countless innocent victims. Ask students to reflect on the ending of Moss' poem:

- *Why do you think he shifts the scene from the Indian Ocean to a beach in the North Atlantic?*
- *Why does he end with the image of the moon a skull in the sky?*

Several of my students suggest that the poem ends very quietly, the "song" is literally over, but poetically, its sadness lives on in our hearts. Others mention that Moss ends on a note of distance and detachment. We are all so far from this disaster, and yet it haunts us with images of death, *the moon a skull in the sky*.

Taken together "Tsunami" and "Tsunami Song" demonstrate for science and English students alike the vast range of poetic evocation. Whether that evocation occurs in the eyes of two individuals, or in the cries of thousands, "Tsunami" and "Tsunami Song" speak to students of possibility, the possibility of human connection and connectivity.

A Brief Digression for the Teacher: To Evaluate or to Value?

What grade, if any, would you give Ben's poem? What grade, if any, would you give to Alex's poem, Anne's poem, or David's poem? Does grading a poem seem challenging, difficult, or problematic to you? If you did not give a grade, how would you assess or evaluate your students' science poems? Would written comments or oral feedback solve this problem for you? Would rubrics solve this problem for you? Would portfolios solve this problem for you? (See Chapter 12, "How to Assess Student Science Poetry: The Art of Response," for approaches and strategies to assessment and grading.)

PART THREE: THE ISSUE OF SCIENCE POETRY AND ACCESSIBILITY

The poetry of a practicing scientist is basically a dialogue; consequently, it should be clear enough to be understood and strong enough to lead somewhere in human terms. Science in poetry should shed some relatively new light.

– Miroslav Holub
"Rampage or Science in Poetry"
(Holub, 2006: 24)

The issue of science poetry's accessibility for the non-science reader remains a debate within science poetry writing circles. Some science poets question the use of highly technical concepts or terms, fearing their work will be too esoteric for the average reader. Edwin Morgan, Scotland's national poet, explains the dilemma:

Sometimes as a writer you are not sure how familiar the fact is, and you have to take a risk. In a recent poem I referred to "black smokers," and I remember when I was in the mid-throes of composition, I had a nagging doubt at the back of my mind as to whether I should use a term that would be well known to oceanographers and zoologists but maybe not to the average chap who had never been to the bottom of the sea. Anyway, I did use the words, in a benignly educational spirit. You only have to look up the *New Shorter Oxford English Dictionary*, which defines a smoker as a 'hydrothermal vent from which water and mineral particles issue.' (Morgan, 2006: 42)

Edwin Morgan does not compromise; he uses the technically accurate term in his poem, "Submarine Demon" (see Chapter 9). Similarly, Miroslav Holub, Czech immunologist and poet, admits to using highly technical vocabulary in his poetry as well: "I am much less cautious now about the reaction of editors and reviewers who would regard fibrins and cytokines as a scientific arrogance and obfuscation, especially when compared to those oxymorons, metonymy, palimpsests, and reincarnations that must be familiar to any cultured consumer of poetry and poetics" (Holub, 2006: 22).

As high school teachers, my science partner and I think Holub's point is well taken. Scientific allusions in poetry are no more difficult for our students than the many esoteric literary allusions we expect them to decipher, research, and understand. Enter the heavily annotated poetry or literature textbook. Has anyone ever read Milton, Dante, Chaucer, or Shakespeare's poetry in school without reference notes? And when it comes to difficult or esoteric vocabulary, English literature can hold its own with science any day. Once a word is unfamiliar and needs to be researched, noted, or referenced, we tend to see the text as less accessible. Why not see the text as intriguing, the poem an instrument of education rather than obfuscation.

For pedagogical value, my science partner and I encourage our high school students to use as much as possible specific, technical vocabulary as well as quantitative data and numeracy in their science poems. We solve the dilemma by suggesting they use a reference note at the end of the poem to explain or clarify the use of highly technical vocabulary or complex scientific concepts, theories, laws, or phenomena not commonly known beyond high school science.[6]

PART FOUR: RELATED SCHOLARSHIP AND PEDAGOGY

POETRY AND THE PHYSICAL SCIENCES

Among the prominent scientist-poets writing poetry today, my science partner and I have chosen to feature the science poems of Roald Hoffmann (see Chapters 4, 6, and Chapter 10). We do so, first and foremost, because his poems have proven highly accessible, instructive, and inspirational for vast numbers of our students in both science and English courses. After engaging with Hoffmann's poetry, our students have written exceptional science poetry of their own. Secondly, we do so because Roald Hoffmann himself serves as a model of the renaissance sensibility we hope to encourage in all our students.

Science teachers, in particular, chemistry and physics teachers, will find in Hoffmann's poetry a wealth of material useful for teaching chemistry and physics principles, concepts, and theories in poetry form. Mark Alber, chemistry teacher at Darlington School in Rome, Georgia, uses Hoffmann's poem, "The Devil Teaches Thermodynamics," as a model for science instruction as well as a model for a science poetry writing exercises in his AP Chemistry class. Alber interviewed Hoffmann and recorded a reading of the poem for his classes.[7]

Related pedagogy of particular interest to teachers in the physical sciences includes two interdisciplinary collaborations: Mark Alber's collaboration with poet and English teacher Rena Patton at the Darlington School ("Creative Writing and Chemistry," Alber

2001) and David H. Tamres' collaboration with English professor, W. John Coletta at the University of Wisconsin, Stevens Point ("Robert Frost and the Poetry of Physics," Coletta and Tamres, 1992). Both collaborations offer model science poetry lessons for both the high school and university classrooms. Other model lessons using Robert Frost's poetry to teach physical science include: Gil Abisdris and Adele Casuga's use of Frost's poems in their physical science classes at Westmount High School, Quebec, Canada ("Atomic Poetry: Using Poetry to Teach Rutherford's Discovery of the Nucleus," Abisdris and Casuga, 2001). Most importantly, they demonstrate the value of the interdisciplinary collaborations that are at the heart of this book.

Notes

1. My science partner and I assume students have prior knowledge of the following concepts: *quantitative data, qualitative data, figures of speech, metaphor, and allusion.* We do not teach these concepts at this point in the lesson. If you are teaching more basic students, you may have to further explain some terminology or concepts.

2. Most science poets, as all poets, embed within their poems stated definitions, descriptions, or contextual clues to clarify the meaning of technical vocabulary, concepts, and allusions for the reader. It is always an artistic choice on the part of the poet when to provide an explanatory reference note for the reader. Generally, most science poets do not provide explanatory notes. In Hoffmann's case, he has stated the definition of *soliton* that he wants the reader to bring to the poem. No further definition or research is required to engage with the poem within the poet's intention. On the other hand, a reader well-versed in solitons and the complexity of wave theory may certainly bring to the poem additional scientific and mathematical insights as well as poetic levels of interpretation.

3. This fact was confirmed in an interview with Roald Hoffmann on April 5, 2008. He explained that he was watching a soliton on film, a YouTube video. Hoffmann added that solitons are extremely difficult to observe in science and nature, referencing the work of Gerhart Ertl on platinum atoms (Gorrell, 2008).

4. *Fourier analysis* is defined by the *New Lexicon Webster's Dictionary* (1989) as a mathematical method used in the solution of physical problems that involves the development of a complex periodic function into a series of sine and cosine functions whose coefficients are computed by integration. The method is widely used for the solution of analytic expressions associated with electrical circuits, heat transfer, and atomic vibrations.

5. In *Leaping Poetry: An Idea with Poems and Translations*, Robert Bly (1972: 3–4) explains poetic *leaping*: "My idea, then, is that a great work of art often has at its center a long floating leap, around which the work of art in ancient times used to gather itself like steel shavings around the magnet. But a work of art does not necessarily have at its center a single long floating leap. The work can have many leaps, perhaps shorter. The real joy of poetry is to experience this leaping inside a poem. A poet who is 'leaping' makes a jump from an object soaked in unconscious substance to an object or idea soaked in conscious psychic substance. What is marvelous is to see this leaping return to poetry in this century."

6. My science partner and I concede that science poetry can theoretically move out of the range of accessibility for the non-science reader when the poem centers around a scientific concept so complex that it would take the highest levels of scientific knowledge and mathematics to understand: for example, poems about chaos theory, wave theory, uncertainty theory, or quantum physics. A case in point is the science poetry of Jorie Graham and Leslie Scalapino, where the poems themselves become *thought experiments*, thinking through a scientific problem (Morris, 2006).

7. A videotape containing examples and interviews is available and can be obtained by contacting Mark Alber at the following address: Darlington School, 1014 Cave Spring Road, Rome, GA 30161 USA; alberm@aol.com.

5 How to Teach Science Poetry Writing

Teacher as "Chemical Artist"

Combining science and the arts…makes pedagogical sense. Both disciplines rely on observation, pattern recognition, problem solving, experimentation, and thinking by analogy. Both artists and scientists observe, record, imagine, and create.

– Pamela Michael,
"Helping Children Fall in Love with the Earth"
(Michael, 2005: 116)

OVERVIEW: ART OR SCIENCE?

Although, as Pamela Michael confirms, much common ground exists between science and the arts making "pedagogical sense" to combine them, few teachers in either discipline have experienced or explored with their students the value of such vital interdisciplinary connections. The aim of Chapter 5 is to offer for science and English teachers alike practical strategies for teaching one of the most challenging skills – the art of poetry writing in general, and the art of science poetry writing in particular. Why is this teaching such a challenge? For many in the field, the writing process, and most certainly the poetic process, remains far more art than science. William Stafford in *Writing the Australian Crawl* acknowledges the mystery:

> I must insist that I am often baffled about what "skill" has to do with the precious little area of confusion when I do not know what I am going to say and then I find out what I am going to say. That precious interval I am unable to bridge by skill. What can I witness about it? It remains mysterious. (Stafford, 1978: 19)

If you are a teacher of science or a teacher of English, you may be wondering, how? How can we, as teachers, so practiced in teaching skills, launch any poem, if that process remains a mystery? Enter you, the teacher as "chemical artist," open to Stafford's "precious intervals," and willing to serve as the "bridge" between not knowing and knowing. If we think of Stafford's "precious intervals" as *teachable moments*, if we think of ourselves as guides providing bridges of understanding, then the "how to" of writing science poetry starts to become clearer – a process fusing the *science part* of the poem with the *poetry part* of the poem, creating something at once "mysterious" yet knowable and, we might add with conviction, <u>teachable</u>.

Yes, teachable. Although my science partner and I recognize the mysteries involved in the poetic process, we firmly believe that we as teachers, or as "chemical artists," if you prefer, can teach science poetry writing with effectiveness and inspiration. This chapter, devoted to that end, explores the following core questions:

- *Is there a formula or recipe for science poetry writing?*
- *What are the most effective methods for teaching science poetry writing?*

To further our pedagogy, we offer the following working metaphor for your consideration.

A Working Metaphor: Teacher as "Chemical Artist"

Alchemy: "n. a medieval chemical art whose principal objective was to find the panacea and to transmute base metals into gold."

(*The New Lexicon Webster's Dictionary of the English Language* 21)

Alchemy, a medieval "chemical art," suggests a possible metaphor for science poetry writing instruction when the student poet, informed, inspired, and empowered by science, transforms something "base," or literal language, into something "gold," or poetic language. The working metaphor "chemical artist" supports the image of transformation that is central to science poetry writing – the "mixing" of the two disciplines or "parts," the *science part* and the *poetry part*. For instructional purposes, this concept of "mixing" may seem at first mechanical, but it has proven useful for novice, student poets. Later, in advanced science poetry writing, this working metaphor gives way to a new one, the more artful concept of *fusion* or MacDiarmid's *perfect fusion* (see Overview: Section Three).

WHAT'S AHEAD

Chapter 5 offers teaching tips, methods, approaches, and strategies for teaching poetry writing in general, and science poetry writing in particular. The chapter is directed to both science and English teachers and those familiar and unfamiliar with poetry writing and poetry writing instruction. Most importantly, Chapter 5 offers an effective, proven, and accessible pedagogy for science poetry writing instruction adaptable for both the science and English classrooms.

Chapter 5 at a Glance

Part One: Teaching Tips for Science Poetry Writing

Part Two: Methods for Teaching Science Poetry Writing

Part Three: For English Teachers
How to Teach the Science Part on Your Own

Part Four: For Science Teachers
How to Teach the Poetry Part on Your Own

Part Five: The Teacher as Chemical Artist
How to Teach the Writing Part
Teaching the Five Poetic Stances

Part Six: Student Handouts
Student Handout #1: How to Identify a Science Poem
Student Handout #2: Data Gathering Chart for Science Poetry Writing

Section One Conclusion

PART ONE: TEACHING TIPS FOR SCIENCE POETRY WRITING

TIP #1: TAKE COURAGE! YOU DO NOT HAVE TO BE THE POETRY WRITING EXPERT

Every classroom-based, poetry-writing lesson should be as true as possible to the art form, or as true as possible to how poets write poetry. That of course, is all in theory. In actuality, no one knows exactly how poets write poems. Even if we delude ourselves into thinking poetry can be defined by its form (*"I've written 14 lines; it must be a sonnet"),* none of this is going to help the teacher new to teaching science poetry writing. Yet, all is well and good. Why? Because science poetry is so unfamiliar, so different, and so unique a genre that you and your students can come together in a common ground of ignorance, journeying together to discover the art form. So tip #1 is to take courage! You do not have to be the poetry-writing expert.

TIP #2: JOIN YOUR STUDENTS AND BECOME A SCIENCE POET

This is a no-fail proposition. If you are an English teacher, your students are not going to expect much science from you for a science poem; and conversely, if you are a science teacher, your students are not going to expect much poetry. Tip #2: Why not surprise them? Write your own science poem along with your students as a response to a given prompt or lesson; or, better yet, write your own science poem modeling for your students a science poetry lesson that you particularly prefer. In this way, you will be able to discuss and share science poetry writing with greater authenticity and insight (see the science poetry of one such teacher in Chapter 11).

TIP #3: BE TRUE TO POETRY

Be open, receptive, and sensitive to the powerful mystery of ambiguity. In the world of poetry writing there are no right, and there are no wrong, answers; rather than answers, there is the wonderful world of possibility unfolding as the poet's imagination, images, and inspiration flow onto paper. In that flow, words rub against each other, and new meanings arise: A digression? No! It could be a delightful surprise! In teaching poetry writing tell your students to go with the flow of their thoughts, impulses, and associations.

TIP #4: BE TRUE TO SCIENCE POETRY

Yes, be open, receptive, and sensitive to the powerful mystery of ambiguity that is the poetry part of the poem, and yet, at the same time, be accurate, methodical, and correct when it comes to the science part of the poem. In the world of science poetry, there may be a wrong answer if the science is not scientifically "true." Challenge your students to research and fact-check their science before, during, and after they write their science poems. Why? Because the process of science poetry writing clarifies thinking, leading to greater understanding that opens windows of possibility. The science that students see and know before they write a science poem may not be the science they see and know after they write a science poem. Ideally, there should be a qualitative difference, one that deepens their understanding of science as they see and experience it from a different perspective.

TIP #5: TEACH PROCESS OVER PRODUCT

It is the process of creation and the enlightenment it brings that is most important in teaching science poetry writing, not the product per se. Here's the paradox: if you teach process over product, creativity over formula, the dynamic quality of poetry as a *work in progress*, you will paradoxically find your students writing much more inspired and authentic science poems.

TIP #6: BELIEVE IN YOUR OWN CREATIVITY AND THE CREATIVITY OF YOUR STUDENTS

Above all else, believe in your own innate creativity and the innate creativity of your students. If you do so, your students will discover the creativity within themselves. To write a science poem is, without question, an act of creative challenge. As such, it is an intensely pleasurable act, involving a focused intensity and commitment to task that results in the creator losing all sense of time in the *flow* of creation. Csikszentmihalyi defines it as "an almost automatic, effortless, yet highly focused state of consciousness" (Csikszentmihalyi, 1996: 110).[1]

As a teacher of science poetry writing, your task is to keep that creativity and *flow* alive. Encourage your students to play with words, experiment with form and shape on the page, follow their ears to "hear" as one word suggests another, and to take risks as they forge a universe of verse. Most importantly, believe in and foster your students' creative potential. If they ask when writing a science poem, "Is it ok if I...?" In the spirit of honoring creativity, the answer should be a resounding "yes." You never know where that creative flow will go.

TIP #7: TEACH THE CREATIVE PROCESS AS RECURSIVE

The creative process remains one of the cornerstones of common ground shared by scientists and poets alike. Mihaly Csikszentmihalyi (1996) identifies five steps in the process: a period of *preparation* (immersion consciously or not with the subject); a period of *incubation* (churning of ideas); a period of *insight* ("Aha!" moment); a period of *evaluation* (is the idea worth pursuing?); and finally, a period of *elaboration* (the hard work itself). He points out, however, that this classical analytical framework must not be taken "too literally," the creative process being much more recursive than linear (Csikszentmihalyi, 1996: 79–80). We would add that the creative process is much more personal and individual than formulaic. Keeping this in mind, you will want to offer your students a variety of modalities for writing and creating: in the classroom, in the laboratory, in the field, in solitude, and in community.

TIP #8: TEACH THE POETRY WRITING PROCESS AS RECURSIVE

Possibly you have been taught or have experienced writing as a linear process: pre-writing, data gathering, outlining, organizing, drafting, revising, redrafting, editing, proofreading, and publishing. In this familiar linear approach, the poet or writer does not go back to a previous step in the process. This is in fact unlikely, impractical, impossible, unrealistic, and not how poets and writers write. They are continually going back, or looping, to earlier phases, and all writers know that writing is, as a result, a messy endeavor, one full of surprises and inspiration, but essentially, the "99% perspiration" of Edison's famous aphorism.[2] Once again, after presenting a science poetry model or prompt, let your students freely write. Do not direct the entire class in required stages of writing. Some students, once inspired, may have their idea and may be able to jump into poetry writing rapidly. Others may need to reflect, gather data, collaborate, or research before their writing starts to *flow*. Remember: There is no one way to write a science poem, and it is definitely not a prescribed formula or linear process that can be the same for all.

TIP #9: DISTINGUISH BETWEEN REVISION AND EDITING

Writing teachers teaching writing as process make a clear distinction between revision and editing, the former involving the entire process of substantively improving a piece of writing, the latter involving mechanical corrections of grammar, spelling, and punctuation, or the end stage of writing (Bizzaro, 1993: 14–38). This distinction applies as well to science poetry writing. Revision, the writing of multiple drafts in response to specific feedback, defines the teaching of science poetry writing as process. Teach science poetry writing as process, providing suggestions for revision in the form of four types of feedback: reactive, descriptive, prescriptive, and collaborative. (see Alan Ziegler, "Midwifing the Craft: Teaching Revision and Editing" for in-depth discussion of these four types of feedback).[3]

TIP #10: DISTINGUISH BETWEEN FEEDBACK AND GRADING

Writing teachers generally make a distinction between feedback and grading, the former a means of giving specific suggestions for revision on a poem in progress, the latter as a means of giving a numerical grade on a finished poem (Bizzaro, 1993: 192–219). Whereas feedback emphasizes writing as *process*, grading, whether letter or numerical, emphasizes writing as *product*. Writing teachers for decades have recognized the problem of putting a grade on a poem: the student may then regard the poem as "finished" with little motivation to revise for improvement. When teaching science poetry writing, give students ample opportunity to substantively revise before they receive a final grade at time of submission.

FINAL TIP: SHARE THE VOICES OF YOUR STUDENTS

Provide opportunities – open readings, performances, and publication – where student science poets can raise their voices; share their poems with their peers, parents, and community; do something important for a local cause; or just have "poetic fun" (see Appendix C for science poetry contests, competitions, and publication resources).

PART TWO: METHODS FOR TEACHING SCIENCE POETRY WRITING

Keeping in mind that there is no one way to write a science poem, there is also no one way to teach how to write a science poem. In the spirit of multiple perspectives which is the essence of our pedagogy, Chapter 5 offers multiple approaches that have proven effective in engaging and instructing student poets in both science and English classes.[4] My science partner and I use all of these approaches individually as well as in combination to teach science poetry.

METHOD #1: THE MODELS APPROACH

This approach is not only the most traditional, academic, and yet artistic approach to teaching any form of poetry writing, but it is especially important for science poetry when the genre is new and unfamiliar to students. In the models approach, the teacher presents a poem as a model for reading and writing instruction. The success of this approach depends upon the interplay of three critical factors: (1) the model must be accessible to students; (2) the model must teach craft; (3) and the model must inspire students, prompting them to write their own poems. For the models approach, inspiration remains the key factor, for without inspiration the resulting poem may be more derivative, imitative, or academic than authentic. Yet given the right model, as in "Tsunami" by Roald Hoffmann, students will move readily from practice exercises to authentic poetry, establishing ownership over their science poems (see Chapter 4). For teachers unfamiliar with poetry or poetry writing of any kind, the models approach is the place to begin. By shifting authority from the teacher to the poet via the poem, the poet or poem provides the "answers" to the "how to" questions. How and why one poet's work inspires another poet's work remains a mystery; regardless of how and why, the fact of that influence remains clear, defining the essence of the discipline.

Although this approach may seem more applicable to the literature classroom, science teachers may use this approach effectively as an anticipatory set to introduce a scientific principle, topic, or theory. Conversely, science poetry models may also bring closure to a course of study, inspiring students to express creatively what they have learned about a given scientific topic from a lecture, lesson, or unit of study.

METHOD #2: THE IMITATION APPROACH

The imitation approach, a variation of the models approach, asks students to intentionally imitate a given model's structure: for example, the same number of lines, syllables per line, stanzas, or exact meter, rhyme scheme, or phrases. If the poem is in a closed form, the student closely imitates the sonnet, villanelle, quatrain, or tercet form. If the poem is in open form or free verse, the student imitates similar grammatical constructions, phrases, line breaks, and number of lines. The imitation poem may be considered a genre of poetry in its own right. Ron Padgett includes the imitation poem in his *Handbook of Poetic Forms* (Padgett, 2000: 89), tracing the origin of the term to Robert Lowell's *Imitations* (Lowell, 1961), a collection of poems based on Lowell's translation of poems into other languages. "What resulted were poems that couldn't really be called translations, nor could they be called original poems: they were halfway between. Lowell called them 'imitations'" (Padgett, 2000: 89). Many authorities advocate the strategy of imitation in poetry writing as a vital teaching tool for beginning poetry writers. Poets Stephen Dunning and William Stafford advocate teaching the imitation poem in *Getting the Knack: 20 Poetry Writing Exercises* (Stafford and Dunning, 1992: 195–198).

If students question whether such imitations are plagiarism, my science partner and I point out the art form, but we also stress the need for student poets to credit the source for their imitation or inspiration either in a citation, title, or acknowledgment. Such credits are necessary for close or exact imitations and inspirations: for example, "Upon Reading 'Tsunami' by Roald Hoffmann," or "For Roald Hoffmann." If the inspiration is loose and the poem clearly becomes the student's own, then credit does not have to be given (see for example, student science poems in Chapter 4). Although we do not directly teach the imitation approach in this book, students at times will closely imitate a model poem.

METHOD #3: THE ACTIVITIES APPROACH

In the activities approach, teachers prompt poetic responses by providing an actual activity, usually hands-on or experiential which inspires students to write science poems. These activities may be in the classroom, in the laboratory, or in the field. For example, in class students may be given naturalistic objects, minerals or gems, or sensory field data to observe, prompting poetic responses (see Chapters 6, 7, and 8). The success of this approach depends upon the interplay of four critical factors: (1) the activity must be engaging; (2) the activity must enable students to gather and/or experience scientific data; (3) the activity must inform student's scientific knowledge; (4) the activity must provoke student's thinking; and (5) and the activity must evoke students' emotions or feelings. An alternate strategy common to the activities approach is simply to make an open suggestion prompting poetic response. For example, instead of presenting a model poem "about bees," a teacher might suggest writing a poem "about an encounter with bees" or "about getting stung by a bee."

The activities approach finds common ground in both science and English pedagogy that holds that students learn more effectively by doing or active learning rather than by the more passive, lecture method. Science teaching, with its emphasis on laboratory and field experience, naturally lends itself to the activities approach. In science class, students might write a science poem to complement their lab reports or field notes. Similarly, in English and creative writing classes, students might respond to open-ended prompts recalling memories of science teachers, science classrooms, and scientific encounters.

METHOD #4: THE MODELS-AND-ACTIVITIES APPROACH

Combining models and activities capitalizes on the strengths of both approaches. My science partner and I use the models and activities approach in all of our Science Academy English lessons (see Chapters 6 and 7) as well as in our science poetry expedition (see Chapter 11). Generally, there are two methods: beginning with models followed by an activity, or conversely, beginning with an activity followed by models. For example, teachers may begin with an activity to engage students in their own thinking and original responses, and then offer model responses by professional poets; or teachers may begin with models by professional poets and then proceed with an activity to inspire further poetry. The combination approach offers variations. For example, in our summer science poetry field trip, my science partner and I began each day with model science poems by professional poets, then we proceeded to the field activity, and we concluded with a sharing of student science poems in progress, another type of model to inspire additional science poems.

TEACHING SCIENCE POETRY WRITING: ON YOUR OWN OR WITH A COLLEAGUE?

Regardless of the writing approach you choose, every science poem will have two parts: a science part and a poetry part, which, when fused together, make the science poem. Given the cross-curricular nature of science poetry, you must decide if you are going to teach on your own or with a colleague. Consider: if you are an English teacher, will you provide the science part yourself, or will you invite a science colleague to team teach with you or guest lecture in your classroom? Conversely, if you are a science teacher, will you provide the poetry part yourself, or will you invite a poet or English teacher colleague to team-teach with you or guest lecture in your classroom? Although we advocate team-teaching whenever possible, my science partner and I offer the following suggestions for teaching science poetry writing on your own.

PART THREE: FOR ENGLISH TEACHERS

HOW TO TEACH THE SCIENCE PART ON YOUR OWN

If you are an English teacher and choose to teach on your own, here are some tips for teaching the science part:

- Borrow pertinent specimens (living, non-living, preserved), charts, graphs, field guides, instruments, equipment, and 3-D models from the science department in your school. This is an effective method for teaching technical vocabulary.
- Borrow pertinent Power-Point lectures, scientific worksheets, and data from the science department in your school. This is an effective method demonstrating for students the transfer of knowledge from one discipline to another.
- Have your students research scientific information relevant to the science poem they want to write. For example, if they are writing a poem on tsunamis, they might research the science behind the subject. This is an effective method to teach relevant research skills that result in a creative outcome.
- Do your own field research and data gathering for science poetry writing. For example, gather your own specimens for writing while beachcombing, walking in parks, or gardening. Bring into your classroom unusual naturalistic objects – shells, rocks, minerals, gems, lava, crystals, mounted butterflies and insects. Use these objects for sensory observation and poetry writing prompts (see Chapter 8 for teacher-gathered data)

PART FOUR: FOR SCIENCE TEACHERS

HOW TO TEACH THE POETRY PART ON YOUR OWN

If you are a science teacher and choose to teach on your own, here are some tips for teaching the poetry part from our book:

- Teach the "Poetic Stances" presented in this chapter.
- Teach the "Rhetorical Progression" presented in Chapter 4. Use professional models from this book to define and illustrate the genre.
- Pair poetry-minded students in your class with non-poetry-minded students for collaborative poetic responses.
- Try writing your own science poem as a model for instruction (see Chapter 11 for a science teacher's poems)

PART FIVE: THE TEACHER AS CHEMICAL ARTIST

HOW TO TEACH THE WRITING PART

Regardless of the science part and the poetry part, ultimately there will be a process, the writing part, fusing the two parts together. How much science should be "fused" into the poem? How much poetry? Is there a recipe or formula for writing a science poem? Enter you, the science poetry teacher as "chemical artist." I like this metaphor for the teacher's role because it suggests that poetry writing is more art than science, and that the process is more intuitive and organic than mechanical and formulaic. That is to say, once the student poet begins to write, drawing on all of the scientific resources at hand, something else takes over, the poetic process itself, which suggests to the student poet, either consciously or subconsciously, direction, movement, and meaning within the poem. This aspect of writing – magical, mystical, and difficult to teach – is the essence of the art form, and in a science poem, the essence of the fusion. It comes from the associative power of language itself; it also comes from the associative power of the sound of language itself, one word in context suggesting another. These aleatoric effects, coming by chance, need to be noticed, encouraged, and applauded by you, the chemical artist.

In addition, you as "chemical artist" will also have to decide just how much science is sufficient to make a science poem as well as how much poetry is sufficient to make the language poetic, not just scientific (see Chapter 2 for the Poetry Litmus Test). Just as poetry may be viewed on a continuum from less poetic language (see found poetry in Chapter 2) to highly poetic language, so too may science be viewed on a continuum from low-level or elementary science, to higher level or high school science, and then finally to advanced science. Kurt Brown's anthology of science poetry presents science poems reflecting this continuum: some like Billy Collin's "Earthling" (Collins, 1988) or William Stafford's "What If We Were Alone?" (Stafford, 1987) reflect elementary science, while others like the poetry of Roald Hoffmann, Alice Jones, Pattiann Rogers, and A. R. Ammons reflect more advanced science.

Here are some basic guidelines to follow in determining just how much science to require in your students' science poems:

- **The level and ability of your students**. If the level and ability of your students is average, you may have to instruct and require students to infuse more quantitative data and specific scientific terminology into their poems, to take the place of the general and generic vocabulary they will tend to use. If the level and ability is advanced, you will still have to challenge your students to further clarify and specify scientific and poetic meaning with pertinent facts and vocabulary.
- **Your particular objective in teaching science poetry**. Is your objective to teach creativity, poetry in general, or science and scientific knowledge? Depending upon your

emphasis and subject (either English or science), you may be more inclined to emphasize the poetry part of the poem versus the science part, or vice versa.

- **The requirements of your particular course of study**. Depending upon your curriculum, you may want to use science poetry as a tool or vehicle to support particular skills: creative, critical, and metaphoric thinking as well as language, vocabulary, writing, and research skills. Such factors may determine just how much science you will require for your students' science poems as well as just how much poetry.

Most importantly, keep in mind that although there is no formula for writing a science poem nor any measure for determining just how much science to fuse into a poem, our working definition provides a standard to follow: the poem must be inspired and informed by some level of science, and it must move from the scientific or literal use of language to the poetic, metaphoric, symbolic, or figurative use of language. Thus, the writing part of a science poem requires the fusion of science and poetry, and perhaps, some "magical" alchemy.

The Five Poetic Stances: A Universal Poetry Writing Strategy

Every introductory poetry-writing lesson I teach includes instruction in the five poetic stances common to poetry. High school students of all levels and abilities easily conceptualize these stances. Use of any one or several of the stances moves literal language to the realm of the poetic. For demonstration purposes, I prefer to use simple, clear, concise, and accessible stance models that say to students, "You can do this, too!" Often I write stance models on the subject of the poetry at hand: for example, minerals and gems (see Chapter 6 for basic examples of the stance models based on the subject of minerals). Other times, I will use student and professional models as examples. Whether you are a science or English teacher, I encourage you to try writing your own instructional models of the poetic stances in the box below.

The Five Poetic Stances

1. Describing the Subject
2. Addressing the Subject
3. Taking on the Identity of the Subject (Persona Poem)
4. Reflecting or Meditating on the Subject
5. Blending Two or More Stances in a Single Poem

Stance #1: Describing the Subject

Stance #1 employs the linguistic devices and figures of speech common to poetry: in particular, sensory imagery as well as sound-based devices such as alliteration, assonance, consonance, onomatopoeia, rhythm, repetition, and rhyme. For examples of stance #1, see Chapter 6, The Four Poetic Stances, and stanza two of "Fluorite" by Roald Hoffmann.

Stance #2: Addressing the Subject

In stance #2, the speaker or poet addresses the subject. I point out to students that the "you" in the poem is the subject addressed. For examples of stance #2, see Chapter 6, The Four Poetic Stances, and Chapter 9, stanza one of "The Wellfleet Whale" by Stanley Kunitz.

Stance #3: Taking on the Identity of the Subject (Persona Poem)

In stance #3, the poet takes on the identity or persona of the subject, giving the subject voice. I point out to students that the "I" in the poem is the subject speaking, not the poet. The poet simply imagines what the subject might be feeling and thinking and then lets that subject speak. To clarify the speaker, students should use the subject as the title of the persona poem. For examples of stance #3, see Chapter 6, The Four Poetic Stances, and Chapter 12, "This is your Geode Talking" by Carter Revard, an entire poem in persona form.

Stance #4: Reflecting or Meditating Upon the Subject

In stance #4, the poet thinks about the subject, reflecting, meditating, and speculating. In its purest form, reflection remains the expression of abstract thought, idea, and opinion. When combined with other poetic stances, reflection fulfills the universal rhetorical pattern, the movement from description or narration to thought or meditation. For examples of stance #4, see: (1) Chapter 6, The Four Poetic Stances; (2) Chapter 7, the poem "Genetic Sequence," beginning with line 4, which reflects on the question: "*If every cell / contains the entire sequence / constituting what or who the creature is / how does a certain clump of cells / know to...*"; and (3) Chapter 10, the last lines of A. R. Ammon's poem, "Cascadilla Falls." Often poems end with the poetic stance of reflection.

Stance #5: Blending the Stances

In stance #5, the poet blends multiple stances often separated by stanzas. Movement from description to reflection, the universal rhetorical pattern identified in Chapter 4, is one of the most common forms of stance blending. I strongly encourage beginning student poets to use stance blending because it naturally "moves" the poem to say more and to say more poetically. For examples of stance blending, see Chapter 6, The Four Poetic Stances, and Chapter 4, "Tsunami" by Roald Hoffmann (Description, Address, Reflection).

PART SIX: STUDENT HANDOUTS

USE OF INSTRUCTIONAL HANDOUTS

In teaching science poetry reading and writing as well as the skills of data gathering and poetry revision, science and English teachers alike may find the use of handouts such as those on the following pages a practical instructional tool. Although I generally do not use handouts for poetry writing in creative writing and English classes, I do find handouts useful for data gathering and the revision process. My science partner, in particular, has found handouts useful in her science classes for identifying what is a science poem as well as for data gathering and distinguishing between quantitative and qualitative data. Although I do not generally use these handouts for poetry writing in advanced English or creative writing classes, I do see their value for students who may need more structure and guidance in the science poetry reading and writing process. Given the success of this approach in our Science Academy English classes, my science partner and I offer the following handouts for identifying a science poem, gathering data for science poetry writing, and assessing and revising one's own science poetry and a peer's science poetry.

STUDENT HANDOUT #1: HOW TO IDENTIFY A SCIENCE POEM

Use this handout to determine if a poem is a science poem by our working definition. Students may fill in the chart as you read the science poem, or they may fill in the chart after they read the science poem to themselves. This handout is useful for science poetry reading, analysis, and explication. Use the last two questions to open discussion and debate after reading a science poem.

How to Identify a Science Poem

Poet's Name	
Title of the Poem	
Identify all the senses in the poem (sight, sound, smell, taste, touch)	Sight:
	Sound:
	Smell:
	Taste:
	Touch:
How does the poet describe each sense? Be specific. For example: smell: fresh grass; hear: blue bird song. Identify sensory details.	Sight:
	Sound:
	Smell:
	Taste:
	Touch:
What area(s) of science does this poem relate to? Are there any scientific allusions?	
Does the poet refer to or describe any scientific concepts, principles, theories, or processes? If so, what are they? Be specific.	
Does the poet use any quantitative data in the poem? (If so, what is the data, and how is that data used?) Reference specific lines, images, or phrases.	
Does the poet express any qualitative data in the poem? (If so, how is that data expressed?) Reference specific lines, images, or phrases.	
Could the poet have written the poem more scientifically? If so, how? (Be specific)	
Could the poet have written the poem more poetically? If so, how? (Be specific)	

STUDENT HANDOUT #2: DATA GATHERING CHART FOR SCIENCE POETRY WRITING

Use this simple handout to facilitate students' data gathering for science poetry writing. More advanced students may not need to use this handout, but it serves as a reminder to all student poets to infuse both types of data.

Data Gathering Chart for Science Poetry Writing

Quantitative Data: (Identify)

1. _____

2. _____

3. _____

4. _____

5. _____

Qualitative Data: (Identify)

1. _____

2. _____

3. _____

4. _____

5. _____

Subject of your poem: _____

Title of your poem: _____

Write the first draft of your poem: (use the back if necessary)

SECTION ONE CONCLUSION

At the conclusion of Section One, your students will be ready to embark on the next phase of their voyage of discovery. They will have experienced multiple ways of seeing art, nature, science, and poetry (Chapter 1). They will have developed an awareness of their poetic and scientific eyes (Chapters 2 and 3). And, they will have explored writing their first science poems (Chapter 4). Now, with eyes wide open, they will be prepared to discover the fundamentals of writing science poetry with the science subjects most familiar to high school students – earth science and biology. In Section Two of this book, my science partner and I open our classroom doors to you and your students as we share our own voyages of discovery teaching the fundamentals of science poetry writing.

Notes

1. See Chapter 5, "The Flow of Creativity," in *Creativity: Flow and the Psychology of Invention* by Mihalyi Csikszentmihalyi for the nine main elements that describe the process of *flow* (Csikszentmihalyi, 1996: 110–113). The creative state of flow remains one of the most significant aspects of common ground between scientists and artists.
2. Edison's aphorism is: "Creativity consists of 1 percent inspiration and 99 percent perspiration" (Csikszentmihalyi, 1996: 80).
3. See Alan Ziegler's "Midwifing the Craft: Teaching Revision and Editing" (Ziegler, 1989: 209–211) for a useful discussion of four types of feedback highly effective in responding to student science poems: reactive, descriptive, prescriptive, and collaborative. These types of feedback do not assess a poem in progress, that is, measure it against some standard, but rather provide specific reader-response information to the student poet to facilitate that student's revision process. I highly recommend adapting Ziegler's writer-friendly approach to your revision and editing lessons.

4. Lucky Jacobs identifies three approaches to teaching poetry writing: the *models approach*, the *activities approach*, and the *models-and-activities approach* (Jacobs, 1977). He does not assess these methods or privilege one over the other. Our approach incorporates these methods along with others.

Section Two: Fundamentals

Basic Lessons for Science Poetry Writing

SECTION OVERVIEW

Section Two offers three fundamental lessons designed to develop basic science poetry writing skills for all students, both in the classroom and in the field. All three fundamental lessons originated in Science Academy English III as a result of the team-teaching of my science partner and myself. They form the core of Morristown High School's Science Academy English III science poetry unit. In each fundamental lesson, students observe with scientific and poetic eyes, beginning with the world of the non-living ("Gems" in Chapter 6) and the living ("Bugs" in Chapter 7), and then going into the field in Chapter 8. Each fundamental lesson offers both an activities approach and a models approach to poetry writing instruction. Emphasizing process over product, the opening activities in the classroom engage students in simultaneous hands-on science and poetry writing practice, developing their confidence and writing skills as well as their understanding and appreciation of science poetry. Most importantly, the model science poems that follow each opening activity demonstrate for students the art form inspiring the more complex and advanced student science poems that follow in Section Three: Fusion.

SUGGESTIONS FOR USING THIS SECTION

Although there is a sequence of development, from the classroom to the field, each chapter in Section Two stands alone as a composite lesson and may be taught in any order or sequence. In addition, each chapter complements courses of study commonly taught in high school science in the United States:

- *Chapter 6, "It's a Gem," aligns with earth science (grade 9);*
- *Chapter 7, "What's Buggin' You?" aligns with biology (grade 10); and*
- *Chapter 8, "Into the Field," aligns with research and environmental science.*

Science teachers will find Section Two a creative approach to the teaching of minerals, gems, arthropods, and environmental science. English teachers will find these basic lessons effective science poetry writing prompts for students in both mainstream and advanced English classes. Both English and science teachers will find the student model responses in each chapter instructive and inspirational. Taken as a whole, Section Two serves as an ideal introductory unit plan in science poetry writing for students of all levels and abilities.

6 It's a Gem!

Rocks and Minerals

Doing science, whose essence is to understand nature, inspires awe. As a geologist, I plant one foot (metaphorically) in the present day and the other foot in Deep Time.

– Leon E. Long
Professor of Geology University of Texas
Letter to the Editor, *New York Times*
(Long, 23 April 2008)

OVERVIEW: FUNDAMENTAL LESSON ONE

The aim of Fundamental Lesson One is to introduce students, step by step, to the basic skills of science poetry writing, thereby preparing them for the more advanced science poetry writing to follow. Rocks, minerals, and gemstones offer an effective and engaging way to begin basic science poetry writing for several reasons. First, rocks, minerals, and gemstones are familiar territory for most students. Nearly all have had some personal encounters with these treasures of the natural world; such encounters serve as sources for poetic inspiration. Second, nearly all students enjoy gemstones. Many have personal favorites and are familiar with folklore about gems and gem symbolism. Third, the basic science of rocks, minerals, and gemstones is highly accessible to hands-on pedagogy in the classroom. Students readily enjoy observing, touching, identifying, and studying different minerals and gemstones. Fourth, minerals offer a concrete approach to science poetry writing, one that lends itself to distinguishing between the science part and the poetry part of a poem. Fifth, most high school students in the United States as well as other countries will complete a basic course of study in earth science, geophysics, or physical science by grade nine.

Fundamental Lesson One consists of four parts consisting of two basic activities: the first, a practice exercise in science poetry writing in response to first-hand observation of rocks and minerals; the second, an exercise in response to a model mineral poem, "Fluorite," by Roald Hoffmann, followed by an extension

---

Fundamental Lesson One at a Glance

Part One: **Practice Science Poetry Writing Exercise**
Activity #1: It's a Gem!
Model Student Responses
"My Geode" by Cori Connolly
"Amber" by Meghan Crippen

Part Two: **Model Mineral Poem**
Activity #2 "Fluorite" by Roald Hoffmann
Model Student Response
"Aquamarine" by Maggie McArdle

Part Three: **Extension Activity**
Advanced Mineral and Earth Science Poems
Model Student Responses
"Quakes of the World" by Rebecca Ozarow
"Plate Tectonics" by Rachel Needle
"The American Dream" by Karley Murphy

Part Four: **Related Scholarship and Pedagogy**
Poetry and the Earth Sciences

activity in advanced mineral and earth science poetry writing. The chapter ends with Part Four, a discussion of related scholarship and pedagogy in poetry and the earth sciences.

Students begin with an opening activity in basic science poetry writing. First they gather data on gems for the science part of their poems, and then they study gem poems demonstrating the poetic stances to inspire the poetry part of their poems. After responding with their own practice gem poems, students explicate a model mineral poem, "Fluorite," by Roald Hoffmann (Hoffman, 1988). Here, my science partner and I demonstrate a team-teaching approach to science poetry explication whereby students see Hoffmann's poem first through the eyes of the science teacher, my science partner, Erin, and then through the eyes of the poetry teacher, myself. Such multiple viewing prompts from thoughtful and authentic poetic "gems" from many students. Fundamental Lesson One concludes with a more advanced extension activity in further mineral and earth science poetry writing with model poems by Loren Eiseley and Carter Revard.

Materials Needed

Science Materials

Jones, Adrian (2006) *Rocks and Minerals: Get to Know the Natural World*. Collins Wild Guide: Harper Collins Publishers.

Oldershaw, Cally (2004) *Guide to Gems*. Firefly Books Ltd.

Mineral trays customarily found in most high school science departments

Rock specimens customarily found in most high school science departments

Semi-precious stone jewelry (optional)

Poetry Materials

"Fluorite" by Roald Hoffmann (provided)

"Notes of an Alchemist" by Loren Eiseley

"This is Your Geode Talking" by Carter Revard

Writing Materials

Handout #2, Data Gathering Chart for Science Poetry Writing (see Chapter 5)

SUGGESTIONS FOR USING THIS LESSON

Both science and English teachers will find Fundamental Lesson One an essential step in teaching basic science poetry writing skills to students of all levels and abilities. Although we recommend allowing time in class for students to practice writing and sharing their science poems in progress, students may be assigned the science poetry writing as homework. In addition, activities #1 and #2 may be conducted in one class period or block of 60-75 minutes, depending upon the time allocated for data gathering, discussion, and poetic response. Most advanced science and English classes complete both activities in one class period.

Suggested Time Allocations

Time allocations for each activity will vary depending upon the level of the students, length of follow-up discussion and writing response time as well as curriculum needs.

Activity #1 (30 minutes)
Activity #2 (30 minutes)
Extension Activity (30 minutes)

PART ONE: PRACTICE SCIENCE POETRY WRITING EXERCISE

ACTIVITY #1: IT'S A GEM

Writing the Science Part

To prepare our Science Academy English III students to write the science part of the gem poems, my science partner and I begin with an activity designed to engage students in the process. We display for observation and identification rocks, minerals in trays, geodes, and gemstones along with field guides, raw and polished stones, and semi-precious jewelry. Students generally enjoy observing, touching, browsing, and admiring the beauty of the raw minerals and the polished and semi-precious gemstones. My science partner overviews the general science behind rocks, minerals and gemstones, covering properties used for identification: color, form, cleavage, hardness, specific gravity, luster, transparency, locale, and abundance. She defines rocks and the relationship of rocks and minerals, covering in particular the classification of rocks by their fundamental origin: igneous, sedimentary, and metamorphic. Next, she familiarizes students with mineral forms, cleavage, and reviews the Moh's scale of hardness. She further explains how to use field guides for identification purposes.[1] She draws students' attention to the Collins Wild Guide, *Rocks and Minerals,* which offers for each mineral a composite "ID Fact File" in the left-hand margin of the page along with a clear, color photograph and detailed description of each mineral. She also points out the technical terminology, encouraging its use for the science part of students' poetic responses. This basic science, coupled with the resources of field guides, serves as sufficient introductory knowledge to enable the Science Academy students to begin data gathering for the science part of their gem poems.

Writing the Poetry Part

For the poetry part of the gem poems, I begin with a review of four of the poetic stances (see Chapter 5). I present four poems I have written on the fossil resin, amber, to demonstrate the five poetic stances of description, address, persona, reflection, and stance blending. First, I overview the scientific facts, data, and vocabulary of amber so that students will be well aware of how I apply those facts, data, and vocabulary in my demonstration of the poetic stances. Then I present examples of raw amber and amber jewelry. To illustrate my address to "the cricket inside the amber," I pass around amber *Insect N side,* edible candy with a real cricket "fossilized" inside. Students seem to enjoy this tasty

touch of humor. Then I read my poems modeling the poetic stances
selected for illustration.

The Scientific or Quantitative Data: ID Fact File

General Description: Amber $C_{10}H_{16}O$ (variable)

*Amber is a fossil resin that is frequently clouded and can contain
fossil insects or parts of plant debris; it is the fossilized resin from
pine trees. It occurs in young sedimentary rocks of estuarine origin
or beach deposits. It is found in countries around the Baltic Sea,
Romania and Siberia.* (Jones, 2006: 159)

ID Fact File

Crystal System: Amorphous
Color: Orangy yellow to brown
Where: Sedimentary
Abundance: Restricted
Form: Nodular
Cleavage: None
Hardness: 2–2.5
Specific Gravity: 1.1.–1.3
Luster: Greasy, resinous
Transparency: Transparent to Opaque
Tests: Conchoidal fracture. White streak
Look Alike: None; Unlikely to be mistaken

(Jones, 2006: 159)

The Poetic or Qualitative Data: The Four Poetic Stances

Describing

A fossil resin frequently found
Around the Baltic Sea or young sedimentary ground,
Frequently clouded, orange-yellow or brown,
Amber has secrets inside which abound…

– *Nancy Gorrell*

Addressing

To the Cricket in the Amber

Oh, how does it feel to be inside
The resin walls of amber tide?
Hidden in its transparency
A fossil from here to eternity.
Do you wish you could escape
Back to the pines when the earth did quake?
To sing your song to the Baltic Sea
Once again a cricket free.

– Nancy Gorrell

Persona

Amber

I am amorphous, resinous and greasy,
I flow from piney trees
Catching insects and plant debris,
With nodular ease.

Some think I am quite wicked;
Others think I am good luck
Whatever you might think of me,
If you're in my way you will get stuck.

– Nancy Gorrell

Stance Blending

The Cricket in the Amber

The cricket
would like to fly back
into the piney wood.   **[Reflection]**
weary of all the gazers
he would shout, if only he could…

I am not a fossil resin
Frozen in ancient time
I have a voice of my own   **[Persona]**
And it can cry and rhyme
Oh cricket in the amber!

How sad it seems to be,   **[Address]**
That only those with empathy
Can hear your soulful plea.
                    – *Nancy Gorrell*

The Symbolism of Minerals and Gemstones

After reading these playful poems as demonstration models of
poetic stances, I point out the literal use of specific scientific facts,
vocabulary, and descriptions. Then I suggest that students select
a particular rock, mineral, or gem that appeals to them to use as a
subject for their practice gem poem. Before going to the field guides
and hands-on tables, I introduce an additional element to further the
poetry part of the poem – the use of symbolism – in particular, the
symbolism of minerals and gemstones. I discuss ancient beliefs in
the mystical and healing power of gems along with the association
of astrological signs with particular gems in the Western and
Chinese traditions. I call students' attention to several resources
on the tables providing gemology, "gemlore,"[2] and the symbolism
of minerals. Most students are excited to research the symbolism
of their birthstones as well as the symbolism of minerals. Now I
distribute the following instructions to guide students a practice
gem poetry exercise.

Practice Exercise: Student Instructions

Writing a Gem or Mineral Poem

General Directions: Select a rock, mineral, or gem as the subject of your exercise. Using the Data Gathering Chart for Science Poetry Writing (Handout #2), record the *quantitative data* (the science part) and the *qualitative data* (poetry part). Then fuse the science with the poetry to create your mineral science poem.

The Science Part: Gather Your Quantitative Data and Scientific Vocabulary

Crystal System
Color:
Where Found:
Abundance:
Form:
Cleavage:
Hardness:
Specific Gravity:
Luster:
Transparency:
Tests:
Look Alikes:

The Poetry Part: Gather Your Qualitative Data and Poetic Strategies

• Observe and sense the properties of your mineral or gemstone.
• Reflect on how you feel about this mineral or gemstone.
• Consider the memories this mineral or gemstone may prompt for you.
• Research the symbolic meaning(s) associated with your mineral or gemstone.
• Choose a particular poetic stance.

The Writing Part: Write Your Gem Poem and Choose an Approach

• Approach #1: Describe your mineral or gemstone (quantitative data) first and then leap to another world or level, the level of self or the human level.
• Approach #2: Address the mineral or gemstone in your poem.
• Approach #3: Take on the identity of the mineral or gemstone in your poem.
• Approach #4: Fuse the scientific description of your mineral or gemstone with its symbolic meaning.
• Approach #5: Blend stances to make a more complex and poetic gem poem.

Model Student Responses: Practice Gem Poetry Exercise

Several students address their minerals of choice. Cori Connolly, a Science Academy III English student and self-proclaimed mineral enthusiast, addresses her geode with passion and intensity. Here Cori fuses the science of *vugs* with her emotional plea: *Tell your story / show your beauty.*

"My Geode" by Cori Connolly

My Geode

Covered by limestone you hide,
Sedimentary formation, your outside, pied
> [*pied*: part-colored, mottled, and flecked]

Tell me, show me,

What you hold deep within.
Could it be those vugs you're in?
> [*vug*: n. a cavity in rock, lined with minerals]

A shell, a blockade,

Maybe I have to open you up to see,
What treasures you keep in your cavity.

A sound, a crack,

Oh my geode, why did you keep hidden,
A site that one should not call forbidden?

Tell your story, show your beauty.

> *– Cori Connolly*, student

Inspired by observing fossilized amber in class, Meghan Crippen takes on an unusual stance, criticizing the amber, *You selfish sediment.* She ends her address on a thought provoking note of possible concession.

"Amber" by Meghan Crippen

Amber

Lurking within trees
Hiding in the pines
You trap the innocent
In your orange cement
Your resinous luster
Enticing to the eye
Catch the defenseless
Ensnare the harmless
You hold on for years
Never letting go
You selfish sediment
Almost justified
By the secrets that await
Inside.

– Meghan Crippen, student

PART TWO: MODEL MINERAL POEM

ACTIVITY #2: "FLUORITE" BY ROALD HOFFMANN

Once students have completed Activity #1, they are better prepared
to understand and appreciate model poems written by scientists
and poets utilizing rocks, minerals, and gems as metaphor to say
something more about self, human nature, humanity, and science.
In Science Academy English III, my science partner and I take
the opportunity to demonstrate for students two different ways of
seeing a science mineral poem: first, through the eyes of a science
teacher and then through the eyes of a poetry teacher. We emphasize
to our students that our "eyes," although somewhat specialized –
the scientist and the poet – are also uniquely our own.

We select for this purpose "Fluorite," an early poem written by
Roald Hoffmann. Although the poem appears on the surface to

be about the mineral, *fluorite,* Hoffmann moves from the matter-of-fact scientific description of fluorite in the first two stanzas, to the world of self as a scientist in the last two stanzas. His rhetorical progression, from matter-of-fact scientific description to highly emotional personal reflection, raises one of the most important moral questions for science, nature, and the natural world: "Why destroy?" Most importantly, Hoffmann's poem models for students the emotional intensity in both conducting science and writing poetry, all in a poem about an inert, non-living thing, a mineral, yet something amazing in its provenance and beauty.

Observing Fluorite and Reading the Poem

First, we circulate samples of fluorite from mineral trays as well as enlarged photographs of fluorites from mineral field guides and photography books. After students have observed natural fluorite, we read aloud Hoffmann's poem.

Fluorite

I was asked about my hobbies.
"Collecting minerals" I said and
stopped to think.
"Minerals in their matrix
are what I like best."

           Fluorite wears a variable habit.
Colorless when pure, it is vodka
in stone. More commonly
it brandishes shades of rose to blue,
occasional yellow. A specimen I have
tumbles in inch-long cubes,
superimposed, interpenetrating,
etched on all their faces.
The cubes have a palpable darkness,
a grainy darkness, texture

blacker than black.
Solid yet fragile, when held
up to the incandescence of light, the
darkness deposited in this ordered
atomic form a million years ago
allows some rays through.
But only on the thin edges,
in sinister violet.

Struck with a chisel and mallet,
unhesitatingly the cubes cleave
and octahedra emerge.
I have seen it done, but my hands tremble.
I know why it cleaves so,
but why destroy what took
centuries to grow, then
rested in the earth for millions,
in a cavelet, a cool fissure in the rock?

Eerie crystal.
Were a Martian photograph
enlarged to reveal such polyhedral
regularity, it would be deemed
intelligence at work. But
the only work here, and it is free
is that of entropy.
– *Roald Hoffmann* (*The Sciences*, Sept. 1988: 30)

Explication through the Eyes of a Science Teacher

My science partner begins her explication by defining fluorite as a "mineral that consists of the fluoride of calcium that is often used in making glass." She identifies scientific terms and concepts, in particular, *minerals, matrix, chisel, mallet, cleave, octahedral, cavelet, fissure, incandescence, crystal, polyhedron,* and *entropy* that may be unfamiliar to students. Then she explains to our

Academy students how she sees the poem, "Fluorite," both as a scientist and as an individual reader. In her own words:

As a scientist, I think that the poet in the opening stanza is describing his hobby with a rather serious geological eye. Most *rock and mineral collectors* do not necessarily consider the *matrix* of a mineral when they are looking and collecting. Rather, they search and find a specimen based on its outer appearance from a distance. A gemologist, on the other hand, may with a keen eye look at a specimen more in-depth and analyze it according to its matrices. I also think that the poet's references to *habit* and *vodka* in the second stanza are linked. Nuns, women of a particular religious order, wear a *habit*. The nuns who are considered to be the most holy are those who are the purest, pure in mind, body, and spirit. Similarly, vodka after undergoing a particular distilling process is clear and smooth, pure throughout. Fluorite can be pure, but finding a pure and colorless specimen is rather rare, just as rare as pure vodka, or the pure soul of those wearing a habit; after all, they are human.

The *cube* the poet refers to in the second stanza is an indicator of shape because scientists evaluate rocks and minerals by the shapes of their faces. The *faces* the poet refers to have nothing to do with the anatomical definition of face, rather, the faces of the rock itself. Fluorite more often than not is grainy and black due to the many imperfections that it can possess. It is also a rock that falls on the softer end of a hardness scale. Fluorite is actually a reference rock on Mohl's scale of hardness. Mohl's scale of hardness is a measure of how hard or soft a rock is in comparison to another rock. The scale begins with the softest of rocks, talc, and ends with the hardest of rocks, diamond. I think that the poet is trying to describe in the second stanza the composition of the rock: imperfect, dark in color, and not as hard as other rocks.

The chisel and mallet in the third stanza are two tools used by geologists to extract a rock from its surroundings. As both are used, the rock will surface, showing its eight-sided shape. Fluorite is not often found on the surface; it is found deep within the rocks of the earth. It could be buried for millions of years before materializing. I think that the Hoffmann is trying to give the reader the sense of awe that he experienced looking at the fluorite specimen. Particularly, he could not imagine what could have been the creative force behind such perfect repetitive shapes that one can observe within the mineral, fluorite. The creative force must be greater than humanity; it is an unexplainable organized force rarely found in the universe; but when appropriately applied, the force creates perfection and that perfection he observed in fluorite.

Explication through the Eyes of the Poetry or English Teacher

Next, I begin by telling our Academy students that my poetic eye is captivated by one word in the poem – *cleave*. To me, the entire poem turns on the dual meaning of *cleave*: (1) scientifically, "the splitting of a crystal along certain directions parallel to certain actual or possible crystal faces," (2) or, more poetically, "to be steadfast, adhere, hold fast" (*The New Lexicon Webster's Dictionary*, 1989: 183). As a poet, I admire the precision of a well-chosen word that can move a poem in new and mysterious directions. In "Fluorite," I see the poet, Hoffmann, scientifically "cleaving" the mineral with a *chisel* and *mallet* while at the same time poetically still "cleaving" to the mineral. He admits he has *seen it done*, but his *hands tremble*. He questions: *Why destroy what took / centuries to grow*? I tell my students how much I empathize with Hoffmann's emotional and moral dilemma, especially knowing how much he appreciates *Minerals in their matrix* (line 4), or order over the disorder of *entropy*. Hoffmann's poem ends for me on a note of sadness and irony: *the only work here, and it is free / is that of entropy.*

I tell our Academy students that "Fluorite" does for me what I want from any great poem; and that is, I want the poem to affect my deepest emotions, and I want the poem to make me think more deeply. "Fluorite" does both. I feel sadness over the conflict scientists must feel conducting research that may disturb or destroy nature and the natural order of things; and yet, I know that scientists must conduct such research for the untold and unforeseen benefits science accrues for human progress. I also tell students that "Fluorite," a simple mineral poem on the surface, raises complex moral and philosophical issues for our consideration, challenging the stereotype of the detached and unemotional scientist.

Student Gem Poem Prompt

After explicating Hoffmann's "Fluorite" through scientific and poetic eyes, distribute or project the following poetry prompt.

Mineral Poetry Writing Prompt

After reading Hoffmann's "Fluorite," write your own science-inspired poem about a mineral of your choice, but use that mineral as a means of saying something more about your own "hobbies" or experience with science. Like Hoffmann, you may want to protest something that disturbs you or expose an irony, paradox, or dilemma.

Model Student Response: "Aquamarine" by Maggie McArdle

Maggie McArdle, in her poem of address, "Aquamarine," fuses scientific description, symbolic associations, and emotional intensity to create a poem of protest.

Aquamarine

Chatoyant, ranging from blue to green, but mostly pale,
Iron impurities and iron concentrations provide the range of color,
Being almost transparent emphasizes the dose of color.

You bring goodness to the world, Aquamarine,
History proclaims you provide everlasting youth and happiness,
You give courage and freedom from laziness and insomnia,
Integrity pours from the long hollow tubes unique to your structure.

Yet, Aquamarine, beautiful gem,
Modern ways have defiled you,
Heat treatments remove the green leaving the blue,
Irradiation can return you to your original color, but you will not
be the same,
The world is cruel to you, Aquamarine.

Not accepting you for who you are,
Trying to change you and your ways,
They can only touch upon your appearance,
In spirit you will always be, Aquamarine.

                                        – *Maggie McArdle,* student

PART THREE: EXTENSION ACTIVITY

ADVANCED MINERAL AND EARTH SCIENCE POEMS

After explicating Hoffmann's "Fluorite," my science partner and I
recommend extending the lesson for advanced English and science
classes with additional mineral poems written by both scientists
and poets, respectively: Loren Eiseley, "Notes of an Alchemist"
(Eiseley, 1998), and Carter Revard, "This is Your Geode Talking"
(Revard, 1998). Both Loren Eiseley and Carter Revard's poems
challenge students to draw on mineral and earth science for both
scientific information and poetic inspiration. In "Notes of an
Alchemist," Eiseley demonstrates the use of mineral science as
metaphor. For example, he begins by describing crystals scientifically forming in cubes, rectangles, tetrahedrons, but then he leaps
to the human and poetic realms. Carter Revard, in "This is my
Geode Talking," imaginatively enters the mysterious and hidden
world of the geode, taking on the geode's identity and voice. In
this sweeping persona poem, the geode takes us on a voyage of
memory and dreams through birth, growth, and life. After engaging
with additional model poems, distribute or project the following
advanced mineral and earth science poetry prompts.

Advanced Mineral and Earth Science Poetry Prompts

1. After reading Loren Eiseley's "Notes of an Alchemist," write any mineral poem using that mineral as an extended metaphor.
2. After reading Carter Revard's "This is my Geode Talking," write your own persona poem taking on the identity of a chosen mineral and letting that mineral tell its story – its birth, its life, its possible death.
3. Write any poem informed or inspired by rocks, minerals, gemstones, and earth science in general. Use any aspect of earth science as metaphor in a poem.

Model Student Responses: Advanced Mineral and Earth Science Poems

The poetry of Hoffmann, Eiseley, and Revard inspire original works by many students in AP English Language and Composition classes. Informed by earth science, Rebecca Ozarow composes a thought provoking poem that says something more. In "Quakes of the World," she uses earth science as metaphor to explore *The faults in human nature*. Although influenced by Hoffmann's "Fluorite," especially his rhetorical progression from scientific description to personal reflection, Rebecca clearly makes this earth science poem her own.

"Quakes of the World" by Rebecca Ozarow

Quakes of the World

Earthquakes shake the ground awake,
Creating seismic waves,
Through a release of energy in the Earth's crust.
Measured on the Richter Magnitude Scale,
From 1-10 in order of intensity,
These tremendous fault lines trigger
Landslides, avalanches, volcanic activity, and fires,
Resulting in destruction.

Life has no scales,
No numbers of measured intensity.
Yet still, the ground shakes and tensions build,
Conflicts mount and go unnoticed.
Despite the more common nature of these vibrations,
The faults of human nature cause
Casualties, breakdowns, volatile hatred, and fiery damage,
Resulting in equally terrorizing destruction.

– Rebecca Ozarow, student

Similarly, in "Plate Tectonics," Rachel Needle uses earth science as metaphor to express the parallels of geologic and human movement and interaction.

"Plate Tectonics" by Rachel Needle

Plate Tectonics
Years and years of anticipation
Ever so slowly
Inching further and further
Toward the common intersection
Finally confrontation
The surface buckles
Explosions sound
If only we did not ignore each other
Until the point of no return
And avoid exploding

– Rachel Needle, student

The highly poetic and thought provoking mineral poem, "The American Dream," by Karley Murphy moves from describing a geologic process to saying something important about Americans and American culture. Karley begins by describing the transformation of a rock, *just a rock* into a *crystal lattice of carbon / no longer just a rock.* Although her poem on the surface describes a common geologic process, "The American Dream" becomes highly poetic and thought provoking for several reasons: First, Karley ends her poem with an esoteric word *Adamas*, from mythology, literature, and science that alludes to "the mineral with the greatest hardness," and connotes multiple meanings: *adamant* in mythology refers to a substance of utmost hardness, or an unbreakable stone; diamonds have "adamantine luster," and *adamatoid* is a form of crystal occurring in diamonds bounded by 48 equal triangles. Second, Karley entitles her science poem, "The American Dream," suggesting an original and surprising analogy: the geologic process of movement from an ordinary, common rock to a mineral of great perfection symbolizing this "dream." Third, Karley never actually uses the word *diamond*, creating greater engagement and cause for reflection. (For further interest, note the diamond-like shape of Karley's poem.)

"The American Dream" by Karley Murphy

The American Dream

Just a rock,
Dull, invaluable, unprecious.
Kicked over time and time again.
Stepped on, thrown around, exploited.
Until out of the fraction of a chance,
It is in the right place at the right time:
Fifty kilobars of pressure,
Two thousand degrees Fahrenheit,
In the lithospheric mantle,
Arranged into a crystal lattice of carbon.
No longer just a rock.
It is the boss.
Invincible.
Adamas

— *Karley Murphy,* student

[*adamas* or *adamantas* (in modern colloquial Greek)
from the Greek αδάμας = diamond)]

Karley's Commentary

My poem started out as a poem about a rock transforming into a diamond. I knew it was an intricate process that took immense pressure over centuries, but I never really knew the details, so I looked it up and found the science I needed to write the poem. As I was writing, I realized that the process served as an appropriate analogy to the rags-to-riches ideal of the American dream, which is where the title came from. When I titled my poem "The American Dream," I felt that it was much more profound than I had originally intended, and I liked the ambiguity. However, the most thought-provoking part of the poem is probably not the title but the arcane use of the word Adamas, which I discovered in my Internet research is Greek for "invincible."

PART FOUR: RELATED SCHOLARSHIP AND PEDAGOGY

POETRY AND THE EARTH SCIENCES

For a model lesson supporting the pedagogy in this chapter refer to Audrey Rule's "Using Poetry to Teach about Minerals in Earth Science Class" (Rule, 2004). Rule, a mineralogist and college education professor, collaborates with an earth science teacher from Oswego High School in Oswego, New York, to teach a lesson on minerals to grade 9 earth science students. Rule shares an electronic slide show of poems she has composed about gem minerals (diamond and tiger eye) that incorporates physical properties, formation, uses, and other scientific information. Before students write their own poetic mineral responses, Rule passes around mineral and gemstone specimens related to her poems. She then distributes a list of Internet sites featuring information about minerals. Students choose a mineral, conduct research, and then write mineral poems. Rule (2004) concludes, "The most satisfying part was the sense of accomplishment in producing a scientific poem." She adds that for the students "the most difficult aspect was finding words to express their ideas in rhyme" (Rule, 2004: Internet source). Although she reminded students that poems need not rhyme, most of the students "felt compelled to produce rhyming verse" (Rule, 2004). Teachers taking note of these conclusions might solve the problem by providing models of non-rhyming science poems on the topic.

Notes

1. Many students are unfamiliar with field guides and may need instruction in how to use them. To encourage the use of field guides as a basic scientific tool, we provide multiple mineral field guides for reference. We also review with our students how to read a field guide. Teachers may also want to provide Internet access for similar mineral information.
2. See "gemlore" in *Guide to Gems* (Oldershaw, 2004: 36–37), which identifies Western astrological gemstones, birthstones, as well as Vedic and Chinese astrological gemstones.

7   What's Buggin' You?

Insects and Other Living Things

Close observation – mixed with wonder – is essential for the development of artist, scientist, writer, as well as mathematician, humorist, inventor, and more.

– Kerry Ruef
"The Loupe's Secret: Looking Closely, Changing Scale"
(Ruef, 2005: 207)

OVERVIEW: FUNDAMENTAL LESSON TWO

The aim of Fundamental Lesson Two is to introduce students to the basic skills of science poetry writing through engagement with the life sciences, thereby preparing them for the more advanced science poetry to follow. Insects and other living things provide an ideal way to introduce science poetry writing to students of all levels and abilities for several reasons. First, insects and other living things from the animal kingdom are accessible and familiar territory for most students. Nearly every student seems to have had at some point a personal encounter or experience with an insect. In addition, most students have observed living things and many have personal favorites. Second, most high school students have acquired some background in the life sciences, in particular, biology, which is a required course of study for graduation from high schools in the United States and worldwide. Third, the science required for insect poetry remains accessible for most high school students. Fourth, this insect-subject poetry naturally lends itself to multiple poetic modes: for example, describing the insect, addressing the insect, taking on the persona of the insect, or reflecting upon the insect. Finally, insect-subject poetry engages science-minded or poetry-reluctant students who might otherwise be deterred by more personal poetry.

Fundamental Lesson Two consists of two activities: the first, a basic practice exercise in science poetry writing in response to first-hand observation of insects; the second, a more advanced exercise in response to model insect-subject poems by naturalist, Alison Hawthorne Deming, followed by a closure activity celebrating insects. The chapter ends with discussion of related scholarship and pedagogy in poetry and the life sciences.

Fundamental Lesson Two at a Glance

Part One: **Practice Science Poetry Writing Exercise**
Activity #1 What's Buggin' You?
Model Student Response
"The Grasshopper" by James Murphy

Part Two: **Model Insect Poems**
Activity #2 *The Monarchs: A Poem Sequence* by Alison Hawthorne Deming
Model Student Responses
"The Butterfly Theory" by Jessica McKinley
"O. hannah" by Kaity Duffy
"DNA" by Karley Murphy

Part Three: **Closure Activity, A Joyful Noise**

Part Four: **Related Scholarship and Pedagogy**
Poetry and the Life Sciences

Students begin with an opening activity in basic science poetry writing focusing on the science and poetry of insects. First they gather insect data for the science part of their poems, and then they study insect-subject poetry demonstrating the poetic stances to inspire the poetry part of their poems. After responding with their own practice insect poems, students engage with two model insect-subject poems by naturalist and poet, Alison Hawthorne Deming: "Genetic Sequence" and "Essay on Intelligence: One." Fundamental Lesson Two concludes with a celebratory insect activity based on Paul Fleischman's *Joyful Noise: Poems for Two Voices* (Fleischman, 1988).

Materials Needed

Science Materials

Scientific charts and diagrams of arthropods customarily found in most high school biology departments.

Specimen jars of insects and arthropods customarily found in most high school biology departments.

Poetry Materials

"Genetic Sequence" (originally titled "26") by Alison Hawthorne Deming (provided)

"Essay on Intelligence: One" by Alison Hawthorn Deming (provided)

"A Noiseless, Patient Spider" by Walt Whitman (available online)

A Joyful Noise: Poems for Two Voices by Paul Fleischman

Writing Materials

Handout #2: Data Gathering Chart for Science Poetry Writing (see Chapter 5)

SUGGESTIONS FOR USING THIS LESSON

Both science and English teachers will find Fundamental Lesson Two an essential step in teaching basic science poetry writing skills to students of all levels and abilities. Although my science partner and I recommend allowing time in class for students to practice writing and sharing their science poems in progress, students may be assigned the science poetry writing as homework. In addition, Activities #1 and #2 may be conducted in one class period or block of 60-75 minutes depending upon the time allocated for data gathering, discussion, and poetic response. Most advanced science and English classes complete both activities in one class period if the drafting of poems is assigned as homework. The closure activity may be reserved for a celebratory science poetry reading at the end of the entire unit.

Suggested Time Allocations

Time allocations for each activity will vary depending upon the level of the students, length of follow-up discussion and writing response time as well as curriculum needs.

    Activity #1 (30 minutes)
    Activity #2 (30 minutes)
    Extension Activity (30 minutes)

PART ONE: PRACTICE SCIENCE POETRY WRITING EXERCISE

ACTIVITY #1: WHAT'S BUGGIN' YOU?

The Science Part

To prepare students to write the science part of their insect poems, my science partner and I distribute a set of insect cards that provide a fact file about arthropods. These cards have a picture and an anatomical diagram of an insect on one side of the card and information about the insect on the other side. More specifically, the cards have an internal and external anatomical diagram labeling each part of the insect using scientific language and vocabulary. We also place specimen jars of insects and arthropods on students' desks. Similar materials are customarily available through most high school science departments or can be obtained through science catalogues. Last, we distribute a two-page handout to the students that includes a diagram of the basic anatomical structures of a grasshopper followed by a fill-in-the-blanks series of questions to check for understanding. The handout, though basic, covers information about arthropods and then becomes more specific, concentrating on insects. The handout includes the following information:

- *What is an arthropod?*
- *The body plan of an arthropod*
- *The unique exoskeleton of an arthropod*
- *The specific body plan of an insect*
- *The inner workings of an insect*
- *Metamorphosis as a process*
- *Incomplete metamorphosis, example insects*
- *Complete metamorphosis, example insects*
- *Insect adaptations*
- *Other arthropods*

My science partner begins by asking students to name specific insects in our particular locale (e.g. grasshoppers, beetles, butterflies, crickets, lice, bees). She directs students to look at the examples on their desks and the desks around them. Orally, students identify and describe their specimens. Few students seem to realize the vast number of insects that roam the Earth. Nor do they recognize that despite the many changes an insect undergoes during metamorphosis, at every stage the organism is still considered to be an insect. Focusing on insects native to our locale provides for students a level of scientific comfort and familiarity necessary for writing the "science part" of their insect poem. Most importantly, reviewing the diagrams encourages students to use specific scientific terminology and vocabulary in their science poems. Once students have gathered their scientific facts, they are ready for the poetry part of the lesson.

The Poetry Part

I prepare students to write the poetry part of their insect poems by presenting the four poetic stances identified in Chapter 5 and further illustrated in Chapter 6: description, address, persona, and stance blending. To model stance blending in an insect-subject poem, I read Walt Whitman's famous, "A Noiseless, Patient Spider," which moves from description in stanza one to address in stanza two. Although Whitman's poem effectively models the blending of stances, I point out to students that his poem is primarily a lyrical poem of observation of a spider casting a web, not a science poem by our working definition; Whitman's poem needs more science. To illustrate, I ask students to brainstorm how Whitman's poem might be infused, theoretically, with more science. Students consider the following strategies:

- *add specific quantitative data*
- *add specific scientific terminology*
- *add specific scientific facts and information*
- *add scientific concepts, processes, and phenomena*

Nevertheless, for our particular purposes, Whitman's insect-subject poem serves as an instructive model for student insect poetry. After reviewing the stances, I distribute the following science poetry writing prompt along with Handout #2: Data Gathering Chart for Science Poetry Writing (see Chapter 5).

Practice Insect Poetry Exercise

General Directions: Using at least one of the four poetic stances, write a poem about an insect that intrigues you. You might choose as your subject your favorite insect. Be sure to gather specific scientific data and terminology from the diagrams, charts, and specimen jars provided. Using the Data Gathering Chart (Handout #2) record the *quantitative data* (science part) and the *qualitative data* (poetry part). Then fuse the science with the poetry to create your insect poem.

Suggested Insect Poetry Prompts

1. Describe an insect you have observed and know well. Focus on your insect's appearance, actions, distinguishing features, as well as the insect's sound and possible sense of touch. Add specific scientific facts and terminology.
2. Address your insect in a poem. Talk to that living thing. Be sure to use specific scientific facts and terminology.
3. Take on the identity of your insect in a persona poem. Imagine what that insect is thinking and what that insect might feel. Let that insect talk. Identify the living thing in your title.
4. Like Walt Whitman in "A Noiseless Patient Spider," blend poetic stances in your poem. Begin your poem by observing and describing your insect scientifically and then end your poem by addressing the insect. Or, you could begin by describing your insect – in the world of science – and then end with your thoughts or reflection – in the world of self or humanity. Consider: how are you like your insect?

Model Student Responses: Practice Insect Poetry Exercise

While my science partner circulates to help students identify scientific aspects of their insect of choice, I circulate encouraging students to experiment with multiple poetic stances and ways of seeing. Although our emphasis on fusing quantitative data with the qualitative may seem a mechanical, our science-minded students take to the process with playful enthusiasm. Several students produced grasshopper poems with humor, irony, and parody. James Murphy, a student in Science Academy English III, practiced with stance blending. He begins by addressing the grasshopper; then he takes on the persona of the grasshopper, and he ends with a personal reflection, connecting the grasshopper's world to the world of himself: *That day the Grasshopper and I were one.*

The Grasshopper

Grasshopper *jump* and catch your prey.
Your mandibles chewing,
Your labium tasting.

Grasshopper *jump*, something comes your way.
The fields are green
Use your metathorax and mesothorax wings to fly away.

Grasshopper *feel* with your tarsus and arolium,
Your compound eyes see the world 100 times over.

Night falls so find your perch.
And chirp until the dew of dawn.

I'M A GRASSHOPPER!

As I awake, I bound and jump,
My abdominal spiracles take in the air
My brain calculates my next perch.

My heart and aorta pump
Faster and louder
As I outrun the human chasing me,
My antennae searches for a place to hide,
Until the human finds me,
Grasps me,
And releases me outside.

I hop away, the day is done,
That day the Grasshopper and I were one.

– James Murphy, student

PART TWO: MODEL INSECT POEMS

ACTIVITY #2: THE MONARCHS – A POEM SEQUENCE BY ALISON HAWTHORNE DEMING

Once students have completed Activity #1, they are better prepared to understand and appreciate model poems inspired by insects. To foster a higher level of response informed by scientific facts and knowledge, I present in AP English Language and Composition classes a series of poems by the naturalist, Alison Hawthorne Deming, from her poem sequence, *The Monarchs*: "Genetic Sequence," and "Essay on Intelligence: One." In each poem, Deming presents amazing facts about insect subjects vis-a-vis the human species. For example, in "Genetic Sequence" (originally entitled "26"), Deming describes scientifically the sequence of moving from caterpillar to butterfly, asking the question: *how does a certain clump of cells / know how to line up side by side / and turn into wings, then shut off / while another clump blinks on.*

Reading "Genetic Sequence" by Alison Hawthorne Deming

Before reading the poem aloud, I ask students to consider how much of the poem is *quantitative* science and how much is *qualitative* poetry. Then I read "Genetic Sequence."

Genetic Sequence

A caterpillar spits out a sac of silk
where it lies entombed while its genes
switch on and off like lights
on a pinball machine. If every cell
contains the entire sequence
constituting what or who the creature is,
how does a certain clump of cells

know to line up side by side
and turn into wings, then shut off
while another clump blinks on
spilling pigment into the creature's
emerald green blood, waves of color
flowing into wingscales—black, orange,
white—each zone receptive only to the color
it's destined to become. And then
the wings unfold, still wet from their making,
and for a dangerous moment hold steady
while they stiffen and dry, the double-
layered wing a protolanguage—one side
warning enemies, the other luring mates.
And then the pattern-making cells go dormant,
and the butterfly has mastered flight.

– Alison Hawthorne Deming (Deming, 1989c: 32)

Students initially see Deming's poem as essentially a description of a scientific process. They note the opening simile, *its genes / switch on and off like lights / on a pinball machine* as one of the few moments of poetry in the poem. And yet, with further reflection, many students begin to sense the emotional base of the poem, the poet's sense of awe and respect for the "intelligence" of natural species.

Reading "Essay on Intelligence: One" by Alison Hawthorne Deming

Next, I ask students to consider another poem by Deming that continues in the same mode: presentation of an amazing scientific fact that ultimately resonates poetically in terms of human nature versus the nature of insects. In "Essay on Intelligence: One," Deming describes the intelligence of the female digger wasp who *maintains several burrows for developing offspring* and yet knows exactly which offspring requires *no food*, and which are *pupated offspring*, sealed in for metamorphosis. Taken as a whole, students see Deming's poetry as a powerful, poetic protest, raising controversial scientific and humanistic questions.

Essay on Intelligence: One

The female digger wasp
maintains several burrows
for developing offspring.
As the day begins, she visits
and inspects each tunnel
determining which contain
eggs requiring no food,
which contain larvae
needing two or three
caterpillars to eat, and which
the pupated offspring sealed
in for metamorphosis. On
the basis of her inspection,
the wasp knows how much
prey to capture and where
to deliver the food. If the
occupants of burrows
are switched in the night,
the mother adjusts to the change,
stocking each nursery
according to its need. But if
the offspring are switched
after her inspection,
she will spend the day
stocking with caterpillars
a burrow containing eggs
and will seal off young larvae
to starve. She will touch
and examine an egg many times
without realizing it needs no food.

– Alison Hawthorne Deming (Deming,1989a: 21)

Model Student Responses: Poems on Insects and Other Livings

After engaging with Deming's poems from *The Monarchs* about insects and other living things, students are prepared to respond in kind. I suggest they research amazing scientific facts about any insect or living thing of their own choosing, and then respond in kind (see Deming's "Essay on Intelligence: Three" in Chapter 11 for a model animal-subject science poem).

Writing Prompts: Poems on Insects and Other Living Things

1. After reading a series of poems on the "intelligence" of living things by Alison Hawthorne Deming, research amazing scientific facts about an insect, animal, or any living thing. Write a poem in response to your amazement, wonder, intrigue, or puzzlement. Like Deming, present in a matter-of-fact tone the amazing scientific fact or facts, describe those facts scientifically, and let the facts speak for themselves.

2. Write any poem informed or inspired by biology or the life sciences.

Model Student Responses: Advanced Poems on Insects and Other Living Things

Although many of the insect poems in response to Activity #1 remain practice exercises, insect poems in response to Alison Hawthorne Deming's models inspire a range of highly poetic poems informed by greater scientific literacy. In "The Butterfly Theory," Jessica McKinley responds with a thought provoking science poem informed by her knowledge of the butterfly effect, a term attributed to Edward Lorenz, one of the earliest proponents of chaos theory.

"The Butterfly Theory" by Jessica McKinley

The Butterfly Theory

For every action,
There is a reaction.
From the flap of a butterfly's wings,
a phenomenal transaction?

Theories and studies attempt to convey,
the influence that minuscule recurrences play.
Mathematically analyzed,
a non-linear dynamical system to prove,
seemingly esoteric behaviors which ably move.

What if a butterfly manipulated my path,
or a pebble or a stone expressing its wrath?
These tiny transactions, what role do they play,
in determining whether or not I'd know you today?

– Jessica McKinley, student

Equally inspired by Deming's models, Kaity Duffy's animal-subject poem, "O. hannah," moves to the realm of authentic persuasion. In "O. hannah," Kaity uses science as metaphor and analogy to say something important about the animal kingdom. The analogy, directly presented, underscores our common nature. Kaity transcends her literal subject, *King Cobra,* to lament in her final address, *Oh Hannah, what has the world come to?* Such a question resonates, moving from the species, hannah (lower case), to the personified *Hannah* (upper case), addressed at the poem's end.

"O. hannah" by Kaity Duffy

O. hannah

King Cobra
Animalia. Chordata. Reptilia. Squamata. Elapidae.
Ophiophagus.
The snake, and also the snake eater.

The forked tongue flicks out.
The tongue mimics the hiss.
A threat. Fight or retreat.

The ribs extend, form the hood.
The hood flares wide.
A dare. Prey or be preyed upon.

The snake, and also the snake eater.
The predator, and also the prey.
The child, attacking another child.

A dare. Prey or be preyed upon.
The modern pecking order, prompted.
The child, attacking another child.

Oh, Hannah, what has the world come to?
The snakes have been forgotten.

– Kaity Duffy, student

Kaity's Commentary

Ever since I can remember, I have been both fearful of and fascinated by snakes. As a child, every time I went to the zoo, I insisted on going to the snake room. I was enthralled by the cobras, and in particular, the spitting cobra, or O. hannah. In studying this species, I discovered that they are truly one of a kind. Like other cobras, their hood is an extension of the ribs. Yet they are one of the few snakes that can, and will, prey on other snakes. I thought of how cruel that is, but in reality it is just their reality. As a predator, the cobra will do what needs to be done to survive, even eating its own kind. We might see this as cannibalism, but I wonder, is it really fair to claim it as so? Our society as a whole attacks the weaker, and we eat our competition with no problem. There is not much that a great majority our population wouldn't do to stay alive. We seemingly don't have a problem with this. We are like the snakes, but we have forgotten the many similarities. I decided to entitle my poem "O hannah" because hannah is the species name, and the genus is Ophiophagus, so its name is O. hannah according to the binomial nomenclature. I like that at the end of my poem my title is suggested: "Oh, Hannah," but with another meaning. Another fun fact I like: Ophiophagus means snake-eater, and the king cobra is one of the few snakes given this name.

The simple instruction to write a science poem informed or inspired by biology or the life sciences produces responses demonstrating the fusion of scientific literacy with artful rhyme. In "DNA," for example, Karley Murphy moves from a scientifically technical description to thought provoking irony.

"DNA" by Karley Murphy

DNA

A sequence of four nitrogen bases,
Encoded in our DNA,
Determines the look of our faces,
And the amount that we will weigh.
The pyrimidines and purines
Undergo transcription and translation
Adenine, Guanine, Cytosine, and Thyamine
Produce each unique creation.
Ninety eight percent the same,
As every human on the Earth.
But that two percent is to blame
For every individual given birth.

– Karley Murphy, student

Karley's Commentary

My inspiration for the poem "DNA" came from my amazement that each difference between human beings comes from a simple recombination of the same four nitrogenous bases. Not only is this how differences between individual human beings occur, but DNA also causes the differences between the human race and every other species that exists. My poem is straightforward and scientific; there is not much ambiguity. I tried to make the poem more poetic by using rhyme. The reason I like

this poem is because I thought it was a simple way to describe
something so complicated that scientists have been studying
it for centuries and still hardly understand it.

Clearly, the student models in this chapter illustrate the range of poetic responses inspired by insects and the life sciences. Although more advanced students with greater scientific literacy tend to produce more complex science poems, students of all levels and abilities demonstrate remarkable creativity and inspiration in their practice exercises and responses. In Fundamental Lesson Two my science partner and I see on the part of many of our science and English students the emergence of skills necessary for writing the advanced science poem, specifically defined in Part Three, Section Overview.

PART THREE: CLOSURE ACTIVITY, A JOYFUL NOISE

INSECT POEMS FOR TWO VOICES

My science partner and I enjoy closing Fundamental Lesson Two by engaging our students in a celebration of insects inspired by Paul Fleischman's *Joyful Noise: Poems for Two Voices* (Fleischmann, 1988). In these poems for two voices, Fleischman takes on the identities of multiple insects, poetically re-creating and re-enacting their sounds, behaviors, and spirits. In a sense, these "joyful" poems may be viewed as an enhancement or extension of the persona mode. Through choral reading (these insect poems cannot be appreciated on the page nor can they be read by a single voice), Fleischman engages readers to experience what it might be like to be, for example, a grasshopper, firefly, digger wasp, or whirligig beetle.

Fleischman's insect poems are challenging to read. For practice, we choose two able students to read with us one of Fleischman's simpler poems, "Book Lice." We divide the class, for demonstration purposes, into two sections: The first section, voice #1, reads the left hand column of the poem (led by a student and myself) while the second section, voice #2, reads the right hand column of the poem (led by a student and my science partner). Once students have mastered the choral reading format, we advance to more challenging two-voice poems: "Grasshoppers," "Fireflies," and "Whirligig Beetles." Given the popularity of performance poetry today, there are always students in class willing to collaborate to produce two-voice science poems. These poems are ideal for not only closing Fundamental Lesson Two, but for closing an entire science poetry unit in a celebratory reading.

PART FOUR: RELATED SCHOLARSHIP AND PEDAGOGY

POETRY AND THE LIFE SCIENCES

Several years ago, Clemson University modified its Writing Across the Curriculum (WAC) program to create a Poetry Across the Curriculum (PAC) program (Waldvogel, 2006: 186). As part of the movement, Jerry A. Waldvogel, professor of biological sciences at Clemson University, began teaching poetry in his introduction to biology course to "encourage the development of cross-disciplinary connectivity, creativity, and critical thinking" (Waldvogel, 2006: 187). In "Mating Darwin with Dickinson: How Writing Creative Poetry in Biology Helps Students Think Critically and Build Personal Connections to Course Content," Waldvogel demonstrates for college science teachers the value of poetic response to biological concepts, content, and controversial issues. For example, Waldvogel (2006: 190) encourages his biology students to write poems reflecting upon "how they personally reconcile the scientific description of human origins with their own socio-religious perspectives." In "Mating Darwin with Dickinson,"

Waldvogel offers practical strategies for connecting poetry with biology instruction, including suggestions for evaluation and grading. Further scholarship related to teaching poetry in college science education includes Waldvogel's (2004) "Writing Poetry to Assess Creative and Critical Thinking in the Sciences" and Young, Connor-Greene, Paul, and Waldvogel's (2003) "Poetry across the Curriculum: Four Disciplinary Perspectives."

An exceptional poetic resource for biology and English students studying Darwin is Ruth Padel's *Darwin: A Life in Poems* (Padel, 2009). Padel, the great-great-granddaughter of Darwin, writes biographical and scientific poems based on stories told to her by her grandmother. Padel's extraordinary science poems paint an intimate portrait of Darwin's life.

8   Into the Field

It's Only Natural

Artists and scientists need cross-fertilization or else their isolated endeavors will atrophy, wither, or fall short of their aspirations.
– Gary Paul Nabhan
Cross-Pollinations: The Marriage of Science and Poetry
(Nabhan, 2004: 12)

It [poetry] is an essentially ecological discipline. It teaches us part of the duty of dwelling, it teaches us a necessary awe. This awe is central, is vitally necessary, to any description of the world.
– John Burnside
"A Science of Belonging: Poetry as Ecology,"
(Burnside, 2006: 95)

OVERVIEW: FUNDAMENTAL LESSON THREE

If there is a common ground between science and poetry, it is found in the natural world, and in particular, in field observations and field experiences. In this regard, the aim of Fundamental Lesson Three is to introduce students to in-the-field sensory data gathering as a stimulus for science poetry writing. In prior fundamental lessons, students respond through their powers of observation to non-living and living things primarily in the classroom setting. Fundamental Lesson Three goes one step further, introducing students to sensory data gathering not only in the classroom, but in the field itself. Our teaching of science poetry writing with high school students demonstrates that such in-the-field responses are natural; that is, students and teachers alike, inspired, intrigued, and in awe of nature, will "naturally" respond with poetry if given the occasion, opportunity, and guided instruction.

Fundamental Lesson Three consists of three parts. Parts One and Two, *Icelandic Summer Expedition Model* and *Back in the Research Science Classroom: Icelandic Data and Poetic Response* are both written by my science partner and expedition scientist, Erin Colfax. Here Erin describes her journey to Iceland to gather in-the-field sensory data with her students, her journey back to Morristown High School's Research Science classroom to organize the data, and finally, her journey into science and Science Academy English III classrooms to teach poetic responses to the expedition data. Most importantly, she describes how the field experience itself inspired her first poetic responses, transforming her from an expedition scientist to an expedition scientist-poet.

As an experienced field research leader, Erin had previously participated in expeditions with the expressed purpose of bringing science from different environments back to Morristown High School's Science Academy program. She had previously linked three scientific expeditions – one to Antarctica, one to Mount Kilimanjaro in Africa, and one to Thailand – to the literary works of Jon Krakauer, *Into Thin Air* (Krakauer, 1997) and F. A. Worsley, *Endurance: An Epic of Polar Adventure* (Worsley, 1931) in two respective Science Academy English classes. Captivated by the science poetry unit we were team-teaching in Science Academy English III, Erin began to explore the possibility of a science poetry expedition she could link to the Science Academy English program. After considerable research, she selected Iceland, known for its distinctive and unfamiliar environment, as the focus of her 2007 summer science expedition.

Although the Icelandic expedition presents an exemplary model for writing science poetry in the field, a practical question still remains: *How will science and English teachers replicate such an extensive, expedition model?* In this regard, Chapter 8 concludes with Part Three, *Replicating the Icelandic Expedition Model.* Part Three offers practical suggestions for in-the-field sensory data gathering methods and activities as a stimulus for science poetry writing in science, English, and creative writing classrooms.

Fundamental Lesson Three at a Glance

Part One: Icelandic Summer Expedition Model by Erin Colfax
Description of the Research Protocol
Expedition Planning
In the Field Data Gathering Methods
In the Field Poetic Responses: Erin Colfax and Students
In the Field Reflections: Writing Science Poetry

Part Two: Back In the Research Science Classroom by Erin Colfax
Data Organization in Research Science Class
Icelandic Data and Science Poetry Writing Activity
Model Student Responses: Using Icelandic Sensory Data

Part Three: Replicating the Icelandic Expedition Model
Sensory Data Gathering: The Mini-Field Trip on School Grounds
Sensory Data Gathering: Daily Field Trips Off School Grounds
Teacher-Gathered Sensory Data for Science Poetry Writing

Part Four: Related Scholarship and Pedagogy
Poetry, Ecological Literacy, and Environmental Education

SUGGESTIONS FOR USING THIS LESSON

Unlike previous lessons, all materials needed for in-the-field sensory data gathering to inspire science poetry writing and responses are self-generated by either the students themselves in mini-field trips or daily field trips, or by the science or English teachers themselves, through gathering their own sensory data for science poetry writing in the classroom. Research and environmental science teachers in particular will find the Icelandic Expedition model presented by Erin Colfax an informative and instructive guide to scientific and sensory data gathering and its use for both in-the-field and in-the-classroom scientific investigation and science poetry writing. English and creative writing teachers will find the in-the-field sensory data gathering methods equally informative and instructive for teaching descriptive writing and poetic responses to nature and the natural environment. Most importantly, both science and English teachers will find practical strategies for conducting interdisciplinary field trips and expeditions for the express purpose of connecting science, nature, and the arts through the writing of science poetry.

These data gathering and poetry writing strategies are effective and appropriate for science and English students of all levels and abilities, requiring at a minimum no more than one or two class periods to gather and respond to the data gathered in poetic form. For example, students may gather sensory data on the school grounds during one class period, and then in the following class period, they may respond to the data by writing a science poem; or, they may gather data in a daily field trip, and then the following day or class period, respond to the data by writing individual science poems or class science poems. For a more extensive sensory data gathering and science poetry writing experience, Fundamental Lesson Three opens by offering for consideration the Icelandic Summer Expedition by Erin Colfax as one possible model to follow. By presenting this model, we hope to encourage science and English teachers alike to collaborate in developing their own science poetry writing expeditions inspired by their own locales, students, or courses of study (see Chapter 11, "Walking in This World with Our Students and Colleagues").

Chapter 8 ends with Part Four, *Related Scholarship and Pedagogy: Poetry, Ecological Literacy, and Environmental Science.* Science, English, and creative writing teachers will find here another effective and relevant model of environmental education: the *River of Words* (ROW) project which combines student investigation of local watersheds with student poetic and artistic response.

PART ONE: ICELANDIC SUMMER EXPEDITION MODEL BY ERIN COLFAX

THE RESEARCH PROTOCOL

After eight months of writing, planning, and researching, our team of three educators, four scientists, and four students flew to Iceland to start conducting the research study: *A Scientific Investigation of Iceland through the Eyes of a Poet.* The objective of the expedition was for students, educators, and scientists to gather sensory, environmental, and weather data indigenous to Iceland for the purpose of writing scientific poetry. The poetry was to focus upon the region's unique geography, topography, ecosystem, indigenous fauna and flora, weather patterns, and culture, and to incorporate quantitative and qualitative data. Our research investigation, in alignment with the United States' National Educational Standards, was intended to formulate a connection between literature and science by using poetry to describe scientific concepts, specimens, and data, as well as utilizing various poetic forms to describe the environment of Iceland.

The investigation was conducted in a three part series. In Part One, the Icelandic research team went to Iceland to gather data. In Part Two, the Icelandic research team turned the data over to a group of students to organize and classify. In Part Three, students enrolled in the 2007–2008 Research Science class were introduced to the data and specimens gathered on the expedition and then asked to write scientific poems incorporating the data.

EXPEDITION PLANNING

I sat down with my poetry partner, Nancy, and brainstormed ways in which we could marry science and poetry in the field. We discussed together what types of data needed to be collected in order to inform and inspire science poems from students back in the classroom. Ultimately, we decided that Icelandic sensory data would be the best to gather. We wanted students to write poems in response to data they had never been exposed to or experienced before. As a consequence, the research protocol I developed explicitly stated that the data gathered be indigenous to Iceland and found nowhere else in the world. In addition to sensory data, I decided to gather weather and environmental data to paint a more vivid picture of Iceland in the minds of students not participating in the expedition.

After lengthy discussion with fellow scientists, I decided along with other expedition leaders to use the following methods for data gathering: digital photography to gather visual data; small digital voice recorders to gather auditory data; cosmetic sponges, small zipper lock clear bags, and marking pencils to capture olfactory data; packaged samples of food that would be purchased to gather gustatory data; and hand lenses, magnifying collection boxes, gloves, clear zipper lock bags, and marking pencils to gather physical specimens for tactile data. In addition, an anemometer, light meters, and meteorological data loggers would be used to gather environmental and weather data.

After conducting a thorough search of indigenous sights, smells, sounds, tastes, and surfaces to be accessed by senses of touch, my student assistant and I drafted lists of everything that the research team would need to gather in the field. These lists were then incorporated into the protocol, and the supplies needed were gathered, labeled, and organized. I began to immerse myself in Icelandic culture. I read books about Iceland, listened to Icelandic music, read poems written by Icelandic poets, read topographic maps of the various regions of the country, and spoke with people who had previously been to Iceland for both pleasure and research. Additionally, I began to write grants, looking for sponsors to subsidize the expedition and research expenses. Simultaneously, my travel partner was focusing on finding people to join the expedition and research team. He had already contracted a travel agent and hired a science professor from the University of Iceland to lead our expedition. He also made sure that each of our travel venues in Iceland would coincide with our research objectives.

IN THE FIELD DATA GATHERING METHODS

Upon arrival, we held a research briefing, and I distributed the research materials to each team member participating in the research project. Each team member received:

- A copy of the research protocol;
- A research notebook;
- A light data logger;
- A meteorological data logger to record temperature, barometric pressure, relative humidity, and dew point;
- A digital voice recorder with a set of batteries (for recording sound data);
- A set of ten cotton cosmetic sponges, zipper lock bags that had pre-printed labels on them, and a marking pencil (for gathering smell data);
- A digital camera if they did not own one (for capturing visual data);
- A stipend for the purchase of packaged foods and 10 zipper lock bags with pre-printed labels on them (for gathering gustatory data);
- A set of ten zipper lock bags with pre-printed labels on them, pair of gloves, a hand held magnifying lens, magnifying collection box, and marking pencil (for gathering touch data).

Weather data collection at Seljalandsfoss, Iceland. Reprinted with permission of Erin Colfax.

Each day we met at breakfast and were briefed by the expedition leader concerning the day's activities. I then led a research briefing outlining the type of data to be recorded for the day. I checked to make sure that each team member's equipment was functioning properly and that each team member had sufficient supplies. I then reported the current weather and meteorological conditions: temperature, barometric pressure, humidity, relative humidity, wind speed, wind direction, and dew point. After the morning briefings, team members gathered their personal belongings, research equipment, and instruments for the day, and we departed for the field.

Depending upon the activities and locations, the time spent gathering data in the field varied. We ventured out to new regions, gathered data, and participated in many adventure activities. To cite a few: we toured the city of Reykjavik, swam in the Blue Lagoon, hiked through Skaftafell National Park, toured the Skatftafell Folk Museum and the Historic Turf Chapel in Jupsstaour, visited the Njals Museum, hiked along the edge of Gulfos and Nesjavellir Geothermal Power Plant, rode the Icelandic horse, explored Pingvellir National Park and Continental Divide, hiked around Carter Kerio and Hellnar glacier, climbed Snaefellsnes Glacier, white-water rafted, and toured a fish processing plant. At the end of each day we conducted a de-briefing session reviewing where we had visited and what we had collected. We also exchanged feedback as to the day's activities and the data we had gathered. The de-briefing sessions ended with a preview of the next day's activities and the anticipated weather.

IN THE FIELD POETIC RESPONSES: ERIN COLFAX AND STUDENTS

Although our intentions were not to write poetry on the expedition itself, several expedition members and I felt inspired to write science poetry as we were recording and gathering data. For example, when we were in a lava field near the Rift Valley gathering touch specimens, I came across this one particular piece of lava. Its colors glistened in the sun, which caused me to ask the expedition leader more about the lava and its origins. He told me that it was basaltic lava and told me how it was formed. This was the first time I had ever seen or encountered basaltic lava. Basaltic lava is porous in nature. One side of the lava is black and shiny due to its silica and the other side is dull because of the iron. Its red color comes from the iron and other small minerals that oxidize in the rock itself. The lava on top has greater aeration, and may be foamy and glassy due to the rapid cooling process. Upon learning about the lava's origin, I felt inspired, so I took out my field journal and began to write my first ever poem, let alone, my first ever science poem.

Icelandic Mystique

Her exterior dorsal surface glistens in the midnight sun revealing
the molecular bonds created by the silica she possesses.
Her red ventral surface has a dull exterior resulting from the
oxidation of the iron she possesses.
The divergence of the North American and Eurasian Plates gave
birth to her mother as the Rift Valley was created.
She sits among her brothers and sisters who are also 600 years
young.
She is basaltic lava.

– Erin Colfax, teacher

The expedition leader often spoke to us about the devastation that
volcanic eruptions brought to the people and the land of Iceland. We
regularly drove through fields of moss indicating that the land was
still recovering from a previous eruption. The scientific information
was rather dry and simply writing the facts down to accompany the
data failed to reveal the emotions that I was experiencing. I wrote
in my field journal, "The Land of Laki."

The Land of Laki

In 1783, a volcanic eruption
forever changed Iceland's topography.
Laki's lava flowed to the sea,
creating fires that destroyed each and every tree.
It would ultimately change the atmosphere,
and interrupt the weather of Earth's troposphere.
Famine spread throughout the world
creating chaos for every boy and girl.
But after Iceland's land suffered this great loss,
there was such a surge in bryophitic moss.
Undergoing succession for more then 100 years,
the Eldhraun lava field developed over tears.
Today the flora geneses of Salix and Empetrum
cover the land in hopes of restoring the dreams of the Icelandic man.

– Erin Colfax, teacher

Another science poem, "Gjainfoss," was inspired by spending an afternoon at the waterfalls created after Hekla, the highest volcano in Southern Iceland, last erupted. The land had only recently regained its beauty after the violent eruption. The colors of the water, lush vegetation along the banks, and soft cushioning moss made the area magnificent. I sat for several minutes absorbing the environment around me. Then I had the urge to jump into the waterfalls with my fellow teammates and experience the cool and refreshing water that was filtered by the surrounding volcanic rock on my skin and through my hair. As I emerged from the water, I felt the desire to write about my experience.

Gjainfoss

I sat on her cushioned green bryophytic banks and watched the vibrant flow dissipate into pools of turquoise and white
ENERGY
She spoke to me in watery words of her creation as each syllable clung to the next like molecules cohering to one another because of their hydrogen bonds
LISTEN
Her story was one of imaginable magnitude… centuries ago Hekla's rage spewed poisonous contents down into the surrounding valleys silencing all those that could be reached. Choking the life from all the flora and fauna for centuries
ORIGIN
Gjain emerged from the ground, restoring life to the desolate barren land. Her flow brings the vital life substance that all those living yearn for
REBIRTH
Vegetation growing along her banks replenishing the beauty of the land, nurturing tranquility and romance
OASIS

– Erin Colfax, teacher

Once I started writing poems, I became more confident in the process of bringing science and poetry together. I even found myself sharing my poems with my fellow team members on the bus. After a while, they began to expect a poem out of me after a new or unusual experience. This in turn began to inspire others to become poetic as well. One of the students on the expedition also began to feel inspired after we visited one of Iceland's largest geothermal energy plants: Nesjavellir. Iceland is in a unique position, sitting on a geothermic hot spot. There are well over a hundred volcanoes and several geysers in the middle of the country. As a result, Iceland has a rather porous continental surface that creates a superb atmosphere for harnessing geothermal energy. After learning about and touring Nesjavellir, one of the students on the expedition, Paige Diamond, composed "Geothermal Energy."

Nesjavellir Geothermal Power Plant, Iceland. Reprinted with permission of Erin Colfax.

Geothermal Energy

Hot spots, hot springs
Maze of pipes
Twisting, turning
Convey splendor to 80% of all
Energy, Heat
Energy reigns life
Energy fuels life
Traveling amongst rocky roads
To the 310,000
Underground she boils fierce
Waiting in steamy lines
What purpose she possesses
Such magnificence is inevitable
Such power is obtainable
Energy is Iceland.

– Paige Diamond, expedition student

The data collection process seemed to be fueled by the poems we were writing and sharing. Team members were able to gather copious amounts of data and everywhere we turned we encountered poetic inspiration. Those who participated in the data collection process seemed to enjoy the experience. I was excited and invigorated to head home and sort through the data with my students in Research Science class. At the conclusion of our ten-day adventure in Iceland, I gathered all of the research materials from the team, packaged them in collection containers, and then reflected upon the experience.

IN THE FIELD REFLECTIONS: WRITING SCIENCE POETRY

After participating in a study with students, educators, and scientists in the field, gathering rather unusual data, and writing a series of science poems, I began to think about what I had experienced. I found that writing science poems forced me to pay attention to the accuracy with which I recorded observations, as well as the technical language I used to express what I experienced. I began to see value in acknowledging the emotions that I was feeling when presented with new scientific information. The poetry that I was writing allowed me to balance the two realms I was experiencing: the emotional and the scientific. Science poetry was no longer just an idea in my head or words on paper; it was real – so real that it would forever change how I taught science, ran a research study, and thought about science.[1] I could not wait to get back to the States to tell Nancy!

PART TWO: BACK IN THE RESEARCH SCIENCE CLASSROOM BY ERIN COLFAX

DATA ORGANIZATION IN RESEARCH SCIENCE CLASS

Upon the team's return to America, I found that sorting through the data was going to be a rather lengthy task. Students in my Research Science course and other interested students sat down to classify and analyze the data. The sight data of digital photographs were reviewed, identified, and classified into categories: volcanoes, glaciers, geothermal energy, agriculture, flora, fauna, and waterfalls. Sound data from each of the voice recorders were transferred, listened to, and recorded and compiled onto a compact disk. Smell data that was gathered by immersing individual sponges in the odiferous environment and then placed into a zip lock bag were vacuum-sealed and re-labeled. Gustatory data was re-labeled with identifiable ingredients and then vacuum-sealed as well. Touch data was reviewed, identified, and placed into zip-lock bags. Each set of data was housed separately in a rubber container and labeled with its contents and date. Then data from the anemometer, light meters, and meteorological data loggers were downloaded and transferred onto the computer and archived.

ICELANDIC DATA AND SCIENCE POETRY WRITING ACTIVITY

My Icelandic presentation and science poetry writing activity opens with Icelandic music and sounds playing while students walk into the classroom. To introduce the data and set the stage, I survey the students to see their familiarity with Iceland. I ask students if they have ever been to Iceland before, where it is located, and what they know about the country. Next, I share information about the region's geography, topography, ecosystems, indigenous fauna and flora, weather patterns, and culture.

In order to begin covering the data collected, I transition into a Power Point program that displays the visual data and relays some pertinent facts about the environment of Iceland. At this point, I move into the active portion of the presentation. Before I begin, I make it quite clear to students that when handling the sensory data, they should keep all positive and negative comments as well as facial expressions to themselves, so that everyone can first experience the data for themselves. I begin by playing an audio recording of eight, ten-second sound clips unique to Iceland. Students then guess what they think the sounds are. After confirming each of the sounds and discussing how unfamiliar some of them are, I move onto the sense of touch.

I then distribute the bags of touch specimens for students to feel. Students read a label, touch a specimen, and then pass that specimen to the next student until all of the specimens go around the room. I then ask students to describe their sensory responses. For example, I ask students to describe the touch of basaltic lava. Did it feel as they expected it to feel? Did the black sand feel like any other sand that they had ever touched?

After collecting the touch specimens, I distribute the smell specimens. I instruct students to open the vacuum-sealed bags containing a specimen, waft the odor towards their nose (to avoid over-exposure to the specimen), and then pass the specimen along. I remind students again that when smelling specimens, it is important not to comment or express their feelings toward the specimen. After the last student smells all of the specimens, I open the floor for questions and comments.

After a brief period of discussion, I expose students' palates to the tastes indigenous to Iceland. I begin by reading the contents and ingredients of the food samples, so that students can make an informed decision about allergens. I then open the package, distribute a small portion of the sample to those willing to try the sample, and then have each of the students taste the sample at once. This method proves to be the best way to avoid student comments such as "gross" or "can I have a little more" before other students have a chance to taste the specimens. Once all of the students' senses are simulated, I share some of the weather and environ-mental data and ask students to comment on how they thought the weather and environment may have impacted the specimens that they worked with in the activity.

Next, I share a few of the science poems I wrote in the field. I follow each poem with a brief commentary. Then I lead a discussion about scientific poetry: what it is, what makes it unique, and how students can write their own science poems. At this point, I suggest to students that they borrow samples from the data collection to inspire their poems or that they reflect upon the poetry models already shared. Last, I distribute Handout #2: Data Gathering Chart for Science Poetry Writing (see Chapter 5).

When my poetry partner, Nancy, is teaching with me, she reviews poetic stances and provides additional examples of forms to guide students' science poetry writing process. If I am teaching the activity by myself, I model the expected process and outcome by creating a class practice poem. For example, in Research Science class, I go through the process of creating a science poem by following the instructions on Handout #2 aloud. First, I identify with students an Icelandic science subject that everyone agrees upon as a subject for poetry writing. Then, I discuss qualitative terms (adjectives) that we might use to describe the chosen subject. All students write these down on Handout #2. I proceed by discussing quantitative terms (numerical data, scientific phenomenon and/ or concepts, or scientific processes) that ultimately cause the chosen subject to be in its current state or condition. All students write these down on Handout #2 as well. Next, I transition these descriptors into specific lines in the poem. When students are finished writing, we name our practice poem and review the process we followed to create the science poem. I tell my science students to be creative and express their thoughts in a poetic manner based on their prior poetry training and experience. I also tell them that all poems generated in response to the activity are poems in progress.

Model Student Responses: Research Science Class

The poems the students create in Research Science class proved to be highly inspired. Some of the student poems were so inspired that they could not be distinguished from the poems by students who had actually participated in the expedition. The following are two poems written by students who did not participate in the expedition. These science students responded only to the sensory data presented in the classroom and the instructions on poetic stances provided by my poetry partner. The poem, "Watch Me Float," a persona poem by Morgan Cole, was written after she was moved by one of the photographs from the visual data collection. The photograph was of an image of water moving down a river propelled by a rushing waterfall. The poem, "Pumice," by Anna McCabe, also a persona poem, was written after she felt a small piece of beige pumice. Like Morgan, Anna too gives voice to her subject.

"Watch Me Float" by Morgan Cole

Watch Me Float

i'm coming undone
in your powerful character
you pull me in, down
unwillingly

your attitude remains
cool and smooth
like the basaltic rock you crash me into

I envy the green moss
out of your clutches
able to escape
cutting, teasing, wicked

why build me up
to wash me out,
break me down?
i'm done
I float on, down the river.

– Morgan Cole, student

"Pumice" by Anna McCabe

Pumice

 I weigh all of two grams
And I'm harsh against your fingertips
You stroke me and I rip your skin

Look at me, you think I'm heavy
Hold me gently and close your eyes
Am I even there?
The gaps in me,
Are made by him
And here in Iceland
I am alone.

Out of my home I come
Leaving behind my thousands
of brothers and sisters
As I travel with you
Parts of me are lost.

Your fingers stroke me gently
And all I do is hurt you
Can you even trust me?
When you close your eyes
Am I even there?

                              – *Anna McCabe*, student

When sharing these poems in Science Research class, several students and expedition leaders in the room were surprised at how natural it was for students to express their feelings about a scientific specimen. It was also exciting to see the Icelandic expedition data generate scientific poetry, something that only a few months prior was a mere idea.

PART THREE: REPLICATING THE ICELANDIC EXPEDITION MODEL

Although the Icelandic expedition presents an exemplary model for scientific research and data gathering with students, the question still remains: *How will science and English teachers replicate such a model for science poetry writing?* For the vast majority of science and English teachers seeking in-the-field experiences, the most practical, effective, and natural alternative remains the field trip and its many variations: field trips during class, field trips on school grounds, field trips walking off school grounds, daily field trips, field trips over several consecutive days, and intermittent field trips over a longer period of time. Application of sensory data gathering methods, exemplified in the expedition model, can occur as simply as walking outside onto school grounds. Let's consider for a moment one possible field trip on school grounds, something I like to think of as the *mini field trip*.

SENSORY DATA GATHERING: THE MINI-FIELD TRIP ON SCHOOL GROUNDS

Over thirty years ago when I first began teaching English, I saw a sight on the 50-yard line of our high school's football field that forever influenced my teaching. It was a beautiful fall day, the kind that makes students ache to go outside. There on the field stood a biology teacher and her class of students, journals and binoculars in hand, patiently observing something in the sky and then recording data. I later found out they were watching the migration of hawks; they called it *the hawk watch*. The biology students did this every day during third period over the course of two weeks, while my creative writing students, inside, watched. Naturally, my students wanted to do the same: "Mrs. Gorrell, can't we go outside, too?" My reaction at the time – "Of course, but we will have to 'watch' for poems instead" – began what would become a foundation lesson in sensory note taking and data gathering for all my future writing classes: going outside to "watch" for poems.

Thirty years later, enlightened by science poetry, I now see *the hawk watch* as an ideal mini-field trip model for interdisciplinary/ cross-curricular teaching, learning, and collaboration. Certainly, if that passionate and innovative biology teacher had known about science poetry, I suspect she would have had her students write in-the-field science poems inspired by the hawks and the hawk watch data as well as the required scientific reports. I also suspect she would have been delighted if I had asked to have our students collaborate, the biology students sharing their scientific data with the poetry students to create poems informed and inspired by the hawk watch. I know my students' poems would have benefitted from the concreteness and specificity of scientific facts and quantitative data. I also know the biology students would have benefitted greatly from the opportunity to express their obvious passion for hawks in a form other than reportage. And most importantly, all students would have benefitted from seeing multiple and cross-curricular uses of the field journal, the field experience, and sensory data gathering.

SENSORY DATA GATHERING: DAILY FIELD TRIPS OFF SCHOOL GROUNDS

The daily field trip model offers the most widely practiced method for data gathering in the field for the purpose of writing science poetry. This method, commonly used in science classes, offers students the opportunity to conduct an inquiry, gather data in the field, and then to study and interpret that data back in the classroom, ultimately writing a science poem inspired by the experience. In English class, the field trip method relates data gathering to some aspect of literature or language and writing skills. Recommended field trip sites for science poetry writing include: natural environments such as parks, botanical gardens, woods, rivers, oceans, estuaries, or man-made environments such as landfills, recycling centers, laboratories, hospital operating rooms, science museums, aquariums, and zoos (see Chapter 11, "Walking in This World with Our Students and Colleagues).

TEACHER-GATHERED SENSORY DATA FOR SCIENCE POETRY WRITING

Although you may not be able to participate in an expedition with your students or a class, you may be able to go into the field to gather sensory data to bring back to your class as a stimulus for science poetry writing. Depending upon your objectives, the field could be quite foreign or unfamiliar to your students, or it could be a familiar field in your particular locale. Consider that exposing the hidden secrets of the familiar may be as inspirational for science poetry writing purposes as unfamiliar territory. Our expedition model attests to the effectiveness of teacher-gathered data. Both science and English students enjoyed experiencing the Icelandic sensory data back in the classroom and naturally responded poetically. For my writing classes, I gather naturalistic objects from local beaches to develop students' observation and sensory skills. Students use field guides to identify the natural objects (e.g. shells, stones, bones, seaweed, feathers, pinecones, driftwood, fragments, and fossilized materials); create description inventories; and then write a science poem informed and inspired by their objects. Similarly, science teachers can gather environmental data, affording students the opportunity not only to observe, sense, investigate, quantify, and analyze the data, but to respond to that data poetically as well.

PART FOUR: RELATED SCHOLARSHIP AND PEDAGOGY

POETRY, ECOLOGICAL LITERACY, AND ENVIRONMENTAL EDUCATION

For the purposes of this book, the most significant example of interdisciplinary literacy may be found in the *ecological literacy* movement that draws on science, technology, anthropology, linguistics, poetry, and the arts to forge change for a more sustainable world. Ecological literacy emerged in the last decade as the educational reform movement and the environment movement converged to produce a new pedagogy – *environmental education*. David Orr in *Ecological Literacy: Educating our Children for a Sustainable World* affirms that the goal of environmental education is not just mastery of subject matter but making connections between head, hand, heart, and the cultivation of the capacity to discern systems (Orr, 2005: x). He defines ecological literacy as having a "basic comprehension of ecology, human ecology, and the concepts of sustainability, as well as the wherewithal to solve problems" (Orr, 2005: xi).

On this side of the Atlantic, one of the most noted proponents of ecological literacy is desert ecologist, Gary Paul Nabhan, who is equally comfortable writing poetry in the nighttime deserts of Arizona near his home as he is writing field notes on hawkmoths and sacred datura flowers. Demonstrating how each discipline needs the other, Gary Paul Nabhan, in *Cross Pollinations: The Marriage of Science and Poetry*, documents how his bilingual translation of native American song-poems unlocked the science he needed to find a breakthrough cure for the prevalence of native American diabetes (Nabhan, 2004: 34–35). For Nabhan, "cross-pollination," is more than a topic of study, a scientific fact of the natural world, or a metaphor for marrying science and poetry; rather, it is for him a process by which he works, the source for his inspiration, creative productivity, and ecological advocacy: "My field work…has helped me understand that cross-pollination is not merely a metaphor but a requisite for sustaining the diversity of life on earth" (Nabhan, 2004: 12). If there is one book your students read on the blending of field science and the arts, let it be Nabhan's instructive and inspiring primer, *Cross Pollinations: The Marriage of Science and Poetry*.

One of the most noteworthy models of interdisciplinary pedagogy and community-based environmental education remains without a doubt, the *River of Words* (ROW) program. *River of Words*, an international program, invites K–12 students to explore their own watersheds, discover those watersheds' importance in their lives, and express through poetry and art what they've observed, felt, and learned. Co-founded in 1995 by U.S. Poet Laureate, Robert Hass, and Pamela Michael, ROW's expressed mission has been to "help children fall in love with the earth." According to Michael:

Our strategy was to create rich sensory experiences for students, encouraging them to explore their communities and imaginations – weaving in natural and cultural history – and to synthesize what they had learned and observed into line and verse. We sought to help children become keen observers of their own 'place in space' as Gary Snyder calls it, in the hope that they would develop a sense of belonging to a particular place. (Michael, 2005: 113)

Since its inception, ROW has sponsored one of the most noteworthy, international poetry writing contests for K–12 students, the *River of Words Poetry Contest* (see www.riverofwords.org for contest information). ROW publications include: *River of Words: Young Poets and Artists on the Nature of Things* (Michael, 2008) including teacher poetry writing curriculum guides.

A final, highly recommended resource for science and English teachers interested in fostering observation skills as well as scientific and ecological literacy is *The Private Eye Project* (www. the-private-eye.com) a self-described "K–16 through life" program designed to build the habits of mind of looking closely, thinking by analogy, changing scale, and theorizing, which are all habits of scientists, writers, poets, and artists described by Kerry Ruef in her article, "The Loupe's Secret: Looking Closely, Changing Scale" (Ruef, 2005: 206–212). Ruef's project offers a book, 5X jeweler loupes and classroom kits with specimens for observation.

Note

1. Erin further notes with delight how the Icelandic expedition and science poetry writing experience "changed forever" not only her classroom teaching, but her scientific expedition presentations as well from passive to active audience involvement. In her own words: "My Icelandic presentation became interactive. It had to be because the purpose of the presentation was not only to disseminate the scientific information to a particular community audience or class of students, but also to get that audience or class of students to write scientific poems about a particular scientific phenomenon, concept, or form of sensory data based on the Icelandic research."

Section Three: Fusion

Advanced Lessons for Science Poetry Writing

There are two kinds of knowledge,
Knowing about things and knowing things,
Scientific data and aesthetic realisation,
And I seek their perfect fusion in my work.

– Hugh MacDiarmid
"In Memoriam James Joyce"
Complete Poems Vol. II.
(MacDiarmid, 1978: 782)

SECTION OVERVIEW: OUR GUIDING METAPHOR, *FUSION*

In Section Three, students move from the foundation and fundamental practice exercises and activities to writing the advanced science poem; that is, a science poem that moves from the academic into the realm of the more personally authentic and artful. In doing so, students dig deep inside themselves, writing from the universal emotions that prompt all poetry, but particularly science poetry – *awe*, *wonder*, *reverence*, and *empathy* (Chapter 9); *outrage, protest, perplexity*, and *speculation* (Chapter 10). Most importantly, the process challenges students to enter the essence of the art form, one defined by Scotland's foremost science poet, Hugh MacDiarmid, as searching for the *perfect fusion*. As Edwin Morgan points out, "He [MacDiarmid] was always searching, and genuinely searching for 'The point where science and art can meet'" (Morgan, 2006: 33).

The two fusion lessons incorporating Section Three originated in AP English Language and Composition classes at Morristown High School as a result of a collaboration between myself and my AP English colleague, Jennifer Furphey. In writing the advanced science poem, these AP English students strive to reach MacDiarmid's *perfect fusion*. Yet the question remains: what exactly is this fusion that serves as the metaphoric guide for artful science poetry writing? Let's consider for a moment the scientific definition of *fusion*.

> **Fusion**: *n. a melting together into a fused mass. The union of light atomic nuclei to form heavier ones under extreme conditions of temperature and pressure, taking place with overall loss in mass and resulting in great energy release. This type of reaction takes place in the sun and in hydrogen bombs//a blending together so the component parts are not distinguishable.* (*The New Lexicon Webster's Dictionary of the English Language*, 1989: 386)

If we apply this definition to the process of writing science poetry, the result is a *melting together*, or a *union* under *extreme conditions of temperature* (or emotional intensity), causing *overall loss in mass* but creating *great energy release*, and something substantially new – the science poem. This poem is at once artful in the sense that *the component parts are not distinguishable*, and powerful in the sense that *great energy* is released. In addition, this type of reaction takes place in the sun (think: poetic enlightenment) and in hydrogen bombs (think: poetic power) – and, I would also like to suggest, in the science poetry of many of Morristown High School's students.

DEFINING THE ADVANCED SCIENCE POEM: STRIVING FOR THAT *PERFECT FUSION*

Striving for *perfect fusion* is truly an artistic as well as a scientific challenge for science poets, professionals and students alike. Critics rightfully caution that "the mere importation of a scientific term into a poem" is not enough "to freight the poem with new meaning" (Cherry, 2001: 27). While my science partner and I advocate such "importation" as a basic strategy to learn the fundamentals of science poetry writing (see Chapter 5), we also advocate that students strive to move beyond mechanical "importation" to more artful fusion of science and poetry. And that is the ultimate aim of Section Three: to seek MacDiarmid's *perfect fusion*.

In order to do so, our science and English students must take up the challenge, one clearly framed by critics. Kelly Cherry explains: "The challenge of using science in poetry lies in using it in a way that results in stronger poetry, a poetry that incorporates as much as possible of the real world" (Cherry, 2001: 27). For our purposes, that means a poetry that "incorporates as much as possible of the real world" of students' deepest emotions and personal experience. In this sense, the advanced science poem moves away from the academic or practice poem to writing a more fully authentic poem. This is not to imply that previous student models presented in the foundation and fundamental sections were not creative or inspired; rather, the advanced student poems in Section Three originate in a different place and fuse science and poetry in more artful and complex ways.

In addition, the advanced science poem demands of students greater scientific knowledge and literacy. Alison Hawthorne Deming further explains:

The challenge for the [student] poet is not merely to pepper the lines with spicy words and facts but to know enough science that the concepts and vocabulary become part of the fabric of one's mind, so that in the process of composition a metaphor or paradigm from the domain of science is as likely to crop up as is one from literature or her own backyard. (Deming, 2001: 186)

In essence, the advance science poem moves away from the purely academic poem to writing the more personally authentic, artistic, and complex poem.

Here are some ways to distinguish the advanced science poem from the more basic science poem. The advanced science poem is:

- *More authentic, rooted in the poet's deepest emotions and personal experience;*
- *More likely to begin with the poet's deepest emotions rather than science;*
- *More likely to be a poem that reflects greater energy and intensity;*
- *More likely to be a poem reflecting a complexity of emotions;*
- *More artful in its fusion of the complexity of emotions with science;*
- *More artful in its fusion of the science part and the poetry part;*
- *More artful in its use of scientific terms and vocabulary;*
- *More likely to be a poem that has something important to say;*
- *More likely to be a poem that matters deeply to the student poet;*
- *More likely to be a poem of greater scientific and poetic complexity.*

For both science and English teachers, Section Three offers two fusion lessons in writing the advanced science poem based exclusively on the models approach: Fusion Lesson One, Chapter 9;

and Fusion Lesson Two, Chapter 10. In these lessons, I do not teach any specific science activities, but rather expect advanced level students to draw on their prior knowledge of science or to research the scientific information relevant to their particular poems. This pedagogical strategy is most appropriate to poetry writing that originates more with feeling and emotion than with a scientific idea, theory, or observation as a starting point. Although a science poem may have one dominant emotion, the professional models in Section Three encourage students to respond to a <u>complexity</u> of emotions. For example, in "The Wellfleet Whale," students see the poet, Stanley Kunitz, responding with awe, wonder, reverence, empathy, as well as outrage to the beaching and death of a whale on Cape Cod. Such response enables students to further reach MacDiarmid's *perfect fusion.*

SUGGESTIONS FOR USING THIS SECTION

Although the aim of Section Three is to teach the advanced science poem, this is not to imply that the pedagogy is exclusive to advanced students. In fact, I have used the professional models in this section with Science Academy English students as well as English and creative writing students of all levels and abilities. Stanley Kunitz's signature poem, "The Wellfleet Whale," is highly accessible and a favorite of Science Academy students as well as English students. The qualities that distinguish the advanced from the more basic science poem apply more to the response and end products of the students rather than the pedagogy itself, which remains accessible to all. My science partner and I encourage science and English teachers alike to afford all of their students the opportunity to write from their deepest emotions – awe, wonder, reverence, empathy, outrage, and perplexity. For this purpose, we recommend extensive use of the exemplary student models in this section to inspire your students to write more advanced science poetry. We also recommend that you join your students in responding to the professional models by trying your hand at writing your own advanced science poems (see Chapter 11, where Janyce Trampler, science teacher and expedition chaperone, writes her first science poems).

9   Writing from Awe, Wonder, Reverence, and Empathy

OVERVIEW: FUSION LESSON ONE

What is it to see?
A mechanism wired in the brain
that leads to wonder. What is it
to wonder but to say
what we have seen and, having said it,
need to see farther.

– Alison Hawthorne Deming, "Mt. Lemmon,
Steward Observatory, 1990"
(Deming, 1994: 53–56)

In Fusion Lesson One students explore *what it is to wonder* by saying in their science poems what they *have seen* and, *having said it*, "seeing" still *farther*. They do so by reading and engaging with an extraordinary poem, "The Wellfleet Whale," by Stanley Kunitz. Although not written explicitly as a science poem, "The Wellfleet Whale" exemplifies the genre in its reverence for the animal kingdom and in its artful fusion of scientific facts and vocabulary with and moral and ethical issues. Most importantly, "The Wellfleet Whale" models for students the power of great poetry to express at once the full range and complexity of emotions. Although awe, wonder, reverence, and empathy dominate and prompt the emotional response of the poet, the underlying emotion remains outrage, protesting the death and destruction of something grand and majestic at the hands of nature, humankind, and/or both. As the model student poems in this chapter clearly demonstrate, students reach into their deepest emotions, responding with awe, wonder, reverence, empathy, and for some, underlying protest. If there is one poem you choose to read to your students to inspire science poetry, let it be "The Wellfleet Whale."[1]

Fusion Lesson One consists of a single activity designed to inspire and guide student poets to write from their authentic selves, drawing on their senses of awe, wonder, reverence, and empathy for nature and the universe that is science. In doing so, they will search, like MacDiarmid, for "the point where science and art can meet" (MacDiarmid, 1978: 782). This is the ultimate aim of Fusion Lesson One: to seek that *perfect fusion*, creating the advanced science poem.

Fusion Lesson One at a Glance

<u>Part One</u>: **Activity #1 Model Poem**
"The Wellfleet Whale" by Stanley Kunitz

<u>Part Two</u>: **Model Student Responses**
"Redwood" by David Pitt
"Humming Bird Gone" by Erica DeLaney
"Old Faithful" by Eric Villhauer

Materials Needed

Poetry Materials
"The Wellfleet Whale" by Stanley Kunitz (provided)
Science Materials
Audio Recordings of Wave and Whale Sounds (see Note #2)
Relevant Scientific Textual Resources: Textbooks, Illustrated Science Dictionaries, Field Guides, and Reference Books (see Note #3)

SUGGESTIONS FOR USING THIS LESSON

The professional model in this chapter, "The Wellfleet Whale," is accessible, instructive, and inspiring for students of all levels and abilities. Although more basic students may not respond with science poems comparable to those of advanced students, they often create authentic, heartfelt responses rooted in their deepest emotions and experience. To encourage all science and English students to take up the challenge of *perfect fusion*, my science partner and I recommend sharing the student model responses that follow the reading of "The Wellfleet Whale." These student models will further prompt and inspire responses on similar ecological and awe-inspiring themes: the plant kingdom (see the student poem, "Redwood") and wonders of the earth (see the student poem, "Old Faithful"). For teachers who prefer a thematic approach to poetry writing, the following professional-student pairs remain instructive for an approach to teaching ecological poetry reflecting awe and empathetic response:

Professional-Student Pairs for Thematic Instruction

- Stanley Kunitz, "The Wellfleet Whale" (professional poem), with Erica DeLaney's "Humming Bird Gone" (student poem).
- Stanley Moss, "Elegy for the Ancient Tree," with David Pitt's "Redwood."
- Edwin Morgan, "Submarine Demon," with Eric Villhauer's "Old Faithful."

English teachers will find these professional-student pairs effective for reading, critical analysis, comparative essay writing as well as poetic response. Biology, botany, and environmental science teachers will find the pairs particularly useful for opening discussion and debate regarding students' attitudes and emotional responses to the wonders of nature and the ethical issues involved in the destruction of nature by humans. My science partner and I can attest to the value of such discussions to prompt powerful and empathetic poetic responses in both the science and English classrooms.

Suggested Time Allocations

Time allocations for Activity #1 will vary depending upon the length of follow-up discussion and time allowed for in-class poetic response and sharing works in progress. Be sure to provide sufficient class time for students to begin writing their poems.

Activity #1: "The Wellfleet Whale" (60 minutes)

PART ONE: ACTIVITY #1 MODEL POEM

"THE WELLFLEET WHALE" BY STANLEY KUNITZ

Introducing and Reading the Poem

If there is one poem to read to students of any level or ability that will evoke the deepest emotional responses, touching both the heart and mind, it is without a doubt, "The Wellfleet Whale," a poem about the beaching of a whale that reaches epic proportions. Although some teachers may prefer to introduce the poem's reading with a discussion of the science and mystery behind the phenomenon of the beaching of whales, I have found that little needs to be said to prepare students to engage with "The Wellfleet Whale." As with all great poetry, the poem speaks for itself. I simply read to my students the entry from Kunitz's journal that prefaces the poem. Then I read the poem aloud, without further commentary, other than to say that Kunitz lived for years in Provincetown, Cape Cod, in Massachusetts, and that his poem is based on an encounter he had with a beached whale in Wellfleet Harbor on September 12, 1966 (Kunitz, 1995: 167). I also tell students to take out their response journals so that they will be ready to respond after they hear the poem.

The Wellfleet Whale

A few summers ago, on Cape Cod, a whale foundered on the beach, a sixty-three-foot finback whale. When the tide went out, I approached him. He was lying there, in monstrous desolation, making the most terrifying noises – rumbling – groaning. I put my hands on his flanks and I could feel the life inside him. And while I was standing there, suddenly he opened his eye. It was a big, red, cold eye, and it was staring directly at me. A shudder of recognition passed between us. Then the eye closed forever. I've been thinking about whales ever since.

                                                                – Journal entry

1

You have your language too,
   an eerie medley of clicks
      and hoots and trills,
location-notes and love calls,
   whistles and grunts. Occasionally,
      it's like furniture being smashed,
or the creaking of a mossy door,
   sounds that all melt into a liquid
      song with endless variations,
as if to compensate
   for the vast loneliness of the sea.
      Sometimes a disembodied voice
breaks in, as if from distant reefs,
   and it's as much as one can bear
      to listen to its long mournful cry,
a sorrow without a name, both more
   and less than human. It drags
      across the ear like a record
running down.

2

No wind. No waves. No clouds.
   Only the whisper of the tide,
      as it withdrew, stroking the shore,

a lazy drift of gulls overhead,
    and tiny points of light
        bubbling in the channel.
It was the tag-end of summer.
    From the harbor's mouth
        you coasted into sight,
flashing news of your advent,
    the crescent of your dorsal fin
        clipping the diamonded surface.
We cheered at the sign of your greatness
    when the black barrel of your head
        erupted, ramming the water,
and you flowered for us
    in the jet of your spouting.

        3
All afternoon you swam
    tirelessly round the bay,
        with such an easy motion,
the slightest downbeat of your tail,
    an almost imperceptible
        undulation of your flippers,
you seemed like something poured,
    not driven; you seemed
        to marry grace with power.
And when you bounded into air,
    slapping your flukes,
        we thrilled to look upon
pure energy incarnate
    as nobility of form.
        You seemed to ask of us
not sympathy, or love,
    or understanding,
        but awe and wonder.

That night we watched you
    swimming in the moon.
        Your back was molten silver.

We guessed your silent passage
   by the phosphorescence in your wake.
      At dawn we found you stranded on the rocks.

    4
There came a boy and a man
   and yet other men running, and two
      schoolgirls in yellow halters
and a housewife bedecked
   with curlers, and whole families in beach
      buggies with assorted yelping dogs.
The tide was almost out.
   We could walk around you,
      as you heaved deeper into the shoal,
crushed by your own weight,
   collapsing into yourself,
      your flippers and your flukes
quivering, your blowhole
   spasmodically bubbling, roaring.
      In the pit of your gaping mouth
you bared your fringework of baleen,
   a thicket of horned bristles.
      When the Curator of Mammals
arrived from Boston
   to take samples of your blood
      you were already oozing from below.
Somebody had carved his initials
   in your flank. Hunters of souvenirs
      had peeled off strips of your skin,
a membrane thin as a paper.
   You were blistered and cracked by the sun.
      The gulls had been pecking at you.
The sound you made was a hoarse and fitful bleating.

What drew us, like a magnet, to your dying?
   You made a bond between us,
      the keepers of the nightfall watch,
who gathered in a ring around you,
   boozing in the bonfire light.
      Toward dawn we share with you

your hour of desolation,
 the huge lingering passion
  of your unearthly outcry,
as you swung your blind head
 toward us and laboriously opened
  a bloodshot, glistening eye,
in which we swam with terror and recognition.

  5
Voyager, chief of the pelagic world,
 you brought with you the myth
  of another country, dimly remembered,
where flying reptiles
 lumbered over the steaming marshes
  and trumpeting thunder lizards
wallowed in the reeds.
 While empires rose and fell on land,
  your nation breasted the open main,
rocked in the consoling rhythm
 of the tides. Which ancestor first plunged
  head-down through zones of colored twilight
to scour the bottom of the dark?
 You ranged the North Atlantic track
  from Port-of-Spain to Baffin Bay,
edging between the ice-floes
 through the fat of summer,
  lob-tailing, breaching, sounding,
grazing in the pastures of the sea
 on krill-rich orange plankton
  crackling with life.
You prowled down the continental shelf,
 guided by the sun and stars
  and the taste of alluvial silt
on you way southward
 to the warm lagoons,
  the tropic of desire,
where the lovers lie belly to belly
 in the rub and nuzzle of their sporting;
  and you turned, like a god in exile,

out of your wide primeval element,
    delivered to the mercy of time.

    Master of the whale-roads,
let the white wings of the gulls
    spread out their cover.
    You have become like us,
disgraced and mortal.

– Stanley Kunitz (Kunitz, 1995:133–138)

Freewriting Response: Into the Eye of the Whale

The oral reading of "The Wellfleet Whale" inevitably creates a sense of awe, reverence, shock, and sadness on the part of many students. After hearing the poem, students are often speechless; a palpable silence pervades the classroom. The complexity of emotions, so evoked, creates a teachable moment, one ripe for poetry. This is not the moment to explicate the poem, but rather, to freewrite, and to create poems in kind. To further this aim and to maintain the moment of solitude, I often play naturalistic or environmental music, in particular, the sounds of waves or the sounds of whales.[2] These naturalistic, environmental sounds establish an atmosphere conducive to empathetic reflection. I tell students to write freely in their journals for approximately 15 minutes. Then I project the following freewriting prompts.

Freewriting Prompts

Questions to Get You Started
- *How did the poem make you feel?*
- *What did the poem remind you of?*
- *What did the poem make you think about?*

Writing Instructions
- *Write freely in your journal from one or more of your emotions evoked by the poem.*

                        Or,

- *Write freely in your journal from an image, thought, or association suggested to you by the poem.*

Post-Writing Sharing and Discussion

After students freewrite, I call on volunteers to share excerpts from their poems in progress. If your students are reluctant to share, suggest they share just a line or a favorite part of their poems in progress. My students generally are eager to give voice to their poems. During this sharing phase, students naturally begin to exchange their reactions to Kunitz's poem as well. Those students who have witnessed the beaching of whales or who have seen whales in their natural habitat are especially eager to share their observations. Other students share comparable encounters they have had with animals in their natural states or family pets. Equally eager to share are students horrified at the actions of the souvenir hunters and even at the role of the Curator of Mammals from Boston. Rather than formal explication, I give the students the opportunity to respond to the poem based on their experiences and what matters to them. This "writerly" approach enables students to enter the poem through the eyes of the poet, fostering more authentic poetic responses. If your students are reluctant to discuss their reactions to the poem, the following open-ended questions will encourage discussion:

Discussion Starters for "The Wellfleet Whale"

1. *If you could ask the poet one question about his poem, what would it be?*
2. *What do you think the poet's attitude is toward nature and the animal kingdom?*
3. *What do you think the poet's attitude is toward science or scientists in the poem?*
4. *Have you ever observed a similar event or phenomenon in nature?*

Lead students to debate whether science is helpful, benign, or cruel in the poet's eyes. For teachers interested in bioethics and the role of science, Kunitz's poem is an ideal discussion starter. In fact, the reading of his poem generally elicits many eco-poems, especially from environmentally minded students. Interestingly enough, "The Wellfleet Whale" inspires a multiplicity of natural and scientific subjects on the part of students, crossing many disciplines: biology, botany, geology, astronomy, and physics as well as environmental science and ecology (see the model student responses to follow).[3]

Writing the Advanced Science Poem

After students have completed their freewritings and have thoroughly engaged with the poem, they are ready to write their science poems. For interested teachers, now is the time for more in-depth, formal explication. This may be particularly appropriate and essential for teachers of students who have not fully comprehended the poem. If so, take a moment to formally explicate the poem based on your students' interests and needs before distributing the following guidelines for writing an advanced science poem. Take this moment to point out Kunitz's fusion of poetic imagery with scientifically accurate terminology like *flippers, flukes, blowhole, baleen, lob-tailing, breaching, krill-rich orange plankton,* and *alluvial silt.* Encourage and challenge your students to describe both poetically and scientifically, striving to achieve that *perfect fusion.* Then project or distribute the following science poetry writing prompts:

Science Poetry Prompts: "The Wellfleet Whale"

Student Instructions

Read the following general guidelines before considering the specific science poetry writing prompts. Choose one or more prompts to respond to in any poetic form you prefer.

General Guidelines

- *Write from your deepest emotions and personal experience.*
- *Use that emotion or experience as a starting point.*
- *Feel free to express a full range or complexity of emotions.*
- *Write what deeply matters to you.*
- *Write what you think is important to say.*
- *Use accurate scientific terms and vocabulary.*
- *Strive for an artful fusion of science and poetry.*
- *Let each enlighten the other in that perfect fusion.*

Specific Prompts

1. Recall a time when you observed something in nature that caused great awe, wonder, or reverence for you. Like Kunitz, convey your sense of awe, wonder, or reverence through specific scientific description and vocabulary.

2. Recall a time when you observed something in nature that caused you to feel a great sense of empathy. Like Kunitz, write a poem of address to your subject, showing your empathy with specific scientific description, vocabulary, and imagery. Think of this as entering the heart, mind, and spirit of your subject.

3. Recall a time when you observed something in nature that caused a complexity of emotions, possibly conflicting emotions. Like Kunitz, write a science poem that begins in awe, wonder, and reverence and then moves somehow to sadness, shock, or tragedy. If you want to protest, try to make that protest implicit rather than explicit; in other words, let the story or the facts speak for themselves.

4. Like Kunitz, recall a time when you encountered an animal in its natural environment. This animal may have been alive, dead, or dying. Describe in a science poem the moment of encounter; be as scientifically accurate as possible in describing the animal. Recall how Kunitz, in his journal entry, touches the whale and looks into the eye of the whale. End your poem with reflection – a moment of recognition or realization.

5. Like Kunitz, write a poem about something you observed or encountered in nature or the natural world that caused you "to think about it ever since." Base the poem on an image, like the eye of the whale that you can never forget.

6. Have you ever looked into the "eye" of another creature? If so, write a poem about that moment of "seeing."

PART TWO: MODEL STUDENT RESPONSES

"REDWOOD" BY DAVID PITT

After engaging with "The Wellfleet Whale," David Pitt writes his second science poem, "Redwood," inspired by a personal experience he had in the California redwood forest several years ago. Like Kunitz, David addresses his subject, the redwood tree, imaginatively entering into its *majestic greatness*.

Redwood

Standing tall
    I don't suppose you wonder.

No quickened heartbeat
    pumping H_2O and glucose faster
    through sclerenchyma tracheids
    as you watch your brethren fall.
        No.
You stand hard as lignin.

    You grow
    not aging,
cambium augmenting ageless pith.
    No
I don't suppose you listen
to the axes.

    Majestic greatness
    pays no heed.
You've been here a while.
    And you might stay.

    Although it's getting warmer
        adjust stomata,
        go on growing.

                 – *David Pitt*, student

"Redwood" models Kunitz's emotional progression, beginning with awe and wonder, observing the redwood *standing tall*, and then moving to empathy, *I don't suppose you wonder / No quickened heartbeat…as you watch your brethren fall*. Last, the speaker moves to reverence: *You stand hard as lignin…I don't suppose you listen / to the axes…Majestic greatness / pays no heed*. Like Kunitz, there is an underlying protest directed to the *axes*, and yet, the speaker, projects confidence, *You've been here a while / And you might stay*. David's provocative ending can be interpreted in two ways. The speaker, addressing the redwood, urges the tree to *adjust* and *go on growing*. In conferencing with David, another possible meaning rose to the surface, one David found equally plausible and intriguing. The tree could be contemplating its own mortality, addressing, in interior monologue form, itself: *adjust stomata / go on growing*. David, in his commentary, explains his intention:

David's Commentary

I was trying to capture a botanist's awe with the specimen he is examining, a redwood tree. The poem tries to capture the reverence the speaker feels towards the tree's passivity as other trees are being chopped down. The poem deals more immediately with feeling (poetry), alluding to the botany (science) secondarily. I used my biology notes from 10th grade to fuse the science into this poem.

David certainly has taken up the challenge of fusion. "Redwood" is emotionally intense, rooted in wonder and awe, as well as personally authentic, based on a personal experience he will never forget. Most importantly, David's use of scientific and technical terms serves his poetic purpose, giving the speaker a powerfully credible voice. This speaker knows the tree inside and out. *You stand hard as lignin* suggests not only affirmation but reverence while *adjust stomata* suggests not only encouragement but empathy.

"HUMMING BIRD GONE" BY ERICA DELANEY

Erica DeLaney responds to "The Wellfleet Whale" by recalling an encounter she had with a humming bird. Her poem, filled with emotional intensity, exemplifies the empathetic responses Kunitz's poem evokes for many students.

Humming Bird Gone

Wings beating hundreds of times per minute
Nothing more than a blur to the human eye.
Darting from flower to flower,
Your iridescent feathers
Glint in the afternoon sun.
With great joy you fed
Not knowing the danger before you.

Thud!
To me, inside the house
It sounded like a pebble hitting the window.
But I knew better.
Mesmerized by your graceful flight,
I watched you hit the glass.
Little hummingbird, I saw
Your fate sealed

Your destiny set as your course had been.
But I attempted to change your fate.
Gingerly I lifted you into a box
Cushioned by both blanket and pillow
And held water and flowers full of nectar
To your needle-like beak.

As you lay on your side,
Your one perceptible eye closed
You took your last labored breath.
Only the splash of my tears disturbed
The ensuing peace.

                                        – *Erica DeLaney*, student

Erica's poem of address begins in awe and wonder, *Wings beating hundreds of times per minute / Nothing more than a blur to the human eye*, and then climaxes in tragedy, *Thud!... Your fate sealed*. Like Kunitz, she concludes her empathetic response looking into the eye of the dying hummingbird: *Your one perceptible eye closed*. Erica explains in her commentary: "I was very pleased with this poem because I feel it very accurately captures the emotion and empathy I felt at the moment of the event." Although Erica's poem does not infuse scientific terminology, "Humming Bird Gone" exemplifies the first necessary step in writing the advanced science poem, and that is, writing from intense emotion, personal experience, and empathy.

"OLD FAITHFUL" BY ERIC VILLHAUER

Eric Villhauer's poem of address exemplifies sheer awe at the sight of the giant geyser, "Old Faithful," in Yellowstone National Park, Wyoming. With an explosion of exuberance, almost parallel to Old Faithful itself, he connects in conversation with his subject.

Old Faithful

You will never abandon me,
as every 90 minutes you speak.
Spurting 8,000 gallons of boiling water,
to heights I strain my neck to observe
(half a football field high),
You reach out to me.
Eternal hot breath whistling with your water
a symphony even Woodward could not have described.
You are Mother Earth's gem,
not just Yellowstone's.
You are the stomach of nature,
bellowing, groaning, and whispering.
I wait for our next conversation.

– Eric Villhauer, student

Eric's poem, a first-hand observation, clearly exhibits the emotional intensity and authenticity that mark the emergence of the advanced science poem. The scientific facts serve his purpose well, confirming his amazement as well as lending power to his desire in the last line to personally connect to nature: *I wait for our next conversation.*

Clearly, the universal emotions of awe, wonder, reverence, and empathy inspire and prompt students to connect the world of self to the world of nature and science, producing highly authentic and powerful science poems. In the following chapter, students move one step further, responding to their empathy with outrage in the face of injustice, and to their wonder with perplexity and speculation.

Notes

1. For a lyrical poem that compares beautifully to the "The Wellfleet Whale," the former about the animal kingdom, the latter about the plant kingdom, see "Elegy for the Ancient Tree" by Stanley Moss (Moss, 2009). There Moss decries the cutting down of the oldest living thing on earth at the hands of an arborist. Like Kunitz, he writes from awe, reverence, and empathy for the tree, at the same time protesting the tree's tragic destruction. Additional science poems accessible to students that demonstrate awe, reverence and wonder include: Alison Hawthorne Deming's "Mt. Lemmon, Steward Observatory, 1990" (Deming, 1994) and Edwin Morgan's "Submarine Demon" (Morgan, 1999).
2. There are many available sources that reproduce the environmental sounds of nature, in particular, waves, wind, ocean, surf, and whales. One such source is Dan Gibson's *Solitude* series accessible online at: http://www.silverlakemusic.com/art/agibson.html.
3. Relevant scientific textual resources for Chapter 9 are biology, botany, and astronomy textbooks available in any science department, illustrated science dictionaries, anatomy charts for animal species, scientific photographic collections that inspire awe and wonder like *Planet Earth* and *National Geographic*.

10 Writing from Outrage, Protest, Perplexity, and Speculation

Each glittering point of light / beckons: 'There is something beyond.'

— William Stafford, "What If We Were Alone?"
(Stafford, 1987: 115)

OVERVIEW: FUSION LESSON TWO

In Fusion Lesson Two students continue to write not only from their deepest emotions and most authentic experiences, but from their deepest and most perplexing thoughts as well. In this regard, they respond with intensity to what outrages them, what provokes their thinking, and what makes them question, speculate, and reflect. If writing from the heart dominates the emotions in Chapter 9, writing from the mind, or as Roald Hoffmann frames it in "Giving In" (Hoffman, 1991) *trying to imagine* and to understand dominates the poetic responses in Chapter 10. In this chapter, students confront controversial issues, wrestling in their poems with the nature and role of science and their own ethical, moral, and religious beliefs.

For some, outrage prevails and their poetic responses become openly political in their protests. For others, reflection and speculation prevail. Students not only express their authentic emotions, they connect their emotions to their thoughts and experiences, clarifying their thinking as well. For students, these poems become important, saying something that truly matters to them. In this sense, the ultimate aim of Fusion Lesson Two is to inspire and encourage student poets to explore the depth and complexity of their thinking about their relationship with and response to the universe of science. In making such connections, as the student models in this chapter demonstrate, we see the emergence of the *perfect fusion* that is the essence of the advanced science poem.

Fusion Lesson Two consists of two parts. Part One, *Writing from Outrage and Protest*, centers on Activity #1, a model science poem by Roald Hoffmann, "Giving In." Part Two, *Writing from Perplexity and Speculation*, centers on Activities #2 and #3, model science poems, "Cascadilla Falls" by A. R. Ammons and "What If We Were Alone?" by William Stafford. Part Two concludes with four model student responses demonstrating perplexity and speculation.

Fusion Lesson Two at a Glance

Part One: Writing from Outrage and Protest
Activity #1 Model Poem, "Giving In" by Roald Hoffmann
Model Student Responses
"Gasp" and "Sadako" by Anne Schwartz
"What am I Doing, Ant?" by Eric Villhauer

Part Two: Writing from Perplexity and Speculation
Activity #2 Model Poem, "Cascadilla Falls" by A. R. Ammons
Activity #3 Model Poem, "What If We Were Alone?" by William Stafford
Model Student Responses
"Versus" by Anne Schwartz
"O Asymptote" by David Pitt
"Nerves" by Alex Davis

Writing the Advanced Science Poem: Striving for that Perfect Fusion
"The Butterfly and Me" by Sarah Ryan

Materials Needed

Poetry Materials
Science Poem, "Giving In" by Roald Hoffmann (provided)
Science Poem, "Cascadilla Falls" by A.R. Ammons (provided)
Science Poem, "What If We Were Alone?" by William Stafford
(provided)

Science Materials
Relevant Scientific Textual Resources: Textbooks, illustrated science
dictionaries, reference books, science journals, magazines, and news
articles[1]

SUGGESTIONS FOR USING THIS LESSON: FOSTERING SCIENTIFIC LITERACY

Both science and English teachers will find that writing a science
poem in response to current and controversial scientific issues is
a highly effective and creative pedagogical strategy to challenge
and develop students' scientific literacy. My science partner and
I recommend engaging students with current scientific articles,
highlighting moments of scientific discovery, or focusing on current
controversial issues. Use of the student models in this chapter, in
particular, the poem, "Versus" by Anne Schwartz, inspired by a
science news article, will encourage students to respond in kind
to their readings.

Science teachers, especially physics and chemistry teachers,
will find the models in this chapter particularly instructive for their
disciplines. The life work of science poet, A. R. Ammons, reflects
his fascination with all areas of the Third Science paradigm – chaos,
complexity, and field theories. Many of his poems, like "Cascadilla
Falls," are studies in chaos and order. Such poems are instructive for
students studying aspects of motion, and may be used to set up or
close a scientific unit of study. Similarly, the protest poem, "Giving
In," by Roald Hoffmann centers on chemical transformation and

experimentation, and raises current issues worthy of discussion in any science class.

English and creative writing teachers will find the student and professional models in this chapter inspirational for prompting authentic and thought provoking responses regarding ethical and moral as well as scientific issues. Once again, the protest poems of Anne Schwartz on capital punishment and the atomic bomb will encourage students to respond in kind. Any readings or units of study on the literature of genocide, the Holocaust, Hiroshima, World War II, or the death penalty will find the models in Fusion Lesson Two ideal additions to enrich the curriculum. My science partner and I firmly believe science poetry offers one of the most effective vehicles for affording high school students the opportunity to express their attitudes and opinions regarding scientific issues and controversies of local, national, and global concern.

Suggested Time Allocations

Time allocations for Activity #1 will vary depending upon the length of follow-up discussion and time allowed for in-class poetic response and sharing works in progress. Be sure to provide sufficient class time for students to begin writing their poems.

> **Activity #1 (50 minutes)**
> **Activity #2 (20 minutes)**
> **Activity #3 (20 minutes)**

PART ONE: WRITING FROM OUTRAGE AND PROTEST

ACTIVITY #1: MODEL POEM, "GIVING IN" BY ROALD HOFFMANN

"Giving In" is a challenging poem to understand without some background knowledge. In my Interview with Roald Hoffmann, he explained to me the origin of the poem that appears on the surface to be about xenon, a gas, turning metallic at 1.4 million atmospheres but then leaps to the human and societal realms. Hoffmann explained to me that the poem drew on two sources. He had just read some experiments (disputed) claiming to make hydrogen metallic, and he was also reading at the same time a memoir by Jacobo Timmerman on his torture as a political prisoner during the military dictatorship in Argentina (Interview with Roald Hoffmann; Gorrell, 2008). Hoffmann could not separate, as he calls them, "these two realms," the realm of matter and the realm of emotion. These two realms converge in "Giving In," giving us two painful images to *try to imagine*: the terrible squeezing of the gas between the two diamond anvils, which Hoffmann describes as similar to the "pressure at the center of the earth" (Gorrell, 2008), and the squeezing of a hand in a press in a cellar in Buenos Aires. Although "Giving In" on paper appears to be a poem that rhetorically begins in science and then leaps to the personal and political, we need to remind our students that in its origins, this is not the case. The poem's distinction is that it originates in both realms simultaneously; the scientific and the personal are <u>one</u>, in *perfect fusion*, in the poet's heart and mind. As such, Hoffmann's poem of outrage and protest serves as a powerful and instructive model of advanced science poetry writing.

Introducing and Reading the Poem: *Trying to Imagine* the Unimaginable

Introduce the poem to your science and English students by explaining the background of its origin. Ask your students to "try to imagine" the unimaginable, that is, political torture. Also ask your students to try to imagine being a scientist, doing an experiment, one difficult to imagine that evokes images of such torture. Finally, ask your students to take up the challenge that Hoffmann's poem poses: try imagining "giving in." Before you read the poem aloud, tell students to take out their journals. Then read the poem aloud.

Giving In

At 1.4 million atmospheres
xenon, a gas, goes metallic.
Between squeezed single-bevel
diamond anvils jagged bits
of graphite shot with a YAG[2]
laser form spherules. No one
has seen liquid carbon. Try
to imagine that dense world
between ungiving diamonds
as the pressure mounts, and
the latticework of a salt
gives, nucleating at defects
a shift to a tighter order.
Try to see graphite boil. Try
to imagine a hand, in a press,
in a cellar in Buenos Aires,
a low-tech press, easily
turned with one hand, easily
cracking a finger in another
man's hand, the jagged bone
coming through, to be crushed
again. No. Go back, up, up
like the deep diver with
a severed line, up, quickly,
to the orderly world of ruby
and hydrogen at 2.5 megabar,
the hydrogen coloring near
metallization, but you hear
the scream in the cellar, don't
you, and the diver rises too fast.

                    – *Roald Hoffmann* (Hoffmann, 1991: 189)

Freewriting in Response to "Giving In"

After hearing the poem, my students are usually silent and deeply moved. Allow students time for reflection before explication and discussion. Instruct them to freewrite in their journals for 10 minutes to one of the following open-ended prompts:

Freewriting Prompts

- *What emotions does the poem evoke for you? Freewrite or write a poem starting with those emotions.*
- *What does the poem remind you of or make you think of? Freewrite or write a poem starting with those thoughts?*
- *What images does the poem evoke for you? Freewrite or write a poem suggested by those images.*

Post-Writing Sharing and Discussion

After students have completed their freewriting, open discussion by asking for volunteers to share their thoughts, reactions, or poems in progress. Such free exchange quickly gets to the heart of Hoffmann's poem and what matters to the students. I find my students react not only on an emotional level to the pain of Hoffmann's images, but on an intellectual level as well. For many, "Giving In" makes them think seriously of controversial issues for which the ethics and morality of science converges with their own personal values and beliefs. After students share poems in progress, guide further explication by asking your students the following questions:

Discussion Starters for "Giving In"

1. What do you think the title means?
2. In the poem, who or what "gives in" literally or scientifically?
3. In the poem, who or what "gives in" poetically or on a human level?
4. What does the poet mean by *No, go back up, up...to the orderly world*? Who or what is "giving in" here?
5. Do you see Hoffman's poem as a protest? If so, what is he protesting, and how does that protest relate to the title?

For advanced English students the title "Giving In" resonates. They see the chemical transformation and the hand in the press as literally "giving in" to another form with all the connotations of pain that both transformations, under extraordinary conditions of "pressure," suggest. They also see the poet's instruction, *No, go back up, up...to the orderly world* to suggest perhaps how we all prefer not to face the reality of political torture; one student mentions how we do not want to see torture, and in that sense, we "give in," doing nothing about it. Together we agree that this point may be the heart of Hoffmann's protest. Once students have reached this level of understanding, I am able to lead them to a final, more philosophical understanding, one they usually do not arrive at themselves.

I ask my students: In what sense may science or the scientist be "giving in?" Knowing Hoffmann's attitudes toward the practice of science and scientific writing, I imagine that he is indirectly affirming the struggle of the scientist doing experimental research to remain objective or unemotional in the face of many possible factors, the foremost being his own personal associations and humanity.[3] Although there is not literally a scientist in the poem conducting chemical transformations, theoretically scientists have experimented with such transformations. I speculate that perhaps the speaker or Hoffmann himself performed such chemical experiments in the past. If so, does the speaker or Hoffmann "give in" to the emotional recognition of an intervening association – the hand in the press – another type of transformation? Although the chemical experimentations in the poem have not aided or abetted the torture, nevertheless, "Giving In" leads me to consider experimentation that has done just that: science gone awry or science put to unethical purposes; in other words, science or scientists "giving in."

After your students have completed sharing and thoroughly discussing their reactions to the poem, distribute or project the following science poetry writing prompts.

Science Poetry Prompts: "Giving In"

1. Write a science poem in which you are observing or performing an action – a scientific experiment or investigation – or having an encounter with or experience with some aspect of science while thinking of or recalling something else quite different. Juxtapose your external observations or actions with your internal thoughts and associations. Like Hoffmann, you could begin in the world of science by describing your observations, experience, or experiment, and then leap by association to the personal and human worlds of self and society. You do not necessarily have to explain the connection. Let the juxtaposition make the point.

2. Write a science poem observing or describing any scientific experiment or investigation. Let your description show your attitudes toward the experiment. Entitle your poem, "Science" or "The Experiment."

3. Like Hoffmann, write a science poem protesting a controversial issue that affects you deeply, or means something to you or science.

4. Like Hoffmann, write a science poem asking your readers to *try to imagine* the unimaginable.

Model Student Responses

"Gasp" by Anne Schwartz

In "Gasp" Anne Schwartz takes up the challenge to try to imagine the unimaginable – capital punishment by electrocution. Sensitive to the cruelty and graphic nature of the subject, Anne explains her intent in her commentary:

Anne's Commentary

I wanted to portray the evil of the death penalty – more importantly, the value of a person's life – as clearly as I could, with little ambiguity. I thus relied on more shocking contrast than usual and a harsher tone – choices that I do not usually make, but that I felt was necessary. This poem is different from some of my others; more protest than art.

Gasp

Not so long ago a family
Gathered in the glow of wonder
Watched the sparkle and fizz of an electric light bulb,
As the current flowed and with a gasp
The light goes on.

Cathode to anode,
Negative to positive.
It seems so simple
To watch the childlike grins on the family's faces,
To watch everything light up.

Not so long ago a group of people
With dour faces, in need of a lamp
Gathered to watch the fizz of a man's life.
Shackled in a chair,
Kept alive by the rushing flow of electrons,
Of memories and thoughts
Of life,
His light glows,
dimly.

Anode to cathode,
Cathode to anode.
Who even remembers anymore?
With a gasp, the current flows and
The light goes out.

– *Anne Schwartz*, student

"Sadako" by Anne Schwartz

Anne Schwartz explains the inspiration and intention of her second
protest poem, "Sadako," as a blur of explosions in her mind:

> *I wanted to write a poem about the atomic bomb, because I realized
> that poetry is best created out of real emotion. I had to look up the
> scientific aspect of the bomb itself, and was completely shocked at*

how tragically poetic I found the chain of events that causes the explosion. I wanted to make the sickening, tragic spiral the center of the poem, especially given the years following Hiroshima and Nagasaki; years that I see as an equally terrifying spiral of new bombs and threats, especially between the United States and Russia. I named the poem "Sadako" after the title character in a book I had read, Sadako and the One Thousand Paper Cranes. Sadako, the protagonist of the story, is a girl who gets leukemia in the aftermath of the explosion. I chose to name the poem after her in an attempt to underscore the humanity that is inherent in the event that always seems to be a blur of explosions in my mind.

Sadako

One neutron
Hurtling not very far
But frighteningly fast
Collides with a neighboring nucleus
The explosion shatters the world
In miniature.
The fragments,
No larger than a whisper
Ricochet,
Causing a rapid chain of explosions.

Moving faster and faster out of control,
Past neutrons and electrons and protons
Bypassing molecules and centimeters and inches
And humans until everything
Lies in waste, until the roaring forest fire
Of collisions and screams and mushroom clouds
Collapses into the aftermath of
Emptiness.

And one thousand paper cranes rise into the air
Weeping.

– Anne Schwartz, student

"What Am I Doing, Ant?" by Eric Villhauer

Eric Villhauer, in the following protest poem, questions the morality of his childhood "experiment" peering through a magnifying glass at a *tiny victim*, the ant. In his poem, another type of laser, *driven by the sun*, causes the cruel transformation, leading to destruction, at the hand of the poet and his "accomplice," little Johnny. At the end of his poem, Eric clearly takes a position: ironically questioning *our progress*, he smashes the glass across the sidewalk.

"What Am I Doing, Ant?"

Little Johnny and I sat in the sandbox,
peering through a magnifying glass,
Gawking at our tiny victim.
A merciless laser beam,
driven by the sun,
pierced the metasoma of our dear ant,
and poisonous fluid colored the sand beneath it.

What am I doing, ant?
No answer.

The ant's antennae grinded like hands trying to warm.
They were already warm, though.
The ant's legs danced in the air,
allowing us to see the bottom of its alitrunk,
crisping under the smoke.

What am I doing, ant?
No answer.

Our work was done,
but I felt unsatisfied.
My stomach hurt,
and so did my chest.
I peaked one last time into the glass to see our progress.
What progress?
And then, without hesitation,

I took the glass, threw it, and watched it smash
across the sidewalk.

What have I done, ant?
Still, no answer.

– Eric Villhauer, student

The student poems in Part One reflect the emergence of the advanced science poem. Some students, like Anne Schwartz, write thought provoking poems responding to controversial or scientific issues that deeply affect their own personal morality and ethics. Others, like Eric Villhauer, write from their own authentic experiences, questioning ethics and morality that relates to science and humanity.

PART TWO: WRITING FROM PERPLEXITY AND SPECULATION

ACTIVITY #2: MODEL POEM, "CASCADILLA FALLS" BY A.R. AMMONS

Of all the emotions fundamental to the practice of science, *perplexity*, the struggle to understand, and *speculation*, the struggle to imagine, remain perhaps the most relevant. What scientist, driven by an abiding curiosity, has not questioned, reflected, and struggled to understand the unknowable and seemingly unimaginable in the practice of science? The model poems in Part Two illustrate writing from the emotions of perplexity and speculation. Responding to perplexity, the poem itself may become a "thought experiment," clarifying the thinking as well as expressing the emotions of the science poet or scientist-poet. A. R. Ammons is one such science poet, deeply thoughtful, who uses poetry as an instrument of scientific and poetic enlightenment, reflecting his fascination with motion, order and chaos.[4]

For advanced science poetry writing purposes, A. R. Ammons' poem, "Cascadilla Falls," offers an inspirational model of writing from perplexity – the struggle to understand, in this case, the paradoxical wonders of the universe – in particular, the concept of motion and the apparent appearance of lack of motion, or stillness. Although his poem is driven primarily by thought or the quest to understand, it is also rooted in the emotions of awe and amazement in the first three stanzas and a complexity of emotions in the last stanza as his thoughts cause a rush – like the stream itself – that overwhelms him. This is a poem that requires explication and discussion before students respond in kind.

Introducing and Reading the Poem

To foster engagement with the poem, ask your science or English students: "How many of you have ever picked up a stone or an object of nature that perplexed you – causing you to think, question, or reflect. What is it? Where did it come from? What happened to cause it to be the way it is?" Most students readily recall responding to such impulses of curiosity, often while walking in natural settings. Before reading the poem to your students, tell them the poet or speaker in the poem does just that: he walks down by Cascadilla Falls one evening to the stream below and there picks up a stone. That simple, inert stone causes him to think, and he reflects, scientifically, upon its meaning; in this case, *all its motions*. At this point, tell your students to pay special attention to images and references to motion and/or lack of motion, or stillness, in the poem. Then read the poem aloud to your students.

Cascadilla Falls

I went down by Cascadilla
Falls this
evening, the
stream below the falls,

and picked up a
handsized stone
kidney-shaped, testicular, and

thought all its motions into it,
the 800 mph earth spin,
the 190-million-mile yearly
displacement around the sun,
the overriding
grand
haul

of the galaxy with the 30,000
mph of where
the sun's going:
thought all the interweaving
motions
into myself: dropped

the stone to dead rest:
the stream from other motions
broke
rushing over it:
shelterless,
I turned

to the sky and stood still:
oh
I do
not know where I am going
that I can live my life
by this single creek.

– A. R. Ammons (Ammons, 1987: 62)

Explicating the Poem

To many of my English students, Ammons' poem, on the surface,
seems simple. When I begin by asking them what happens on a

literal level in the poem, they can easily paraphrase the narrative: the poet or speaker goes down to a stream, picks up a stone, reflects scientifically about all of the "motions" in it, drops the stone back into the stream, and then becomes overcome with emotion, *I do / not know where I am going.* Yet, when I guide them to delve deeper into the poem, (e) *motion* and all its layers of meaning begin to resonate. To further such explication, ask your science or English students the following critical questions:

- *What is moving or in motion in the poem on the scientific level?*
- *What is moving or in motion in the poem on the poetic level?*
- *What is moving or in motion in the poem on the micro or subatomic levels?*
- *What causes the poet or speaker to be so perplexed?*
- *Does the poet or speaker reach an understanding?*
- *How do you interpret the ending of the poem? Is there clarity or confusion?*

Next, lead a discussion pointing out first the scientific and numerical references to motion in stanzas two and three, and how the images of motion there, on the *macro* level, crescendo to the point of spinning out of control, causing the poet or speaker to further action – *thought all the interweaving motions into myself.* At that thought, the motions stop in his mind, and he drops *the stone to dead rest.* The sudden stillness at this moment in the poem is scientifically inaccurate (note for your students the continual motion on the micro or subatomic levels). Here, in stanza four, the poetic levels of emotion emerge. Ask your students to find the line where the poet or speaker recognizes this reality. My students quickly reference *the stream from other motions broke* and, *shelterless, I turned / to the sky and stood still.* They also mention how the poet might appear still on the outside, but that inside, he is both scientifically and poetically in motion.

Students find the ending to Ammons' poem ambiguous and debatable. Some interpret *I do / not know where I am going* as a moment of confusion and despair. Others sense a more complex emotional response, one in which the poet, overwhelmed with awe and amazement, stands in recognition of the paradoxical nature of the universe: the experience of motion and lack of motion simultaneously.

ACTIVITY #3: MODEL POEM, "WHAT IF WE WERE ALONE?" BY WILLIAM STAFFORD

To inspire students to speculate and imagine, ask your students to think of a compelling *what-if* question related to science or nature. Then mention to them that science poets often embed *what-if* questions in their poems, and that the poems themselves become the "answer." To illustrate, read aloud William Stafford's poem, "What If We Were Alone?"[5]

What If We Were Alone?

What if there weren't any stars?
What if only the sun and the earth
circled alone in the sky? What if
no one ever found anything outside
this world right here?—no Galileo
could say, "Look—it is out there,
a hint of whether we are everything."

Look out at the stars. Yes—cold
space. Yes, we are so distant that
the mind goes hollow to think it.
But something is out there. Whatever
our limits, we are led outward. We glimpse
company. Each glittering point of light
beckons: "There is something beyond."

The moon rolls through the trees, rises
from them, and waits. In the river all
night a voice floats from rock

to sandbar, to log. What kind of listening
can follow quietly enough? We bow, and
the voice that falls through the rapids
calls all the rocks by their secret names.
                    – William Stafford (Stafford, 1987: 115)

Writing the Advanced Science Poems of Perplexity and Speculation

---

Science Poetry Writing Prompts

1. Like A. R. Ammons, write a science poem expressing your perplexity or struggle to understand and appreciate a scientific concept, phenomenon, or aspect of nature as it relates to the universe and the universe of self. Like Ammons, you can take a walk, observe something, touch it or pick it up, and then reflect about it.

2. Write any science poem expressing your struggle to understand a scientific concept, theory, or phenomenon; in other words, write a science poem from perplexity. This poem may be sheer thought and reflection, or it may be a poem rooted in a deep sense of wonder as you struggle to understand.

3. Write any science poem inspired or prompted from your reading of news articles, scientific journals, and/or scientific magazines. If you read something that causes you to react strongly – to think, wonder, wrestle with perplexity, or to speculate – write that science poem.

4. Write any science poem speculating about a scientific issue or question that causes you to wonder and imagine. Like William Stafford, pose a *what-if* question and then answer that question in your poem. Think of this poem as a *what-if* science poem. Like Stafford, consider placing your *what-if* question in your title.

Model Student Responses: "O Asymptote," "Versus," and "Nerves"

"O Asymptote" by David Pitt

In "O Asymptote," David Pitt addresses a mathematical concept[6] with personal authenticity and a complexity of emotions – wonder, perplexity, and imaginative speculation.

O Asymptote

O asymptote
the noting I can never reach
   for ever.
However infinite I am.
I stretch, I pull myself
   so thin.
      Approaching zero.

It's silly
To be so close.
(less than 1 away!)
And nearing
   rapidly.

      And I can strive forever.
        Obsessively augmenting x or y.

But past a certain point
The more I try
   the less a point
     at all.
       O asymptote.

                  – David Pitt, student

David may not be able to reach the unreachable asymptote, but he has certainly reached the artful fusion of the advanced science poem. Remarkably, he takes an abstract, literally unattainable concept, *infinity*, and engages us in his perplexity. How infinite he is when he acknowledges: *The more I try / the less a point / at all.*

Here, irony prevails as David cleverly puns on the word *point*. Like A. R. Ammons in "Cascadilla Falls," David leaves us to reflect upon his deeply authentic expression of emotion – *O asymptote*.

"Versus" by Anne Schwartz

In response to her reading of a science news article *that another path to an AIDS cure had failed*, Anne Schwartz also reacts with a complexity of emotions – outrage, protest, and perplexity – as she struggles to understand, *why can't we?* She comments:

> *It was a hard article to read because it clearly set up the contrast between the tiny and cowardly duplications of one virus and the efforts of the science community. It was also so hard to think that such a small virus – not even alive – could somehow be winning the war."*

Versus

Yesterday I read
That another path to an AIDS cure had failed.
No good.
That another trail of hope,
that catches your breath in your throat,
that forces out a prayer
even when you try not to care
is gone.

How does that even make sense?
That the best minds of the world
cannot beat this virus, this
Acquired
Immune
Deficiency
Syndrome,
in reality nothing more than a tiny mutation,
nothing more than a lifeless coward,
spinning into cells, slipping out again,
ducking out of what is to come.

How does it make sense,
that the work of this one pollutant,
this one seed,
can do all this?
Twenty-five million dead.
How can it,
by quietly creating duplicates,
hold on to so many?

And why can't we,
quietly making experiments,
and making prayers,
have the same effect?

– Anne Schwartz, student

"Nerves" by Alex Davis

"Nerves" by Alex Davis exemplifies the emergence of the advanced science poem rooted in the effort to thoughtfully connect scientific and poetic meaning. Alex explains in his commentary the origin of his poem of perplexity.

Alex's commentary

The writing of this poem coincided with study of the nervous system in biology. Biology is one of the most interesting classes I've ever had. The material does not just pass from the book through my head and to the test, it fills my head and spreads through everything. When I began to think of poems to write, this came to me quickly and easily. Turning the material from my class into poetic inspiration was not difficult at all. I like this one a lot. It feels very professional.

Nerves

Nerves feel, and the brain thinks, in that order.
When I see her, it is chemistry. The cytoplasm depolarizes.
The threshold is reached, and the action potential is transmitted.
The receptor doesn't know that it hurts.

The brain cannot remind it of her distance,
And it doesn't listen when somewhere in the cerebrum,
A connection is made to the beauty of the night sky.
No thought can silence a feeling.
My eye doesn't know how it would burn to touch a star.

– Alex Davis, student

Clearly, Alex's poem is rooted in his deepest personal emotions and experience. His use of science and scientific terminology is artful; it serves his purpose and seems to flow in his natural voice. The poem also matters deeply to Alex; he acknowledges its importance not only because he "likes this one a lot," but because it also "feels very professional" to him. Most importantly, Alex's poem embodies the artful fusion of his passion for biology with his passion for "her." He makes meaningful connections – from his academic studies to the real world of his experience, and finally to his appreciation of *the beauty of the night sky*. Furthermore, he expresses those connections with a complexity of emotions – wonder, amazement, and perplexity. The poem begins in science, and then moves with a series of imaginative leaps, ending with a striking image: *My eye doesn't know how it would burn to touch a star.* Alex's poem took nerve, as it explores the wonderous connections between thinking (science) and feeling (poetry).

Writing the Advanced Science Poem: Striving for that Perfect Fusion

CLOSURE SCIENCE POEM: "THE BUTTERFLY AND ME" BY SARA RYAN

For closure, share with your students Sara Ryan's thought provoking poem, "The Butterfly and Me." Sara's poem reflects the ability to meaningfully connect the self with a scientific phenomenon, theory, or fact. In "The Butterfly and Me," she fuses her scientific knowledge, struggling with the knowledge of its significance for herself and her life. In this sense, her perplexity rises to the level of moral decision-making, as she questions, imagines, and speculates: *If I live, could I ruin life?*

The Butterfly and Me

Breath in
Breath out
Oxygen flows in
I give carbon dioxide back
Part of respiration
Part of life.

A butterfly's wing
Can change
Atmosphere
.506
Is different than
.506127
One flap
Can bring
Or prevent
Destruction.

Breath in
Breath out
Breath
Can it change the world?
Should I hold it in an extra second?
Should I breathe faster?
Can I make the world better?

I am part of life.
If I worry about life I do not live.
If I live, could I ruin life?
Life
Live
The butterfly is not bothered by this.
I am my own destruction.

– Sarah Ryan, student

Sara's answer to her moral question results in a deeply affecting and authentic poem that powerfully recognizes the connectedness of all things and the consequences of one's actions. "The Butterfly and Me" offers a mature and important message. Most importantly, it exemplifies the artful fusion we want to encourage in the advanced poetry of all of our science and English students.

Notes

1. Relevant scientific textual resources for Chapter 10 include chemistry and physics textbooks available in any science department, illustrated science dictionaries, scientific charts of animals and plants, scientific photographic collections like *Planet Earth* and *National Geographic*, and scientific journals, news articles, and magazines exploring current and controversial issues of scientific interest. My science partner and I use the science section of the *New York Times*, the magazine *Science*, and *Science News*.
2. *YAG* (yttrium aluminium garnet) is a crystal used for solid state lasers (Interview with Roald Hoffman; Gorrell, 2008).
3. See Roald Hoffmann, "On Poetry & the Language of Science," where he calls upon his fellow scientists to "humanize" the publication process: "The community should relax its strictures against expressing emotions and personal motives" (Hoffmann, 2002: 139). Decrying what he calls the "ritualistic," "mind-deadening monotony" of scientific writing with its "general use of the third person and passive voice," Hoffmann (2002: 139) argues "we have much to gain from acknowledging more directly in our scientific papers the personal and emotional elements in our struggle to discover, and create, the molecular world."
4. For critical understanding of A. R. Ammons' poetry as it reflects the new science or the Third Paradigm, refer to Daniel Tobin, "A. R. Ammons and the Poetics of Chaos" (Tobin, 2001). Tobin argues that Ammons' poetry reflects "at every turn its profound sympathy with the new science," in particular, chaos theory, complexity theory, and the field concept. Through analysis of "Corson's Inlet," and the longer pieces, *Sphere,* and *Garbage*, Tobin demonstrates how Ammons' poetry embodies in substance and style "what Gleick might call a vision of 'chaos and

order together'" (Tobin, 2001: 127–128). See James Gleick, *Chaos: The Making of a New Science* (Gleick, 1987: 8).

5. For interested teachers, "Cascadilla Falls" and "What If We Were Alone?" serve as ideal poems for comparative analysis. To challenge English students' comparative and critical essay writing skills, assign an essay response comparing Ammons' and Stafford's use of the images of river, rock, and stone each in of their respective poems.

6. *Asymptote*: A line that approaches but never meets a plane curve within any finite distance. It would be tangential to the curve at infinity (*The New Lexicon Webster's Dictionary of the English Language*, 1989 Edition: 58)

Section Four: Forging Common Ground

Interdisciplinary Curriculum

Imagination is more important than knowledge.

– Albert Einstein

(Isaacson, 2007: 7)

Knowledge is not to be transferred from teacher to student. It is to be constructed.

– Lei Bao

Professor of Physics, Ohio State University

Interview (Gorrell, 2009)

SECTION OVERVIEW

In Section Four, my science partner and I forge common ground first as we walk in this world with our students and colleagues on a summer science poetry writing expedition (Chapter 11) and then in our respective classrooms, as we respond to our students' science poems in progress, evaluating, assessing, and grading the results of our universe of a different kind (Chapter 12). Thus Chapter 11 offers multiple voices and perspectives, including those of my science partner, Erin Colfax; our science colleague, Janyce Trampler; and myself. The underlying premise that informs the pedagogy of this book is Einstein's often quoted observation: *Imagination is more important than knowledge.* In Section Four, students and teachers together use their collective imaginations to construct knowledge from the common ground of their shared experiences in the urban field and back in their respective classrooms. In the process, many students and teachers become transformed, writing science *walk poems* that connect knowledge of science and nature to the universe of self. One such science teacher, our colleague, Janyce Trampler, a chaperone on the expedition, began to write her first science poems, forever changing her teaching of biology.

In Chapter 11, "Walking in This World with Our Students and Colleagues," science-minded students of all ages, levels, and abilities engage in a summer science poetry writing expedition to urban venues in the New York metropolitan area: the New York Museum of Natural History, the Bronx Zoo, the New York Botanical Gardens, the New York Hall of Science (Queens, New York), and the Liberty Science Center and State Park (Jersey City, New Jersey). On the expedition, our students begin with natural and life science venues and then move to the more conceptual and abstract sciences represented by the science museum experience. In each venue, they simultaneously gather scientific data, take notes, and freewrite, composing science poems prompted and inspired by their observations and encounters. In some venues, students become fixed observers, studying a subject and then composing a science poem. In other venues, students become moving observers, walking through a location, composing poems in their journals as they walk along. In the process, students write remarkably powerful and authentic poems, literally and figuratively forging common ground. Chapter 12, "How to Assess Student Science Poetry: The Art of Response," guides teachers in assessing and grading student science poems.

SUGGESTIONS FOR USING THIS SECTION

The aim of Section Four is to forge common ground between the arts and sciences, in particular, poetry and the life sciences, developing an interdisciplinary pedagogy that is at once practical, adaptable, and highly relevant to existing science and English curricula. Both science and English teachers will find the summer expedition model an easily adaptable and replicable one-day or one-week science poetry writing field trip or mini-expedition experience for students and teachers. In addition, this model serves as an ideal interdisciplinary in-service workshop, affording the opportunity for science and English teachers to forge together common ground. My science partner and I advocate this inter-department model to open eyes, foster communication, and transform teaching, the ultimate objective of any model of educational reform.

11 Walking in This World with Our Students and Colleagues

Walking is the basic discipline of science of belonging, for this science is based almost entirely upon field work. On foot, we are able to imagine an accord between poetry and ecology.
– John Burnside, "A Science of Belonging: Poetry as Ecology"
(Burnside, 2006: 105)

OVERVIEW: WALKING IN THIS WORLD WITH OUR STUDENTS AND COLLEAGUES

Imagine walking in this world with your students and colleagues to write poems through the eyes of science. Imagine walking together through city parks and botanical gardens, and through natural history and science museums. Imagine seeing at once the past, present, and future in the bones of dinosaurs or the buds of flowers. Imagine seeing your students become science poets and your science colleagues become scientist-poets. Imagine seeing education in its most fundamental sense, *educere*, from the Latin meaning "to bring forth." Imagine seeing science poetry, the subject itself, educing poetry from scientists and science from poets. Imagine seeing students and teachers sharing and airing science poems in view of the Statue of Liberty and New York City harbor, or similar impressive sites and sights in your own town or region. Imagine walking, feet to pavement, feet to earth. Imagine just walking in this world with your students and seeing through the *eyes of science* and the *eyes of poetry*.

All of this my science partner and I actualized during our summer science poetry expedition to venues in the New York and New Jersey metropolitan area, July 21–25, 2008. The success of the 2007 Icelandic poetry expedition prompted my science partner to consider another expedition, but this time, one more accessible to Morristown High School's students and faculty in terms of costs, time frame, and locale. In contrast to the Icelandic expedition, Erin organized this time an urban expedition to five science venues: the Museum of Natural History (New York, New York), the Bronx Zoo (Bronx, New York), the New York Botanical Gardens (Bronx, New York), the New York Hall of Science (Queens, New York), and the Liberty Science Center and State Park (Jersey City, New Jersey). Each venue represented a different aspect of science, beginning with the natural and life sciences, and then proceeding to the more conceptual and abstract sciences.

Our major objective was to confirm the value and the power of science poetry to engage, inform, and transform science-minded students of varying ages, ability levels, and scientific backgrounds. To this end, we chose twelve science students and three high school science-teacher chaperones to participate with us in the expedition. The twelve, highly diverse Morristown High School science students represented incoming sophomores, juniors, and seniors (grades 10-12) of average ability and average science background from the Science Academy or mainstream science classes. Only three of the students had Advanced Placement or Honors science background, and none of the students had background in poetry or poetry writing. With the exception of three self-identified renaissance students and one humanities student, all students considered themselves science rather than arts students.

In addition, we wanted to test our science poetry pedagogy in an in-the-field immersion writing experience, one enabling intensive writing over a concentrated period of time. Such writing, typical in summer writing workshops, frequently inspires work that becomes authentic and transformative. Could our science poetry expedition do the same for our basic science students and science colleagues? The answer, as we will see, is a resounding, "yes." All of our students wrote informed science poetry. That much we expected. What we did not expect was the ease of their engagement, the intensity of that engagement, and the ability of several to reach the authentic, connecting the world of science to the world of self. Perhaps the greatest surprise of the expedition was the metamorphosis of our science chaperone and colleague, Janyce Trampler, from confirmed scientist to inspired scientist-poet. This fact alone spoke volumes to our students, literally bridging the cultural divide before their very eyes. *Ms. Trampler writing poetry?* It also spoke volumes to us, confirming once again the power of science poetry to inspire not only our students but our colleagues and ourselves.

For if the concept of the expedition (in contrast to the field trip) is true to the spirit of adventure and mystery inherent in the process, then something must happen unexpectedly and unpredictably, something that reaches beyond stated objectives, something that becomes transformative, defining and reflecting the very essence of the expedition model itself. That something occurred quite spontaneously on day #3 when Erin and a student in need demonstrated the power of the collaborative *walk poem* to transform.

WHAT'S AHEAD

Chapter 11 consists of an introductory overview and description of the science poetry writing expedition followed by Parts One, Two, and Three, descriptions of the instruction, activities, experiences, and student and teacher writing responses occurring on three consecutive days: Day #1, Day #2, and Day #3 of the expedition, respectively.

Chapter 11 at a Glance

Summer Science Poetry Expedition

Part One: Science Poetry Observing the Non-Living
Day #1: The Museum of Natural History
Model Student and Teacher Responses: Fossil Hall
"Reflections on Fossils" by Jocelyn Burney
"Agate Springs" by Catherine Chu
"Bones" by Maya Blades

Part Two: Science Poetry Observing the Living – Animals
Day #2: The Bronx Zoo
Model Science Poem: "Essay on Intelligence: Three" by Alison Hawthorne Deming
Model Student and Teacher Responses: Bronx Zoo
"Red Panda" by Jocelyn Burney
"Lonely Old Man with Wings" by Janyce Trampler
"Snow Leopard Rap" by Jacob Scheer

Part Three: Science Poetry Observing the Living – Plants
Day #3: The New York Botanical Gardens
The Walk Poem and Science Poetry
Model Student and Teacher Responses: New York Botanical Gardens
Collaborative Walk Poem by Erin Colfax and student
"Yellow Pinwheel" by Janyce Trampler

Part Four: Post-Expedition Reflections by Janyce Trampler, Science Teacher

Part Five: Related Scholarship and Pedagogy

A Science of Belonging: Poetry as Ecology

SUMMER SCIENCE POETRY WRITING EXPEDITION

OBJECTIVES

Our main objective of the expedition was to provide an in-the-field-immersion writing experience for science-minded high school students, one enabling intensive science poetry writing over a concentrated period of time. In addition, we wanted to:

- *Demonstrate the power of science poetry to engage, inform, and inspire science-minded students of varying ages, ability levels, and backgrounds;*
- *Demonstrate the value of science poetry writing as process rather than product;*
- *Demonstrate the power of science poetry as an instrument of transformation;*
- *Demonstrate the power and value of interdisciplinary, cross-curricular pedagogy.*

PARTICIPANTS

- Erin Colfax: Science Academy Research Teacher and Expedition Leader
- Nancy Gorrell: Poet and Retired English Teacher, Morristown High School
- Janyce Trampler: Science Academy Teacher and Chaperone
- Robert Kirchmer: General Science Teacher and Chaperone, Vernon Township High School
- Jill Magidson, Science Academy Program Director
- Twelve Morristown High School Students, Ages 15–17

Science Objects Pastiche. Reprinted with permission of Nancy Gorrell.

Materials Needed

Science Materials

A spiral, *Scientific Lab Notebook* (carbonless duplicate set) published by Hayden McNeil (www.labnotebooks.net) to serve as each student's field journal. This particular notebook offers a two-column format on each page – the left column designated for scientific data, the right column for written notes. We suggested students use the left column for field notes and the right column for composing poetry. Students kept their notebooks, but we collected each day the carbon copy.
Science Handout Packets: Relevant Scientific Data and Information

Poetry Materials

Science Poem, "The Fish in the Stone" by Rita Dove
Science Poem, "Fossil Texts on Canyon Walls" by Pattiann Rogers
Science Poem, "This is your Geode Talking" by Carter Revard
Science Poem, "Essay on Intelligence: Three" by Alison Hawthorne Deming (provided)
Poem, "The Wellfleet Whale" by Stanley Kunitz (see Chapter 9)
Poetry Handout Packets: Poetry Prompts and Instructions

Poetry Resource Kurt Brown's *Verse and Universe: Poems about Science and Mathematics*.

PROCEDURES

We began each day at 8:00 a.m. with an hour-long science poetry lesson led by myself, the poetry teacher on the expedition. Our purpose was to prepare students to write science poems particular to each day's science venue. Students explored *what is science poetry*; they read model science poems by scientists, poets, and other students; and they each acquired a science poetry "tool box" consisting of different poetic stances, methods, forms, and techniques. In addition, they acquired the attitudes necessary to enable the writing of science poetry, the ability to open their eyes and see through the eyes of both science and poetry.

At 9:00 a.m., with field journals and "tool boxes" in hand, students boarded the bus for each day's science venue. Since the venues were vast in scale, we began by selecting one particular area in each venue for our students to observe and experience: for example, Fossil Hall in the Museum of Natural History and the Children's Garden in the New York Botanical Garden. Over the course of the expedition, students moved from the concrete world of the non-living, to the world of the living, and then finally to the more abstract worlds of conceptual and physical science:

Museum of Natural History Observing the Non-Living: Fossils and Dinosaurs
Bronx Zoo Observing the Living: The Animal Kingdom
New York Botanical Gardens Observing the Living: The Plant Kingdom
New York Hall of Science Exploring Scientific Phenomena and Principles
Liberty Science Center Giving Voice to Science Poetry

While students engaged with the focus of each venue, science teachers circulated to help with scientific observations, and I circulated to assist poems in progress. Students took intensive notes in their field journals and wrote poems in the venues and on the bus ride back to school.

Each day ended back at Morristown High School with a one-hour closing circle sharing reflections and poems in progress. We required students to submit carbon copies of their notes, and to write one completed poem per day. The expedition concluded with an informal poetry reading during a picnic lunch at Liberty State Park, culminating in a more formal poetry reading back at school to a small, invited audience. The poetry readings were challenges for our science-minded students, who had never shared original poetry before, but our emphasis on process rather than product encouraged them to raise their voices, and in doing so, they surprised themselves and their peers with remarkable poems.

OUTCOMES

The kind of poetry our expedition produced – poetry of observation or poetry of the here-and-now – enabled our students to experience the common ground between scientists and poets: the use of observation, both fixed and moving, the use of multiple ways of seeing, and the use of metaphoric, creative, and critical thinking skills. Students wrote poems using science as a prompt, a point of entry, a way of knowing, and a metaphor to "leap" to other realms. On their walks through the venues, they stopped, producing fixed observations, and then they walked again, producing moving observations, culminating, both literally and figuratively, in the walk poem. For several, the scientific eye enabled authentic, empathetic, and highly inspired science poetry.

The unexpected outcomes of our expedition concerned its transformative value for science teachers and science teaching. Not only did Janyce Trampler use her scientific eye to write inspired science poetry, but she got the "bug." Now she uses her own science poetry as an instructional tool in her AP Biology classes. Seizing a teachable moment in the Botanical Gardens, Erin demonstrated the process of "walking in this world" with our students using collaborative writing strategies to create a science *walk poem*. Another significant outcome with pedagogical implications concerned the difference among venues to facilitate and prompt science poetry writing. We discovered that our students more easily wrote poems in the life science venues – Museum of Natural History, the Bronx Zoo, and the New York Botanical Gardens rather than in the science museum venues, in particular, the New York Hall of Science. Several factors may have contributed to this outcome:

- These science museums were hands-on, active, noisy, and crowded environments full of self-discovery activities. Students were either too busy with self-discovery or too distracted with crowds to pause to reflect and write poems. Their notes reflected a paucity of material in contrast to previous venues.
- The scientific concepts, principles, and demonstration activities were mainly abstract and conceptual, prompting more thoughtful and intellectual responses rather than emotional or empathetic ones. Such responses were more readily prompted in the post-expedition sharing circle under teacher direction rather than in the moment at the science museums.
- Lack of on-site quiet places available for students to write and reflect contributed to students' difficulty in composing poems in the moment.

To rectify this problem, my science partner and I suggest arranging ahead of time with the science museum a room or quiet space for students to write in solitude. As a consequence, this chapter reflects student science poems primarily from the first three venues, which were more conducive to on-site poetry writing.

PART ONE: SCIENCE POETRY OBSERVING THE NON-LIVING

DAY #1: THE MUSEUM OF NATURAL HISTORY

Introducing novice student poets to the art of science poetry writing in a one-hour poetry lesson to prepare for a week-long expedition involved a combination of teaching strategies: the mini-lecture to define the topic, a demonstration of the four poetic stances, and a study of model science poems by poets and scientists relevant to our first day venue. In addition, we needed to get our science students' creativity flowing, dispelling any misconceptions they might have regarding poetry writing that could impede their responses. Most importantly, we had to model and engender a sense of wonder and fun; after all, this was a summer expedition.

Introduced by my science partner as "the poet" on the expedition (none of the students knew me personally or professionally), I realized I had to be a model for the students, but not an imposing one; therefore, I chose to instruct at times, in humorous verse, to help create an atmosphere of risk-taking, informality, and playfulness. I began by making several philosophical points: that our expedition was about making connections, seeing through the eyes of science and poetry, stressing multiple perspectives, the fusion of disciplines, and the primacy of observation, imagination, and creativity as common ground. Then, I asked rhetorically, "How do poets write poems?" And I answered, "Not from definitions," but rather from, "head, heart, and experience." Then I voiced spontaneously:

Don't worry about definitions!
Discard all premonitions.
Think if you want like a physician.
But write like a musician.
Write the poem you want to write.
Don't worry if you did it right.
And just remember…

Every poem that wants to be
Will be the poem that we will see.

– Nancy Gorrell, teacher

I introduced formally *what is poetry* by defining the four poetic stances (see Chapter 5) and modeling the four stances as I observed a cricket fossilized in amber (see Chapter 6). Next, I reviewed with students our working definition of science poetry and general science poetry writing strategies: start with the science and then "leap" to another world or realm. Then, I presented as professional models science poems relevant to Fossil Hall in the Museum of Natural History from Kurt Brown's anthology, *Verse and Universe: Poems about Science and Mathematics* (Brown, 1998: 135–180).

First, expedition students read Rita Dove's "The Fish in the Stone," where she observes a fossil of a fish in a stone and imagines how this fossil would feel (Brown, 1998: 145). I encouraged students to empathize with their subjects, the fossils they will observe, and to imagine how those fossils might feel. Next, students considered part one of Pattiann Roger's "Fossil Texts on Canyon Walls," where Rogers takes on the identity or persona of the fossil on the canyon walls and lets that fossil speak (Brown, 1998: 146). I suggested to students to take on the identity of their subjects, the dinosaurs, fossils, minerals, and preserved animals, and imagine what they might say if they could talk. Then, students considered Carter Revard's "This is your Geode Talking," a science poem fusing specific scientific and technical language – *pterodactyls, archaeopteryxes, chalcedony, siliceated* – with the passion and empathy of poetic persona (Brown, 1998: 138). Here I pointed out that through the eyes of the science poet, even rocks have feelings. Again, I encouraged students to be as passionate and scientific as they could be in their observations. Last, I distributed the following specific science poetry writing prompts for the Museum of Natural History and General Science Poetry Prompts for the entire expedition:

Science Poetry Prompts for the Museum of Natural History

1. Observe dinosaur bones and artifacts. Write a dinosaur poem using one or more of the poetic stances; address the dinosaur or let the dinosaur speak in a poem.
2. Observe fossils of non-living plants and animal remains. Write a poem addressing the fossil or taking on the persona of the fossil. Be scientific <u>and</u> empathetic.
3. Write a poem based on your observation of any non-living thing using science as metaphor to say something else.

General Science Poetry Prompts for the Expedition

1. Observe something that "blows you away." Feel that sense of amazement, wonder, or awe. Write a science poem from wonder and awe.
2. Observe something that causes your heart to skip a beat; feel sympathy or empathy for fossils, bones, dinosaurs, animals, plants, insects, and artifacts. Write an empathetic science poem.
3. Observe something that causes outrage, shock, or protest. Write from that emotion. Put on your poetry "eco-hats." Write a science poem about what disturbs you.
4. Observe something you appreciate in terms of its beauty; it arouses your sense of *biophilia*, or love of the earth and all living things. Write a poem of *biophilia*, respecting, honoring, and appreciating what you have observed, whether it is a living creature, a mineral, a sculpture in a garden, or a botanical.
5. Observe and record your observations while walking in any environment. Create a *walk poem* from your walk.

As students bordered the bus for the day #1 expedition, I handed each student, in scroll-like form, a copy of an envoy poem I wrote as a "pep talk" to launch the journey.

Envoy Poem from Ms. Gorrell to Science Expedition Students

Ok, don't moan
It's only a science poem
All you have to do
Is find some science glue
Words that stick to science
Quantitative compliance
But not complete reliance
Poetry can be defiant
Or any one of the emotions
To stir up a commotion

Yes science poems can get green
They may even be quite mean
If humans destroy all living things
The air we breathe; the birds that sing
Then eco-poets write with might
Science poems to set things right
So all we really want from you
Is a science poem…maybe one or two
That sets just right inside of you

So write it just for yourself
Otherwise it will sit on the shelf
A fossil relic to preserve
For no one will read or observe
A poem that's dead, not loved or read,

Now on the bus when we return
We hope you will share what you've learned
And we will hear to our hearts delight
Science poetry from morning to night!

– Nancy Gorrell, teacher

Model Student and Teacher Responses: Fossil Hall

Day #1 in Fossil Hall of the Museum of Natural History produced sensitive, inspired, and empathetic science poems from many of our students. Jocelyn Burney responds with awe and empathy.

"Reflections on Fossils" by Jocelyn Burney

Reflections on Fossils

Caught up by the snare of Time,
The ancient remains of a terrible reptile that,
Ten million years ago,
Stood transfixed, fascinated, horrified
By the inevitable sleep that is Death
Knew the animal feeling shared by all living creatures
That have slipped away from all we know,
Silently remind us that Time is not our own.

– Jocelyn Burney, student

One particular exhibit in Fossil Hall, a jumble of bones from Agate Springs, Nebraska, captivated the imaginations of students and my science partner, Erin. This jumble of bones contained fossil remains of animals piled atop of one another as a result of a severe drought that occurred in the region 20 million years ago. Animals that normally fed and drank along the riverbed came to the banks of the river, and when they saw there was no water and food, they were unable to survive. The bodies were then buried under years of sediment, creating the Agate Springs fossil bed. Catherine Chu records the following observations in her lab notebook:

"Agate Springs" by Catherine Chu

Agate Springs

what gave life
dwindles
the rhinoceros comes to sneak
a drink
but leaves feeling thirsty
as ever
20 million years ago.

searching for water
they die in a mudhole
day by night
laying to rest
the river of bubbles
the springs give life
once more
sweeping away
the sad bodies
burying stories in a puzzling
cacophony of bones
until the day they are found
again.

The dawning image
of the fossilized remains
of great creatures does not speak
the volumes of what happened
then. The death of one
caused the death of many.

– Catherine Chu, student

For one of our students, Maya Blades, Fossil Hall brought back vivid memories of an Earth Explorer Expedition she took in 2002. When she was a sixth grader, she went on an expedition to the Wyoming Dinosaur Center. In her poem of address, "Bones," Maya uses science as metaphor: *take the skeletons out of your closet* and *fossilize this memory* to create a science poem that is highly poetic and personally authentic.

"Bones" by Maya Blades

Bones

Like Morgan Freeman,
I've come to collect your bones.
New bones, old bones, decaying bones.
Take the skeletons out of your closet
And fossilize this memory.
With the beauty of a mosquito entrapped in amber
Keep this in the back of your mind,
But never let it go.
Moments once so vivid
Leave their footprints in time.
Slowly you crack,
crumble,
And fade away.
Buried further from thought,
Yet closer to the core,
Years, upon years, upon years,
Layers, upon layers, upon layers,
The sediment hides your presence.
The bones that once kept you on your feet
Become nothing but dust in the wind.
Yet one day,
Some curious wanderer
Will rediscover you,
And piece your history back together.

– *Maya Blades*, student

In her commentary, Maya reflects upon the origin and meaning of her poem.

Maya's Commentary

I was sitting in front of a few different skeletons or dinosaur casts. What fascinated me the most about the exhibit was not the whole that the parts created, but the individual parts themselves, every little detail. One meaning of my poem is that, like dinosaurs, we all have our own memories that we don't wish to forget, but sometimes we let slip from our grasp. We keep them in the back of our minds, and then eventually, what we once forgot is somehow brought to the surface. The past can always be dug up. Just like bones. Otherwise, the ability to study history would not be possible.

PART TWO: SCIENCE POETRY OBSERVING THE LIVING – ANIMALS

DAY #2: THE BRONX ZOO

To prepare students for their zoo experience observing living animals, I presented two model poems for consideration: the first, Alison Hawthorne Deming's science poem, "Essay on Intelligence: Three" (Deming, 1989b), and the second, "The Wellfleet Whale," by Stanley Kunitz (Kunitz, 2000; see Chapter 9). Deming's poem, set in the Yerkes Primate Laboratory, sees the primate, Sherman the Chimp, as a subject of experimentation. In "Essay on Intelligence: Three," the scientific eye prevails, presenting the chimp essentially as subject-to-be-studied by those in the lab. The second poem I read, Stanley Kunitz's "Wellfleet Whale," sees the subject, the beached whale, in a natural setting, Wellfleet Harbor. In this poem, the poetic eye prevails, seeing the whale not only as subject, *when the Curator of Mammals arrived*, but in its full humanity: *Master of the whale-road /...You have become like us.*

Model Science Poem, "Essay on Intelligence: Three" by Alison Hawthorne Deming

Essay on Intelligence: Three

After many years of language training
in the Yerkes Primate Lab (*our animals*
have indoor/outdoor access and may
withdraw from lessons at will) Sherman
the chimp, after correctly categorizing

> socket wrench
> stick
> banana
> bread
> key
> money
> orange

as either food or tool,
used the incorrect lexigram
to classify a sponge.

The chimp has one hundred keys
to choose from. First, he was
asked to sort food and tools
into two bins. Later,
instead of bins, to press
the lexigram for food or tool.

He could string lexigrams to say

> please
> machine
> give
> piece
> of banana

Sherman's apparent mistake
was subsequently read
as the interpreter's
misunderstanding of the animal's
intent. An active eater,
Sherman is prone to
sucking liquids from a sponge,
often chewing and swallowing
the tool as if it were food.

           – Alison Hawthorne Deming (Deming, 1989b: 34-35)

Deming's deceptively simple and highly accessible poem – it reads like a report on a scientific experiment – immediately engages our science-minded students. Given Deming's title, "Essay on Intelligence: Three," irony abounds. Students readily see Deming's poem protesting the arrogance of science that gives human intelligence primacy over that of animals. Although the language of all her "Essays on Intelligence" is clearly literal, informational, and scientific (see additional Deming poems in Chapter 7) Deming's awe, empathy, and respect for all living things touched the heart strings of many of our expedition students as well as eliciting their wonder and outrage. Her poems raise critical questions concerning animal experimentation, the treatment of animals by humans, and the philosophy of zoos to maintain animals in captivity in order to preserve endangered species. After reading Deming's poem, several students share their attitudes and feelings regarding zoos and animal captivity in general. Some mention that it is difficult for them to visit zoos.

Taken together, Deming and Kunitz's animal-subject poems offer dramatically contrasting tones: the first, seemingly objective and matter-of-fact, the second, highly subjective, emotional, and elegiac. I point out to students the vast range of perspectives and voices they may use in response to the animals they will soon observe in the Bronx Zoo. We allow students to explore the zoo in small groups or pairs, instructing them to seek out their favorite animals for observation, scientific description, and poetic response.

Science Poetry Prompts for the Bronx Zoo

1. Choose to observe in action a favorite animal or living thing. Observe that animal for at least 10 minutes. Record in your lab notebook specific details of appearance, actions, and behaviors of the animals in relation to the environment and other animals. Read pertinent zoo data and record specific quantitative information as well as scientific classifications and terminology. Then write a science poem describing your animal subject using one or more of the poetic stances you have learned.
2. Choose to sense as well as observe a favorite animal or living thing. Employ all of your senses, especially auditory, olfactory, and tactile senses (if you are allowed to touch the animal). Record specific details of appearance, actions, and behaviors. Write an animal-subject sensory observation poem.
3. Write an animal-subject poem that reflects your attitudes regarding animals in captivity. Avoid telling or explaining your opinion. Rather, like Deming, let the facts speak for themselves.
4. Like Kunitz, write an animal-subject poem that reflects your empathy and respect for that animal.

Model Student and Teacher Responses: Bronx Zoo

Many of our students were captivated by the Red Panda exhibit. Jocelyn Burney in particular, notices through her poetic eye the juxtaposition of the animal inhabitants inside and the human inhabitants outside the zoo. For Jocelyn, animal rights and human rights converge in ironic complexity.

Red Panda at the Bronx Zoo. Reprinted with permission of Cori Connolly.

"Red Panda" by Jocelyn Burney

Red Panda

Far from Himalayan forests,
Ailurnus fuigens, the "Shining Cat,"
Stares at the blotchy, purple-black sky
Tainted by a million city lights
And blissfully slips into the peaceful ocean of sleep,
Unaware of poverty and joy,
Fear and passion,
That plague creatures of another genus and species
Half a mile away.

– Jocelyn Burney, student

In her commentary, Joceyln explains the thoughts and emotions that prompted her science poem of protest.

Jocelyn's Commentary

If you ride the monorail at the Bronx Zoo, you can see on one side the animals and on the other side the Cross Bronx Expressway. This particular monorail circumvents the Asian Animals exhibit. A fan favorite is the Red Panda. It looks like a fox, but bigger and probably more colorful. The Red Pandas sit on tiny, thin branches ten feet off the ground, close their eyes and sleep peacefully, not a care in the world. And that's interesting, considering, just like its black-and-white cousin, the Red Panda is on the verge of extinction. So this Red Panda just sits there as everyone squeals and coos at it, probably unaware that it is being fed better than some people living half a mile away. People are poor and starving on the outside, yet people are joyful and loving on the inside. For reasons that words cannot express, this Red Panda is safer in the dirty, polluted Bronx than in the silent, clean, uninhabited Himalayan mountains.

"Lonely Old Man with Wings" by Janyce Trampler, Science Teacher

Gazing at a lone stork for over a half hour, Janyce Trampler our science teacher chaperone, was so moved that she wrote her first science poem, one that reflects, not only scientific accuracy and technical language, but deep respect, insight, and empathy for her subject.

Stork at the Bronx Zoo. Reprinted with permission of Cori Connolly.

Lonely Old Man with Wings

Intriguing stork stands alone.

Like a lonely old man with wings.
Bristly, gray hair sticks up out of a wrinkly bald scalp,
Not even enough for a comb.

Magenta head and neck,
Flecked with asymmetrical brown patches,
Like liver spots on a collagen-depleted face.
Scaly, knobby knees
Like aged, sagging skin,
Seems too fragile for support or locomotion.

Uninflated gular sac,
Sometimes engorged to echo an amorous call,
Now hangs like a flaccid penis,
Useless without a mate.

Yet vibrant, alert, and youthful eyes belie the outward appearance,
Reflecting a striking, youthful soul inside,
And memories of a life as long and beautiful as the wing span.

Spread your angelic wings and fly to a place where you look like
The swan
You feel like inside.

— *Janyce Trampler*, science teacher

In her commentary, Janyce explains the origin and inspiration for her first science poem.

Janyce's Commentary

"Lonely Old Man with Wings" was my first science poem, and it was written at the Bronx Zoo while standing outside an enclosure that had many male and female peacocks and a single stork. The peacocks were beautiful, with their colorful plumage, and the males and females seemed to be engaging in mating rituals. Most of the people passing by were expectedly drawn to the peacocks, but this stork mesmerized me. It was certainly not a beautiful bird by any stretch of the imagination, and its outward appearance reminded me of an old man. What I found so sad was that it was the only one of its kind in the enclosure. And although it looked like an old man, its eyes seemed very bright and alert, and for a brief moment, it stretched out its wings. It was then that the true beauty of this creature emerged. I didn't plan on writing a poem at the time I was observing, but as the day went on, I found that I could not get the stork out of my mind. It reminded me that even though our bodies age, on the inside we still feel relatively the same as we did when we were much younger (at least I do). Later that night I was inspired enough to finish writing the poem.

"Snow Leopard Rap" by Jacob Scheer

Although many student science poems were of a deeply serious nature, some of our summer expedition students wrote poems on a lighter note. We all enjoyed hearing Jacob Scheer perform on the bus back to school, "Snow Leopard Rap."

Snow Leopard Rap

Now listen up! Here's the story,
'Bout the big snow leopard in his territory.

Way up high in the Himalayas,
They've got great real estate, what can I say (a)

Ears poppin', blood clottin', rising to the top
To 18,000 feet, the leopards come non-stop.

To Mount Everest, jewel of the crown,
The best spot for a leopard, hands down.

Some leopards have spots, as you can see.
Some are just white, and that's fine by me.

When it comes to speed, leopards are fastest,
Other animals are slow, much slower than molasses.

When it comes to hunting, leopards are the best
Eating ibex, marmots, rodents, and birds from the nest.

Right now, they have a small population,
But we're trying to save 'em, it's a great sensation.

With your help, we can save one at a time,
And thanks for listening to the snow leopard rhyme.

– Jacob Scheer, student

PART THREE: SCIENCE POETRY OBSERVING THE LIVING – PLANTS

DAY #3: THE NEW YORK BOTANICAL GARDENS

The Walk Poem, Science Poetry, and the Botanical Gardens

The New York Botanical Gardens presented a rare opportunity to explore a little known poetic genre, the *walk poem*. I had discovered this genre by reading Ron Padgett's *Handbook of Poetic Forms* (Padgett, 2000). The beauty of the walk poem is its utter simplicity: "The walk poem involves a walk" (Padgett, 2000: 200). Padgett suggests four basic types of walk poems consisting of many variations and blends.

1. *A poem about what the poet sees during a particular walk.*
2. *A poem about a walk that produces a revelation of some kind.*
3. *A poem whose length, style, and shape mirror the length, style, and shape of the walk.*
4. *A poem that reflects the way the mind works during the walk.* (Padgett, 2000: 200–201).

After reading Padgett's definition, I realized the walk poem offered an ideal form for scientific observation and investigation of the natural world. Perhaps our science expedition students could become poetic naturalists, walking in this world while writing science poems in their field journals. In preparing students to engage with the Botanical Gardens on Day #3, I introduced the concept of the walk poem, suggesting to students to take notes as they walked through the gardens, producing at the conclusion of their walk, a *science walk poem*. I described the process as moving to a location, stopping to observe and write (a fixed observation), and then moving to another location and observing once again. I told my students to think of the walk poem as having a chronology from beginning of the walk to the end. They could construct the walk poem as one continuous moving observation or separate, fixed observations as they walked.

Most relevant for our expedition students and teachers, the model poem Padgett offers in his *Handbook,* "Class Walk with Notebooks after Storm," by Bill Zavatsky (Padgett, 2000: 200–201), records a third grade teacher's thoughts while walking with his class down Main Street, *trying to make sense of this town.* We read together this lengthy model in class as one possible way of doing a walk poem.[1] Little did I know at the time that this poem would become the model for Erin's collaborative walk poem with a student-in-need. Erin explains what happened and the ensuing walk poem that grew from her experience with a student-in-need in the New York Botanical Gardens.

Writing a Collaborative Walk Poem by Erin Colfax

I was sitting alone, writing in my field journal the beginnings of a poem when my cell phone suddenly rang. It was a student on the other end saying: "I am lost, all alone, please help." I quickly figured out where she was and told her to stay put; I was on my way. Seeing her in the distance, I noticed her head in her hands, and I realized that something dramatic must have happened. I waved and yelled out, "I'm here. Are you okay?" When she started talking, I soon realized that her feelings of being lost and alone had nothing to do with the gardens. She was talking about something else, something I didn't know about. We walked a little, began to talk, and then sat in a spot where she began to tell me how her father had died after a long illness, and how being in the Children's Garden reminded her of him and the times they shared together. At that moment, her story was more than I could respond to, and then somehow, the thought of the walk poem Nancy had taught us earlier that day entered my mind. Perhaps, I thought to myself, the walk poem could be a way to help this student "walk" through her feelings and memories. So we walked; she talked, and I wrote down her words. The poetic process gave me a means by which I was able at first to just listen to her and write. The result became a collaborative walk poem, one we composed together, as I wrote down the student's words and thoughts and then added some words and thoughts of my own.

"In the Botanical Gardens: A Collaborative Walk Poem in Two Voices" by Erin Colfax and Student

> I sit on your periphery enraptured by your radiant colors;
> Snowballs of pink, lavender, and blue
> Lilies of the day in Easter yellow and tiger orange
> How unique each angiosperm displays her color
> Petals curled like birthday ribbon bows
> Pollen tubes hollow and erect like skyscrapers
> Anthers large and masculine like the antlers of an elk
> Ants crawling, bees buzzing, butterflies flinting –
> And then, a phone call to say…
>
> *I am lost, all alone, please help…*
>
> My teacher waves, I'm here, are you okay?
> Let's walk, let's talk, let's sit…
> She said, Tell me what is wrong.
> He died, January 7th
> He was good, happy, kind.
> He took me to new places.
> He held my hand.
> Outstretched hands
> She asks me,
> Do you want to walk?
> We walk, I talk, she writes.

I told her of his greatness
He would help me climb small trees.
I was lifted up, like now; I smile,
I think of him, she writes.
Purple my favorite color; grapes, plums, delight!
The old lady drawing trees, he loved trees, flowers, parks,
That flower, the big one, Fiji, last summer, alone on a trip
No one on the other end, tears streaming down my face.
Relief, now no tears, someone answered my call.

Another one, big beautiful, hibiscus petals,
With bees, lots of bees, buzzing around
Bees, oh how I fear you, you stung me as a baby,
Crawled into my diaper and stung my soul
I swatted at you with my racquet and said
Never again, but not now, I am at peace with bees.
She tells me of your value, explains how you actually help,
Not harm; bees pollinate, and we walk on.

Hello, he says, nice day, have you been here before?
She introduces us, tells him of our purpose, poetry.
Great! he says.
Great job you have here, she says.
I'm blessed, he says.
We see yellow, shades of yellow, lots of yellow,
Lady in blue shirt near the orange-most yellow.
Excuse our Appearance, Garden in Progress.
Men at work, shoveling rocks, bulldozing
Creating a place for someone who wants to be alone.
Alone in their thoughts, alone in their memories,

We stop; sit in a new garden, on a bench,
Describe orally what we see,
What we like, and what is meaningful.
We look in the field guide, read descriptors,
And write poetry together…

Blue Glow
Spiky fireworks is your display
Dark and purple center with light edges
Your spiny bracts stick out,
Your height of three feet outstretches
over the other beautiful flowers,
You're classified as a weed, a nuisance
but to me your splendor intrigues
I shall call you my blueberry sea urchin.

We look up, observing two plants
Together they lie in one bed growing,
Intertwining, embracing, the good with the bad…
We write…

Petunia: Flowering Tobacco

How odd that you should grow together
something with a name so sweet
in a bed with a name so harsh.
The rabbit comes to nibble at your flowers
entranced by your magnificent magenta.
Bees come to feed on your pollen
wind blows through your petals
causing you to wave at the onlookers
who can't understand your unique marriage…

Coming to an end, the end of our walk.
She asks, What are you thinking about now?
                              I say, "He will not be forgotten."

Post-Writing Reflections by Erin Colfax

Writing a walk poem with my student was originally intended as a
means by which I could just listen to my student, give her a chance
to talk about her father, and write what she said while we walked.
However, the process turned out to be much more than anticipated.
It began as I wished, giving her a chance to recall memories of

her father, but then evolved to simultaneous observations and writing together. The process, quite spontaneous, could not have been planned. It simply occurred, as we walked. We utilized our time in the garden to connect and share thoughts that came to our minds with one another.

Once we began writing, it became difficult to differentiate between my student's thoughts, what I thought my student was thinking, and my own thoughts. The entire process brought us together in a way in which education in its purest form is intended; a teacher helping a student think about something in a new way and a student, conversely, helping the teacher to do the same. The occurrence was truly one of the pinnacles of my career. Never has an experience left me with such an awareness of a *teachable moment*. As I left the Garden that day, not only did I finally write a poem, I connected with a student in such a way that it solidified to me why I became a teacher.

Applications in the Science Classroom: The Walk Poem

I most certainly would recommend to science teachers the use of the walk poem as a means by which pairs of students and/ or teachers could work together to "walk" through or describe a scientific process in a laboratory setting. One of the partners could do the physical observing and verbalize the observations to their partner as the partner wrote them down. Afterwards, the two partners could collaborate to add additional facts, observations, and scientific concepts. This method could in fact serve as an important tool in the science classroom. Experimental observations that are verbalized by one laboratory partner and written by the other could be an effective means by which collaborative science could occur more readily. Students could use this form both to record observations scientifically as well as to record poetically their thoughts and feelings.

"Yellow Pinwheel" by Janyce Trampler

Day #3 proved to be a poetic turning point for both Erin and our science teacher chaperone, Janyce Trampler. While Erin was exploring new poetic voices and forms with her students, Janyce was writing her second science poem observing the pollination of the yellow pinwheel flower. In her poem, Janyce fuses highly technical and precise science with poetic description to give voice to the process of pollination, *Come hither, taste my sweet nectar*. She describes in "Yellow Pinwheel" the process of double fertilization, unique to flowering plants, whereby two sperms enter the ovary:

Yellow Pinwheel

Anthers and pistil
Like outstretched fingers of a beckoning hand,
Welcoming all manner of pollinators.

"Come hither, taste my sweet nectar," they seem to say.
And as your bristles brush up against the phallic-shaped anther,
You unknowingly carry the seemingly delicate pollen,
protector of sperm and tube cells,
to the glutinous stigma,

Whence invisible questing pollen tubes probe deep into the style,
searching for the prize,
the ovary,
protector of the egg,
Flanked by its synergid cells,
which chemically beckon the double sperm.

At last, success,
Fusion of haploid sets,
Creation of living embryo and supporting endosperm,
Patiently awaiting imbibition,
From which germination will come.

– Janyce Trampler, teacher

In her commentary, Janyce explains the origin and meaning of her second science poem, and how she hopes in the future to use her plant-inspired poems to help engage her students more fully with the plant kingdom:

Janyce's Commentary

The inspiration for this poem came while at the New York Botanical gardens. I was wandering around observing various flowers, once again not expecting to write any poetry, but I was amazed at the size of the anthers on some of the flowers. Quite honestly, they were the biggest, most beautiful anthers I had ever seen. After looking at the anthers on several types of flowers in several different parts of the park, I finally came upon these yellow pinwheels whose anthers, while not particularly big, reminded me of a hand that was palm up, with fingers outstretched and slightly curled inward. I started writing, and what began as an ode to anthers became a journey into the process of angiosperm reproduction.

I hope to use this poem to inspire my students to learn about plant physiology. Although I love and appreciate plants, and have tried several different approaches to teach the subject matter, most students have little to no interest in the topic. This year I am hopeful that I have found the answer to inspire more emphatic responses: science poetry.

PART FOUR: POST-EXPEDITION REFLECTIONS BY JANYCE TRAMPLER, SCIENCE TEACHER

When I first agreed to be a part of the science poetry expedition, it was without any thought of actually writing poetry. At the last minute, Erin mentioned that she needed an extra chaperone, so I agreed to go along. Although I had written a few non-science poems in the distant past, I never thought that the week would become so inspiring. It started with our pre-field trip poetry discussion in which Nancy began explaining about various types of poetry, and

I, always eager to learn new things, became interested. When she began describing how science and poetry could mix, and read some models and examples, I became intrigued, and a little excited. It was a whole new concept to me. Was it possible that the emotional and scientific parts of my brain (two very active parts) could be stimulated simultaneously? Later that day, I was inspired to write my first science poem. Since then I have written three others and have ideas in my head for several more. It has become a new intellectual and emotional outlet for me, but I also realized that science poetry may be a whole new way to reach students while teaching science. It may provide a new way of looking at a difficult subject, or may be a way for an otherwise uninterested student to be able to relate to the subject. I am so eager to try out my ideas during this coming school year in my biology classes!

Forging Common Ground

The science poetry expedition literally and figuratively forged common ground for our students and teachers. Students actively engaged with their teachers, peers, and the immediate environment, experienced first-hand the fusion that is the essence of the science poem. As a tool, science poetry writing opened their eyes to new ways of seeing, knowing, and experiencing. Most significantly for our purposes, it opened the eyes of our science colleague, Janyce Trampler, to new ways of teaching science as well. For my science partner and myself, the expedition confirmed the enduring value of science poetry to educate in the purest sense of the word, *educere*, "to bring forth." As we walked in this world with our students and colleagues, we did just that: constructing knowledge together, transforming both hearts and minds, forging a universe of a different kind.

PART FIVE: RELATED SCHOLARSHIP AND PEDAGOGY

A SCIENCE OF BELONGING: POETRY AS ECOLOGY

Ecological literacy inspires what in the past may be thought of as nature, pastoral, or social protest poetry, but now, in the context of the environmental movement, inspires ecological poetry by ecologically minded poets. Such poetry has its own world view, one which John Burnside, a self-described "ecological poet" from the University of St. Andrews, Scotland, refers to as "a science of belonging," a view that is at once scientific, poetic, philosophical, educational, ethical, and political (Burnside, 2006: 94-95). In his thought provoking essay, "A Science of Belonging: Poetry as Ecology," Burnside explains the connection: Poetry is an "essentially ecological discipline. It teaches us part of the duty of dwelling; it teaches us a necessary awe" (Burnside, 2006: 95).

Such poetry seems naturally rooted in what Edward O. Wilson calls *biophilia*–"The innate pleasure [humans derive] from living abundance and diversity, particularly as manifested by the human impulse to imitate Nature with gardens" (Wilson, 1998: 212). In this sense, according to Burnside, walking becomes the basic discipline of the science of belonging: "For this is a science based almost entirely on field work. On foot, we are able to imagine an accord between poetry and ecology," one which reconnects us once again to the earth (Burnside, 2006: 105). In this sense, walking becomes for Burnside, "a political act…out in the open, I participate in the world as it is, in the real" (Burnside, 2006:105). For interested teachers, the convergence of ecological literary and science poetry provide for our students and ourselves a powerful pedagogy for developing a "science of belonging."

In this spirit, Poets House of New York City has launched "The Language of Conservation," a national project aimed at heightening environmental awareness through poetry installations at zoos in the United States. Originating in the Central Park Zoo in New

York City under the direction of leading poet, Sandra Alcosser, the project plan includes poetry installations with science Poets-in-Residence in zoos in Milwaukee, Wisconsin (Pattiann Rogers) and Jacksonville, Florida (Alison Hawthorne Deming). Interested teachers will find these zoos ideal environments for science poetry expeditions and readings. (For poetry and photographs of the Central Park Zoo project see http://www.shapingoutcomes.org/course/cases/centralparkzoo.pdf.)

Note

1. Additional walk poem models accessible to high school students include: A. R. Ammons' "Corsons Inlet," Gary Snyder's "A Walk," and Theodore Roethke's "A Walk in Late Summer." Writing walk poems about a walk has a long history if one considers epic journeys like Dante's *Inferno* a walk poem. Padgett also recommends William Wordsworth's "An Evening Walk" and Walt Whitman's "Song of the Open Road" as exemplary models of the genre.

12 How to Assess Student Science Poetry

The Art of Response

In my everyday dance class I found a new curiosity for scientific endeavors that I never would have discovered without scientific poetry.

> – Sarah Ryan, student commenting upon
> her grade "A" mastery level poem, "An Arabesque"
> at the conclusion of this chapter.

OVERVIEW: HOW TO ASSESS STUDENT SCIENCE POETRY

In the spirit of forging common ground, Chapter 12 guides science and English teachers in responding to student science poems in progress. Given the interdisciplinary nature of the genre, science and English teachers alike must become "chemical artists," fusing the science part of the poem with the poetry part of the poem, helping their students strive to achieve the *perfect fusion* that is the essence of the art form. This is not to say that to teach science poetry, English teachers need to become scientists and science teachers need to become English teachers or poets. Rather, each needs to draw on a variety of intra and interdisciplinary resources, strategies, and collaborations suggested in this chapter. Whether you are a science or English teacher, after engaging in science poetry writing and instruction with your students, you will undoubtedly have to face the critical issues of response, assessment, and grading of your students' science poems. In this regard, Chapter 12 addresses the following pedagogical questions:

- *What are the most effective methods for responding to student science poems in progress?*
- *What are the most effective methods for assessing and grading student science poems?*
- *Will you respond on your own or with a colleague?*
- *Will you assess and grade on your own or with a colleague?*

WHAT'S AHEAD

Chapter 12 offers practical methods, strategies, and approaches for responding to, assessing, and grading student science poems. Part One offers specific examples of how to respond to student science poems that need more science, science poems that need more poetry, and science poems that should be left alone. Part Two offers discussion of how to assess and grade student science poems in the science or English classrooms. Drawing on the best practices in writing pedagogy, this chapter advocates the use of portfolio assessment as well as the contract grading system and check sheet formats for assessment of student science poetry. Part Two includes sample grading contracts and check sheets along with a descriptive rubric for the grading of individual science poems. The chapter ends with an example of a mastery level science poem (grade A) by a grade 11 student.

PART ONE: RESPONDING TO SCIENCE POEMS IN PROGRESS

THE ART OF RESPONSE: STUDENT MODELS

Whether you are a science or English teacher, on your own or in collaboration, you are still a reader, with all the power, integrity, and authority that all good readers possess. Given that there is no exact formula for writing a science poem, how will you, the good reader, respond to your students' science poems in progress? Here you will become the "chemical artist," considering whether a student's science poem requires more or less science, or more or less poetry in order to be: (1) all that an effective science poem can be; (2) all that the student wants the science poem to be; or (3) all that the science poem itself can be. I prefer emphasizing the latter. In essence, your task is to show your student the science poem's *potential meaning*, and then let that student ultimately decide upon the final meaning.

Questions to Ask of the Science Poem

- *Does the poem need more science?*
- *Does the poem need more complex science?*
- *Is the science in the poem accurate, factual, and correct?*
- *Does the poem need more poetry?*
- *Does the poem move from literal to poetic language and meaning making?*
- *Does the poem have a poetic stance?*
- *Could the poem benefit from stance blending?*
- *Could the poem benefit from rhetorical movement or progression?*

A Poem that Needs More Poetry: "Vascular Tissue" by Maggie McArdle

Let's consider for a moment, Maggie McArdle's science poem in progress, "Vascular Tissue," written in an AP English Language and Composition class:

Vascular Tissue

Xylem and Phloem
The components of vascular tissue in plants
Both transport water and nutrients throughout a plant.
Xylem focuses on moving up and Phloem moves down.

Using transpirational pull and root pressure
The Xylem moves water up the stem
The Phloem, with its sieve-tube cells and companion cells
Moves sugars formed in the photosynthetic leaves down to the
roots.

The Xylem and Phloem
Responsible for the continuity of life in a plant
The secret pathways of the plant
Bringing food and helping it grow.

– Maggie McArdle, student

Maggie's poem, a matter-of-fact description of the vascular process of plants, remains essentially literal, scientific language. Given that the science is accurate, is there enough poetry? Maggie has structured her language into a poetic form: three unrhymed quatrains. But as we have seen in Chapter 2, form alone is not sufficient to make a poem a poem. Even if Maggie had rhymed, rhyme alone would not meet our criteria or litmus test for poetry. Yet Maggie's poem does have the seeds of poetic potential. First, she employs the poetic stance of pure description. In her poem she does describe a scientific process. Second, by capitalizing *Xylem* and *Phloem*, Maggie accords these substances the respect of proper nouns, suggesting the possibility of extended personification. Third, Maggie refers at the end of her poem to the *secret pathways of the plant*. The word *secret* holds the potential for imaginative meaning making: What is secretive about this plant process literally invisible to the naked eye? Is there potential here for irony? I tell Maggie her poem has the science, but she needs to explore the poem's untapped, poetic potential. I encourage her to experiment with several possible ways to move the poem further into poetry:

- *Personify Xylem and Phloem throughout the poem.*
- *Use the leaping method to move from description to reflection.*
- *Use an additional poetic stance or stance blending.*

- *Strike a metaphor moving from the world of science to the human world.*
- *Create more than one meaning for the "secret" in the poem.*
- *Consider what might be ironic about this scientific process.*
- *Consider a more poetic title, one that adds levels of meaning.*

Before Maggie revises "Vascular Tissue," we consult with botanist, Steven Handel, to check the poem for scientific accuracy. His reaction resulted in several subtle suggestions: (1) eliminating the word *both* in line three since it seemed to him to imply completely identical functions for xylem and phloem, which is not scientifically true; (2) substituting a more scientifically accurate word for *focuses* in line four; (3) adding the word *stems* along with *roots* in line eight; (4) and substituting the word *hidden* for *secret* in line eleven since, in his opinion, the functions of vascular tissues are not a *secret* to science.

After much consideration, Maggie revises her science poem to infuse more poetry through the major use of address and extended personification. Her new title, "Pathways of a Plant," suggests not only an image but movement from the literal to further levels of meaning.

Pathways of a Plant

Xylem and Phloem
You are the secret to life
The internal pipes that keep a plant alive
Transporting water and nutrients
The means for survival

Xylem, straight to the top
Water droplets march their way through you
From roots to leaves, a water superhighway
Aided by the transpirational pull
Though your cells are dead you bring life

Unlike most, you, Phloem, strive to reach the bottom
Moving the hard work of the leaves
Carrying sugars to the roots
Life is hard at the bottom
But you have sieve-tube and companion cells as friends

Xylem and Phloem
Ever working, ever striving invisibly
Secret pathways of a plant
Responsible for the continuity of life
And all that is green in this world.

– Maggie McArdle, student

Maggie's revision results in a more poetic poem, one with greater emotional depth, empathy, and original meaning-making. "Pathways of a Plant" reflects a sense of awe and wonder that "Vascular Tissue" lacks in its matter-of-fact science. More important than the product, Maggie's revision process has taught her how to advance her science poetry to higher poetic levels (see Maggie's poem, "Aquamarine" in Chapter 6).

A Poem that Needs More Science: "Your Eye Opens" by Meghan Crippen

Meghan's poem, originally untitled, describes in general terms the process of seeing *the beautiful world*. Her poem is clearly one that would benefit from greater and more specific science.

Your eye opens
the iris contracts
light bounces
in through the pupil
on to the retina
along the optic nerve
into the brain.

Your eye opens
and you see
the beautiful world.

– Meghan Crippen, student

The contrast between the two stanzas in Meghan's poem offers great poetic potential: stanza one, scientific seeing, and stanza two, more poetic seeing. I commend Meghan on presenting or just stating this contrast without explaining it, but I suggest to her to add more science to intensify and strengthen the contrast. I further suggest to Meghan that in strengthening the contrast, she will also be strengthening the poetic potential as well. I mention to her that I noticed that only one eye opens in her poem. I tell her this fact seems particularly intriguing to me. It makes me wonder, where is the subject? In a bed in the morning? After surgery on a hospital stretcher? Or, on the beach at dawn? I ask Meghan to consider whether she would like to introduce a context for this one-eye-opening in her revision. I encourage Meghan to experiment with the following revision strategies to move her poem into greater science.

- *Add more science to this poem by using more specific, scientific terminology.*
- *Describe all the steps in the process of seeing. Review them and make sure they are accurate and precise.*
- *Consider the significance (scientific as well as poetic) of one eye opening rather than two.*
- *Consider the lack of context and whether context should be identified or defined.*
- *Add a title to reflect greater scientific and poetic meaning and/or possible context.*

Meghan's revision results in a highly scientific poem, one that intensifies the contrast between scientific seeing and poetic seeing. Meghan explains her intension: *I am still struggling with the title. I feel that the generality of the poem should be kept. I don't want to give it further context. I believe this will direct the focus of the poem to the technical vs. simple theme.* I agree with Meghan and suggest she make her opening line her title.

Your Eye Opens

Your eye opens,
The levator palpebrae muscle
Lifts the eyelid
Light rushes in
First through the cornea
Then the anterior chamber
The colored iris contracts
To filter the light
The journey continues
Through the pupil, off of the lens
Across the vitreous humor
And finally to the retina
Concentrating on the fovea centralis
Interpreted by rods and cones
Then along the optic nerve
Finally to the occipital lobe of the brain.

Your eye opens
And you see the beautiful world.

– Meghan Crippen, student

Meghan's revision successfully moves her poem to greater science, and I think poetry as well. In strengthening the contrast, the meaning of *beautiful* seems to resonate both in the world of science and the world of nature. At least to me, there seems to be a beauty in the technical description of opening in stanza one, a beauty I had not noticed in the original version of the poem. (See Meghan's poem, "Amber" in Chapter 6).

A Poem that Needs to be Left Alone: "Dancing in the Sky" by Ashish Gupta

Often, in an attempt to write science poetry, a student will write an inspired poem, but one which is not a science poem by our working definition. At times, such poems should be honored as such and left alone. In this case, as a teacher you will truly have to be the "chemical artist," determining whether a poem could benefit from more science or not. In making your decision, you will have to imagine: What would this poem be like given more quantitative, factual, or scientific data? Will such data make the poem more informative, thought provoking, creative, aesthetic, or original? Conversely, will such data destroy the spirit, essence, or art of the poem?

"Dancing in the Sky" is an example of a poem that needs to be left alone. In this poem Ashish Gupta describes the phases of the moon as it "dances" poetically in the sky. Although Ashish uses some scientific terminology, *waxing* and *waning*, clearly more science could be infused in the poem. And yet, adding more science might very well destroy the structure of the poem, a visual suggestion of a half moon on the page, as well as the flow of the poem, a luminous dance across the sky. Given the recognition that "Dancing in the Sky" is a particular genre, concrete poetry, this is a poem that generally achieves its purpose and should be left alone.

Dancing in the Sky

Waxing,

And Waning,

Reflecting the

Light, shimmering,

And glimmering away,

It swims through the sky,

Dancing, circling, twirling,

Providing hope and guidance,

As it rises up during the night,

When everything else is dark,

It reveals itself, it is clear,

Shining and smiling,

But the sun arises,

And it falls, falls,

Out of sight, as

It disappears

For day.

– *Ashish Gupta*, student

TYPES OF RESPONSE

Teacher's Checklist: Responding to Student Science Poems in Progress

The following is a checklist of questions to ask when responding to student science poems in progress. Please note that all of the questions need not apply to a particular poem to make that poem a successful science poem. For example, a science poem may move from science to poetry or use science as extended metaphor throughout the poem but not necessarily both at the same time. A science poem may have quantitative data in terms of specific scientific facts but not necessarily in terms of numbers.

Teacher's Checklist for Science Poem Response

The Science Part (Quantitative Data)
- Is the science accurate? Are the facts correct? Are the theories clear?
- Is the science simplistic? Does the poem need more complex science?
- Is there sufficient quantitative data? Numeracy?
- Does the poem need more scientific or specific technical vocabulary?
- Does the poem need more scientific research?

The Poetry Part (Qualitative Data)
- Is the poem poetic? Does the language move from the literal?
- Is the meaning making sufficient? Is there any ambiguity?
- Is there a clear poetic stance? Is there stance blending?
- Is there sensory imagery and use of figures of speech?
- Is there sufficient qualitative data? (thought and feeling)

The Writing Part
- Does science prompt, inform, or inspire the poem?
- Does the poem move from science to poetry?
- Does the poem use science as metaphor?
- Is there artful fusion of the science and the poetry?

Methods for Teacher Assessment of Student Science Poems

When teaching science poetry writing, provide students with an assessment of their poems in the form of multiple types of feedback leading to specific ideas for revision:

- *Informal oral feedback on the science poem in progress.*
- *Formal oral feedback in a one-to-one conference on the science poem in progress.*
- *Informal written feedback on the student's science poem in progress.*
- *Formal written feedback on the student's completed science poem.*

On Your Own or With a Colleague?

Consider for a moment: Every poem deserves a good reader to provide assessment, but every science poem deserves perhaps two good readers: one with an eye to science, the other with an eye to poetry. Ideally, every science poem should be assessed by a science teacher for accuracy, precision, and correctness of the science, and by an English teacher for mechanical accuracy and the art of the poetry. Although the assessment process may seem at first overwhelming, there are strategies to expedite the conferencing, revising, and editing process. Depending upon whether you are teaching on your own or with a colleague, here are strategies to consider:

- *If you are an English teacher on your own, find a science colleague willing to read student science poems for accuracy; or conversely, if you are a science teacher, find an English colleague willing to read science poems for the poetry.*
- *Place part of the assessment process in students' hands by requiring them to seek out their current English or science*

teacher to read their science poems for either science or language accuracy and correctness.
- *Require English students to provide a scientific reference, citation, or explanatory paragraph substantiating the source and/or accuracy of their science poem.*
- *Team-teach a science poetry writing lesson with a colleague from another department and share the assessment process.*
- *Consider using portfolios to facilitate the assessment process.*

Methods for Student Assessment of Student Science Poems

When teaching science poetry writing, provide students as much as possible with the opportunity to self-assess their own poems in progress as well as the poems of their peers. Distribute Handouts #3 or #4 either before or after conferencing with students during the revision process.

Student Handout #3: How to Assess and Revise Your Own Science Poem

Students can use Handout #3 to assess their own science poems in progress as part of their revision process. The left-hand column poses questions for assessment and revision. The right-hand column provides space for revision ideas and notes.

Student Handout #4: How to Assess a Peer's Science Poem

Students can use Handout #4 when assessing a peer's science poem in progress. The left-hand column poses questions for the peer assessor to consider. The right-hand column provides space for the peer assessor's suggestions. Peers should exchange their poems in progress to facilitate their revision process.

How to Assess and Revise Your Own Science Poem

Your Name	
Title of Your Poem	
Identify all the senses you use in the poem (sight, sound, smell, taste, touch). Consider: does your poem need more sensory images or concreteness? If so, add sensory details.	Sight:
	Sound:
	Smell:
	Taste:
	Touch:
What area(s) of science does your poem relate to? Do you use any scientific allusions? If not, consider adding a scientific allusion.	
Do you refer to or describe any scientific concepts, principles, theories, or processes? If so, what are they? Be specific.	
Do you use any quantitative data in the poem? (If so, what is the data, and how is that data used?) Do you need to add more scientific data?	
Do you express any qualitative data in the poem? (If so, how is that data expressed?) Reference specific lines, images, or phrases where you express feelings, emotions, attitudes, or opinions.	
Identify your poetic stance. Consider: stance blending or incorporating more stances.	
Identify use of metaphor and figures of speech. Consider extending a metaphor or infusing more figures of speech: simile, personification, and symbolism.	
Does your poem need more science? If so, imagine how to add more science.	
Does your poem need more poetry? If so, imagine how to add more poetry.	

How to Assess a Peer's Science Poem

Assessor's Name	
Poet's Name	
Title of the Poem	
Identify all the senses in the poem (sight, sound, smell, taste, touch). Consider: does the poem need more sensory images or concreteness? Explain.	Sight:
	Sound:
	Smell:
	Taste:
	Touch:
What area(s) of science does the poem relate to? Can you identify any scientific allusions? If so, what are they?	
Does the poem refer to or describe any scientific concepts, principles, theories, or processes? If so, what are they? Be specific.	
Does the poet use any quantitative data in the poem? (If so, what is the data, and how is that data used?)	
Does the poet express any qualitative data in the poem? (If so, how is that data expressed?) Reference specific lines, images, or phrases where the poet expresses feelings, emotions, attitudes, or opinions.	
Is there a poetic stance or stances in the poem? If so, identify the stance or stances.	
Does the poet use metaphor, symbolism, or figures of speech. Identify specifically.	
In your opinion, does this poem need more science to be a science poem? If so, explain why.	
In your opinion, does this poem need more poetry to be a science poem? If so, explain why.	

PART TWO: METHODS FOR ASSESSING AND GRADING STUDENT SCIENCE POEMS

In Chapter 4, I posed a question for reflection: What grade, if any, would you give to a science poem? If you did not give a grade within a grade-oriented course, what would you be saying to your students about how you value their poetry writing? Grading, the placing of a value on a finished poem, need not be a conundrum for the high school science or English teacher. Much will depend upon your particular course (graded or not graded), curriculum require- ments (science or English), and specific objectives in teaching science poetry (to foster scientific knowledge, poetic techniques, written expression, or creativity and imagination). Since you most likely will be integrating science poetry writing into an established course with its own established grading system, ask yourself the following questions:

- *How can I grade my students' poems with integrity and value within my current grading system?*
- *How can I adapt or adjust my current grading system to more meaningfully grade student poems?*
- *What are my grading preferences and biases, and how do they impact upon my grading of student science poems?*
- *What constraints, if any, does the grading system in my department or school impose upon my grading of student science poems?*

With the emphasis on competition and grading in most high schools nationally and internationally, you will most likely be teaching poetry writing to students who expect, demand, and at times only want to work for a grade. Given this reality, you should grade student poems, affording those poems the value and respect they deserve within the framework of your particular course. In other words, the grade should be meaningful in terms of time, effort, and achievement; and the grade should be valued, that is, required for the course, not just for extra credit.

METHOD #1: THE CONTRACT GRADING SYSTEM AND CHECK SHEET FORMAT

The contract grading system establishes a contract between student and teacher at the onset of the course by delineating the specific requirements and expectations for each grade in the form of a check sheet. The contract, an agreement between student and teacher, outlines for the student exactly what that student must do to achieve a given grade in the unit or course of study. Under the contract system, you, the teacher, decide the requirements for each grade; your students decide what grade they want to work for; and together, you and your students strive for the highest level of achievement. A contract grading system dispenses with placing grades on individual poems. Instead, your students receive a single grade for the entire poetry unit or portfolio.

This system offers an ideal way to grade student science poems. You establish your own requirements for each grade, emphasizing the content and skills most essential for your course and curriculum. The system can be adapted to any numerical grading system. The following are factors to consider when designing the requirements under a contract grading system:

- Quality of the poems
- Quantity of the poems
- Revision of poems
- Careful editing of poems
- Conferencing over poems
- Workshop participation
- Meeting deadlines

In determining the overall quality of poems, consider the accuracy and complexity of the science as well as evidence of revision and careful editing. When determining the quantity of poems, take into consideration not only the number of poems, but the length and complexity of the poem as well (one long, complex poem may be credited as two poems). If the teacher places value on process writing and participation, students will be motivated to not only revise their own poems, but to help each other. A sense of community will emerge.

How to Use the Check Sheet Format

Distribute the requirements on day one of your science poetry unit or course in the form of a check sheet. Tell students to put a check mark next to each requirement as they complete it. The check sheets should reflect exactly what you are teaching and expecting the students to accomplish. Remember: the requirements are not cast in stone; they may change and evolve as you teach science poetry writing, but they reflect at the outset, what you expect your students to accomplish for each grade given.

Please note: not placing a grade on an individual poem does not imply a lack of assessment. You still will be deciding if that poem meets your expectations for the given writing exercise in terms of content and skills. I use the following simple system:

"S" for Satisfactory
"R" for Redraft and Resubmit

Check sheets may be designed in several ways:

- By content or assignments;
- By mastery of skills; or
- By a combination of content and skills.

Regardless of the method, check sheets logically present requirements in chronological order. The following is a sample check sheet based on teaching the fundamental lessons in Part Two of this book. This check sheet lists a combination of content and skill requirements for a science poetry writing unit plan.

Sample Check Sheet: Science Poetry Unit Requirements

For an "A": Excellent Quantity, Quality, Effort, and Achievement

1. One science poem informed and inspired by minerals or earth science
2. One science poem informed and inspired by insects or biology
3. One science poem informed and inspired by in-the-field data gathering
4. One science poem using science as extended metaphor or symbol
5. One science poem describing a complex scientific process or phenomenon
6. One science poem inspired by your favorite science poet or poem
7. Five additional free choice science poems
8. Substantive revision of five science poems
9. Participation in conferencing, workshops, and peer editing
10. Consistent punctuality; meets all deadlines

For a "B": Good Quantity, Quality, Effort, and Achievement

1. One science poem informed and inspired by minerals or earth science
2. One science poem informed and inspired by insects or biology
3. One science poem informed and inspired by in-the-field data gathering
5. One science poem inspired by your favorite science poet or poem
6. Three additional free choice science poems
7. Substantive revision of three science poems
8. Participation in conferencing, workshops, and peer editing
9. Generally consistent punctuality; meets most deadlines

For a "C": Satisfactory Quantity, Quality, Effort, and Achievement

1. One science poem informed and inspired by minerals or earth science
2. One science poem informed and inspired by insects or biology
3. One science poem informed and inspired by in-the-field data gathering
4. One science poem inspired by your favorite science poet or poem
5. Substantive revision of one science poem
6. Participation in conferencing, workshops, and peer editing
7. Inconsistent punctuality; meets some but not all deadlines

A Note on Numerical Grades and Plus and Minus Systems

The contract grading and check sheet system may be adapted to any numerical grading system. If you prefer a more precise grading system, simply indicate what is required for A+ or A-. One simple way of indicating plus and minus grades is to use them for either merit (extra effort, improvement, or going beyond expectations) or penalty (not meeting deadlines or insufficient participation in workshops) but with the assignment still meeting the basic require-ments within a given grade category.

A Note on Punctuality

Punctuality – meeting deadlines, being prepared for writing workshops, and conferences – remains a critical factor for success in any writing program. All writing requires development over a period of time, and science poetry writing is no exception. Although I place considerable emphasis on punctuality in my contract grading system, I also want to keep the door open at all times for students' delayed creative impulse, that is, the poem that suddenly comes in the dead of night, after the deadline. I want to see those poems, and I want students to know that those poems will be read, valued, and counted. Here's where I often apply the plus/minus system.

METHOD #2: PORTFOLIO ASSESSMENT AND THE CONTRACT GRADING SYSTEM

Writing teachers advocate the use of portfolios to facilitate the assessment and revision process. Whether you are teaching science poetry for one lesson, one unit, or one semester, portfolios provide the most effective, practical, and meaningful approach to teaching writing as process. This approach, supported by decades of writing pedagogy and scholarship (Bizzaro, 1993: 193) sees the portfolio as a flexible, reader-response approach to assessment that encourages conferencing, maintains the integrity of each and every poem, and respects the collaborative authority of both the student-poet and you, the teacher. For example, you and your student may decide together the contents of the portfolio and/or the skills to be demonstrated or mastered on individual poems or on the portfolio as a whole. Although the portfolio assessment process operates in its most ideal form in courses established as writing workshops[1] (e.g. creative writing or poetry writing courses), portfolio assessment offers practical and effective application within any existing curriculum that has a writing workshop component.

At the end of the unit or at given intervals during an entire unit, students commonly write portfolio assessments. These assessments include:

- *Assessment of their most successful poem*
- *Assessment of their most successful revision*
- *Assessment of their science poetry writing progress*
- *Overall assessment of what they have discovered about poetry*
- *Overall assessment of what they have discovered about science*
- *Overall assessment of what they have discovered about the "common ground" of science and poetry*
- *Overall assessment of how science poetry writing has affected, influenced, or transformed them in anyway.*

Under the portfolio assessment system, many writing teachers dispense with placing grades on individual poems, preferring instead to grade the entire portfolio at the conclusion of a unit, workshop, or course of study.

Given this process writing approach, portfolio assessment naturally goes hand in hand with the contract grading system and check sheet format. My science partner and I strongly recommend combining both methods for the most effective mode of assessing science poetry writing lessons and units. Students maintain in their individual portfolios all of their science poems, in chronological order, based on the requirements delineated on the check sheet. The check sheet, based upon the agreed contract, serves as page one of each student's portfolio. As students write and submit their science poems, they place a check mark after each exercise or requirement. Students keep track of their satisfactory "S" poems and the number of their substantive revisions on their check sheets. This record-keeping facilitates subsequent portfolio conferences and portfolio assessments.

METHOD #3: THE DESCRIPTIVE RUBRIC: GRADING OF INDIVIDUAL SCIENCE POEMS

Although the combined method of portfolio assessment, contract grading, and check sheet format remains the ideal process writing approach, you may not be teaching an entire unit of science poetry, and you may not want to teach process writing. The question then is how to grade an individual or occasional science poem within a numerical grading system. Here the strategy of rubrics may prove useful. Rubrics are highly adaptable to any grading system, and they can provide helpful information to the student poet. That information, the standards for each grade, generally falls into two formats: (1) the descriptive rubric and (2) the grid-style rubric. I prefer using the descriptive rubric format when applying a grade to an individual science poem. I attach the rubric to the student's poem along with specific commentary. The following is a descriptive rubric for science poetry grading that may prove useful to science and English teachers.

Descriptive Science Poetry Rubric

The following grades indicate mastery level of skills or degrees of command regarding the fusion of scientific knowledge and poetic skill. Note: a given grade indicates demonstration of <u>all or most</u> of the bulleted criteria.

"A" Mastery Level of Command: Outstanding Science Poem
- Evidence of artful fusion of science and poetry
- Demonstrates advanced and/or complex scientific knowledge
- Demonstrates accurate, specific, and plentiful quantitative data
- Employs specific scientific or technical vocabulary
- Employs a clear poetic stance or stance blending
- Employs science as extended metaphor, symbol, or allusion
- Employs rhetorical movement or leaping from science to poetry
- Evidence of the emergence of an authentic poetic voice
- Highly inspired, creative, and original

"B" Proficient Level of Command: Very Good Science Poem
- Evidence of fusion of science and poetry
- Demonstrates more basic or elementary scientific knowledge
- Demonstrates some accurate and specific quantitative data
- Employs some scientific or technical vocabulary
- Employs a clear poetic stance or stance blending
- Employs science as extended metaphor, symbol, or allusion
- Employs rhetorical movement or leaping from science to poetry
- Inspired, creative, and original

"C" General Level of Command: Satisfactory Science Poem
- Evidence of mechanical fusion of science and poetry
- Demonstrates basic or elementary scientific knowledge
- Demonstrates some accurate and quantitative data
- Employs little or no scientific or technical vocabulary
- Employs a clear poetic stance
- Little inspiration, creativity, and originality

"D" Incompetent Level of Command: Weak Science Poem
- Lacks evidence of fusion of science and poetry
- Lacks scientific accuracy and/or specific quantitative data
- Lacks scientific or technical vocabulary
- Lacks a clear poetic stance
- Little or no inspiration, creativity, and originality

"F" No Level of Command: Not a Science Poem
- Does not demonstrate sufficient criteria for science poetry
- Does not complete the assignment

Model Student Science Poem: "A" Mastery Level of Command

The following science poem, written by student poet, Sarah Ryan, received a grade of "A" for its masterful as well as highly creative fusion of the scientific with the non-scientific. Sarah's poem, "An Arabesque," begins with the instruction in an AP English Language and Composition class to write a science poem, but then quickly moves to the personal and authentic. Sarah explains in her commentary:

Sarah's Commentary

I wrote "An Arabesque" to portray the frustration I felt as I danced. A simple arabesque is such a complex working of muscles and bones. When I danced, I was aware of my muscles working, but I never knew their exact names in relation to what I felt in my body. In order to create a scientific poem, I had to find a diagram of muscles and bones on the Internet. Then I continued doing countless arabesques, comparing the muscles I felt to the figures in the pictures I found online. It was a long process, but it made me appreciate my body, and how each muscle aided me in my quest to perform the perfect arabesque.

"An Arabesque" by Sarah Ryan

An Arabesque

It pushes down,
My toes resist, pushing back,
My hips pull apart,
Muscles straining to turn out.
Iliopsoas helping
I pull up
Abdominal external oblique's contracting,
Holding my stomach,
Striving for the line.

My arm reaches forward
Leg extends back
Quadriceps burning
Both stretching
Striving for the line
I hold in my tailbone,
The unwanted gluteus maximus
My head is tall
Neck straining up
Trapezius
Latissimus dorsi
Holding my spine straight
My muscles start to shake
Reacting against each other
Toes push down
Quadriceps and gastrocnemius holding me straight
Pulling up my stomach
Stretching my neck
Arms up reaching
Leg up, reaching,
Nose, rib cage, hips, toe,
All in line
My muscles shutter
The hips stop pulling
It pushes down too much
Gravity
I lose balance
I fall
Dreams are for the foolish anyway,
But I put down my platform and lift again.

– Sarah Ryan, student

Sarah may not have succeeded in her arabesque, *I lose balance*, but she certainly has succeeded in balancing the scientific with the non-scientific. In her poem, Sarah fuses sheer physicality, emotional intensity, and personal authenticity with the scientific to achieve a better understanding of her body, her spirit, and "an arabesque." She notes the irony of her newly found understanding: "In my everyday dance class I found a new curiosity for scientific endeavors that I never would have discovered without scientific poetry." Grade: "A"

Note

1. The term *workshop* has several possible meanings. It may describe an entire writing course, as "Creative Writing Workshop," or it may be a component within any science or English course. Consider the *workshop* as the laboratory component of any writing class where students receive writing instruction, compose, and then sit around helping each other improve their poems through revision and editing.

Conclusion

Toward a New Interdisciplinary Literacy

Neither science nor the arts can be complete without combining their separate strengths. Science needs the intuition and metaphorical power of the arts, and the arts need the fresh blood of science.

– Edward O. Wilson
Consilience: The Unity of Knowledge
(Wilson, 1998: 211)

Much is to be gained when scientists raid the evocative techniques of literature and when poets raid the language and mythology of science.

– Alison Hawthorne Deming
"Science and Poetry: A View from the Divide"
(Deming, 2001: 186)

MUCH IS TO BE GAINED...

Much is to be gained when we as science and English teachers raid the methods, approaches, and ways of seeing of each other's disciplines. In doing so, we enter a universe of a different kind, forging through our teaching, a new interdisciplinary literacy. If there is one science poem that exemplifies the philosophy and pedagogy of this literacy, incorporating the core objectives of this book, it is Howard Nemerov's "Figures of Thought."

Figures of Thought

To lay the logarithmic spiral on
Sea-shell and leaf alike, and see it fit,
To watch the same idea work itself out
In the fighter pilot's steepening, tightening turn
Onto his target, setting up the kill,
And in the flight of certain wall-eyed bugs
Who cannot see to fly straight into death
But have to cast their sidelong glance at it
And come but cranking to the candle's flame –

How secret that is, and how privileged
One feels to find the same necessity
Ciphered in forms diverse and otherwise
Without kinship – that is the beautiful
In Nature as in art, not obvious,
Not inaccessible, but just between.

It may diminish some our dry delight
To wonder if everything we are and do
Lies subject to some little law like that;
Hidden in nature, but not deeply so.

                    – *Howard Nemerov* (Nemerov, 1977: 472)

In our individual journeys, my colleagues and I have witnessed our students using the interdisciplinary tool of science poetry to make connections in the world of nature, science, and self. We have seen our science and English students alike appreciate *how secret* it is, and we have noticed *how privileged* many of them feel making connections in *forms diverse and otherwise / Without kinship*. But most importantly, we have relished the struggle of our students to engage with ambiguity, realizing *the beautiful in Nature and art is not obvious / Not inaccessible, but just between.* For our students, science poetry has become the means to a greater end – an interdisciplinary literacy that enables them to discover areas of common ground, bridging the cultural divide. These areas include shared methods, approaches, skills, and ways of seeing, feeling, and thinking. Together they form transferable and portable skills to further advancement on the highest levels in both the arts and sciences.

THE COMMON GROUND

Combining science and the arts...makes pedagogical sense. Both disciplines rely on observation, pattern recognition, problem solving, experimentation, and thinking by analogy. Both artists and scientists observe, record, imagine, and create.

– Pamela Michael
"Helping Children Fall in Love with the Earth:
Environmental Education and the Arts"
(Michael, 2005: 116)

OBSERVATION AND SENSE PERCEPTION

Both scientists and poets aim to "see," literally and figuratively, as far as that seeing will go; that is, with the naked eye, or with the eye aided by instruments of technology. Such seeing involves observation and sense perception to discover the nature of phenomena or the nature of the unknown or the unknowable. Both disciplines begin with focused attention, using observation and sense perception to bring hidden realities to light. Both disciplines require the accurate recording of observations and sensory data. Although poets move in their recordings beyond attention to accuracy, to self-observation and emotional response, the basis for much modern poetry remains the concrete, material universe of things. The writing of science poetry requires students to observe, sense, and data-gather for both scientific and poetic purposes.

CREATIVITY AND THE CREATIVE PROCESS

Both scientist and poets engage in the creative process to discover the unknown, to imagine, to invent, and to create. Mihaly Csikszentmihalyi's seminal study, *Creativity: Flow and the Psychology of Discovery and Invention* (Csikszentmihalyi , 1996) defines creativity, the creative personality, and the creative process, confirming the common ground for artists, poets, and scientists alike. The writing of science poetry requires students to use their creative thinking, imagination, and writing skills as well as the creative process to create something new – a science poem.

METAPHOR AND ANALOGY

Both scientists and poets draw on metaphor to express the inexpressible, the unseen, invisible levels of the universe, making them as visible, knowable, expressible, and concrete as possible. In this regard, Roald Hoffmann's observation that "the language of science is a language under stress" is particularly relevant (Hoffman, 1988: 10). He explains how "words are being made to describe things that seem indescribable in words – equations, chemical structures and so forth" (p. 10). He points out the paradox: "By being a natural language under tension, the language of science is inherently poetic. There is metaphor aplenty in science" (p. 10). In this sense, a science poet may be thought of as a word-scientist, and a science poem, a laboratory or linguistic model where the word-scientist, through metaphor and analogy, conducts the word-science experiment.

AMBIGUITY

Although scientists seek to clarify and resolve ambiguity while poets tend to savior it, both wrestle with ambiguity and the unknown and the unknowable, trying to forge clarity. As such, the writing of science poetry requires students to wrestle with ambiguity, applying the test of scientific knowledge with the insights of poetic meaning. In doing so, they must hold two opposing views in their mind at the same time, find coherence in complexity, and employ a multiplicity of points of view. Such thinking skills form the foundation of all creative thinking in the arts and sciences.

EMOTION AND WRITING

Both scientists and poets feel passionately about their disciplines, yet scientists do not always have the opportunity to express their emotions publicly or in scientific writing. According to Norman MacLeod, "All scientists – at least all systematists – respond on an emotional level to their objects of study" (Crawford, 2006: 142). Conceding that "long training in the analytical style of scientific writing squeezes the ability to communicate this emotion, lyricism, and passion out of most of our writing," MacLeod stresses: "Contrary to the scientist's public image, however, that doesn't mean we don't feel these things. Indeed, I believe it is precisely those feelings that make us scientists" (p. 142). The science poem affords science students the opportunity to express in writing the full range of their emotions in regard to science and nature.

WHY TEACH SCIENCE POETRY?

REASON #1: FOR OUR STUDENTS

'If you squander all your time reading poetry and novels,' one mathematics teacher admonished me, 'you'll never be able to master the rigors of science and math, which are the most precise ways of understanding how the world works.'

– Gary Paul Nabhan
Cross-Pollinations: The Marriage of Science and Poetry
(Nabhan, 2004: 11)

We need to teach science poetry for students like Gary Paul Nabhan gifted in both disciplines but ignorant how each can inspire and inform the other. Such creatively gifted students need to know that there is no need to divide the world of knowledge into competing disciplines, and that turning to poetry may be one of the best ways to make a scientific breakthrough. Albert Einstein did it with his visualized thought experiments (*Gedankenexperiments*), a form of deep, metaphorical thinking (Isaacson, 2007: 26). His biographer, Walter Isaacson, describes how Einstein's quest to discover the "harmonious reality underlying the laws of the universe" began when "as a 16 year old he imagined what it would be like to ride alongside a light beam" (Isaacson, 2007: 3). Only a decade after that, in 1915, he "wrestled from nature his crowning glory, one of the most beautiful theories in all of science, the general theory of relativity: Imagine being in a closed elevator accelerating up through space…the effects you'd feel would be indistinguishable from the experience of gravity" (p. 3). Isaacson (2007: 26) points out that "visual understanding of concepts," in the mind, not in the laboratory, "became a significant aspect of Einstein's genius" (p. 26). And yet, many of our students still hold to the stereotypical image of the methodical scientist in the white coat, bent over the microscope or notebook, writing equations.

Did Einstein just dream up thought experiments, or did he have an education that taught him "intuition, conceptual thinking, and visual imagery?" In this regard, Einstein's biography becomes highly significant and relevant to us as teachers of science and poetry. Struggling in the German educational system grounded in rote drills, "impatience with questioning," and "worship of authority," Einstein dropped out of high school and headed for Italy and the Alps (Isaacson, 2007: 21–23). There, he entered a cantonal school in the village of Aarau based on the progressive philosophy of the Swiss educational reformer, Johann Pestalozzi. Pestalozzi believed that students should be allowed to reach their own conclusions "by using a series of steps that began with hands-on observations and then proceeded to intuitions, conceptual thinking, and visual imagery" (p. 27). Isaacson (2007: 27) points out: "It was a perfect school for Einstein"…and he "loved" Aarau, for "it was even possible to learn – and truly understand – the laws of math and physics that way" (p. 27).

Why teach science poetry? We teach it for students like Albert Einstein and all of the potential Einsteins who need to learn in their formative years, not only the subject matter, or fact-based knowledge of science, but also the portable, poetic skills of visualized imagery and metaphoric, imaginative, and intuitive thinking necessary for the advancement of knowledge.

REASON #2: FOR OUR DISCIPLINES

Although teaching the specialized knowledge of English and science remains the paramount objective of English and science teachers alike, we limit educational advancement by not recognizing and teaching our students how to transfer their knowledge from one discipline to another.

Like Einstein, Gary Paul Nabhan was influenced in his high school years by a personally profound experience with cross-curricular teaching that shaped the later direction of his breakthrough scientific research. At age 15, a school nurse told Gary, an aspiring artist, that he was color blind. Despairing, he thought he would have to give up painting. Enter Dorothy Ives: "Paint what you see, that's all…then you and I will become scientific experts on color blindness, to figure out what you see – what you do and what you don't see – so that then we can use that knowledge of science to guide your art" (Nabhan, 2004: 19). That semester under Dorothy Ives' guidance, Gary conducted an independent scientific study of color, developing his own color wheel. He credits his art teacher for enabling him to become a scientist: "It was the first time that I ever felt the excitement that experimentation and scientific discovery could bring, and it happened in an art class in the basement of a rather ordinary high school in Gary, Indiana. Together, Dorothy Ives and I, began to generate new hypotheses which we tested through our own experimental designs" (Nabhan, 2004: 21). Years later, in his desert field work, Gary could attest to the fact that he "encountered fifteen times as many camouflaged cacti as all his 'color-normal' colleagues found collectively" (p. 25).

As English and science teachers, we need to tell the stories of remarkable individuals like Gary Paul Nabhan, scientist-poet, who alternates freely between field science and literary art, recognizing no essential boundaries between the two disciplines. Equally important, we also need to provide opportunities for students to synthesize knowledge and skills from the arts to the sciences and from the sciences to the arts. Only in this way will we be able to affirm the intrinsic, reciprocal, and complementary value of each discipline, thereby bridging the "cultural divide," and in the process, creating new synergies for future discovery and advancement in each discipline.

REASON #3: FOR OURSELVES, TO OPEN OUR EYES TO THE JOYS OF A DIFFERENT UNIVERSE

We need to teach science poetry for ourselves; that is, for our own personal and professional knowledge, growth, and, for some of us, eye-opening renewal. If we look once again at Frost's poem, "The

Secret Sits," we might now consider an additional interpretation. Perhaps the "secret" to the mystery is science poetry itself; not just literally the subject and existence of science poetry, but rather, the recognition that science poetry symbolizes the value of open eyes, multiple perspectives, and interdisciplinary synthesis. Once we recognize this value and make it our own new perspective, we will no longer *dance around* and *suppose*; we will have solved the mystery, and we will *know*.

As this book goes to press, my science partner, Erin Colfax, and our science colleague, Janyce Trampler, know the secret. They continue their true journeys, raiding the evocative techniques of literature to teach their students science. Erin now teaches her biology students human anatomy through Charles Harper Webb's performance poem, "Liver," and Alice Jones' science poems, "The Larynx," "The Lungs," and "The Inner Ear." Janyce Trampler composes original poems, like "Cellular Respiration," to teach her AP biology students the complex and technical process of cellular respiration. Similarly, Jennifer Furphey now teaches her AP English Language and Composition students a science poetry unit in conjunction with the science and nature readings in *The McGraw-Hill* reader (Muller, 2006). Clearly, much is to be gained when we as science and English teachers raid each other's disciplines, realizing the joys of a different universe.

REASON #4: FOR SCIENCE POETRY ITSELF...

And the limitless possibilities that poetry holds as a tool for future exploration of the universe of literature, life, science, and the arts. In that exploration, may that tool lead our student scientists to use poetry for scientific research as well a mode to clarify thinking and express emotion. In a similar vein, may that tool lead our student poets to use science for poetic thought experiments not only to clarify thinking, but to reach, as Stanley Kunitz so eloquently dreams, "an art so transparent that you can look through and see the world" (Kunitz, 2000).

Epilogue
(What is Being Said Last)

Poetry not only gives a voice to the poet, it gives a voice to science when the meaning is deeper than the eye can see.

– Erin Colfax

TEACHERS AND STUDENTS MAKING CONNECTIONS

This book began by making connections. In that spirit, this book ends by asking you to consider the following connections from contributing author and science teacher, Erin Colfax, and student-science poet, Anne Schwartz.

HOW SCIENCE POETRY GAVE ME MY OWN SCIENTIFIC VOICE BY ERIN COLFAX

As a teacher and scientist, I have been taught to present scientific information and knowledge in the third person voice, to remove my emotions from any scientific experience, and to present just the facts. Emotions, I was taught, remain irrelevant to the essential data and observations that scientists make and will interfere with the science being studied, researched, or investigated. On some levels, I agree with this counsel; however, this teaching has created a void in my inner being that has prevented me from connecting my scientific experiences with my gut instincts and emotions. It was not until I was introduced to poetry that my inner voice as a scientist was able to emerge. Poetry gave me a means to connect my emotions to scientific fact, observation, and experience. It allowed me to express in writing what my heart had been feeling, and what my eyes had been seeing all these years.

This occurred when I was paired to co-teach Science Academy English III with Nancy Gorrell. Nancy's first reading in our class of Stanley Kunitz's poem, "The Wellfleet Whale," inspired me to look at the science of the world through new eyes – poetic eyes. This visual clarity came when I heard Kunitz marry his emotions to scientific fact. As Nancy read the poem aloud to the class, I had an epiphany. The moments of despair that I had experienced while trying to convey observations in science to my students without imparting emotion instantly dissipated. Kunitz's poem showed me that poetry could be the means by which I could describe my emotions and connect them to my scientific observations and experiences.

Perhaps Kunitz did not realize when he wrote about the whale's *eerie medley of clicks* that a science teacher reading his poem decades later would be transported back to a college lecture on animal communication. Or that the line in the poem *the crescent of your dorsal fin*, would be used as a reference when one teaches about the anatomical directions of ventral and dorsal. I do not know if Kunitz even recognized that by leading his reader through the fifth verse he would be telling the heartbreaking story of geologic time that is essential to teaching biology and earth science. Nor do I think Kunitz comprehended how intently important it was to connect the line, *krill-rich orange plankton* with *crackling with life*; for few scientists, with the exception of those studying in the arctic waters, know these vital truths on multiple levels.

I have read dozens of poems throughout the years about nature, plants, and animals, and I have been introduced to numerous poets, but never did I think that I would someday become a poet myself. As a student, poetry was introduced to me in small chunks. In courses I took over the years, I was often instructed to read a poem and then provide feedback. It seemed difficult and like a foreign language, one that I would never have a use for. But now, I crave poetry. I build in time after running experiments, learning about a new concept, or making observations to write and reflect. My field journals have poems imbedded with scientific facts and observations. My first poems in Iceland spoke about science at face value. But after some coaching, I have been able to reach a deeper level. My co-teacher and partner, Nancy, has now become my guide, introducing me to various poetic forms and methods that have helped me explore my scientific voice. She has encouraged me to embrace my newfound love, **science poetry**.

Science poetry has enabled me to express my love of science in a way that is different from the way my students normally *hear*. For me, it is the voice that tells the story of what my scientific eyes see.

ENVOY POEM: "US" BY ANNE SCHWARTZ, STUDENT-POET

Us

There's something comforting about evolution.
The notion that I
did not begin to live a mere sixteen years ago,
but three or four billion,
with the shock of life into that first cell.

I like the idea of a continuum;
A cycle of creatures, of steps along the way,
and I like my part in it.

My skin is not mine, but ours;
of prokaryotes and eukaryotes,
vertebrates and invertebrates,
amphibians and fish,
mammals and primates and humans
and
me.

Think of it! All of us connected,
Ancestors, brothers, sisters, cousins,
All children of that one cell.
That makes you feel a little less lonely,
doesn't it?

The thing I like best, though, is
Natural selection.
The idea of someone, somewhere,
Who's on our side.
Who creates miracles
of camouflage and opposable thumbs
and wings and fingers
Who raised me up to walk on two legs,
And will continue to do so,
in order to watch the world
Unfold.

– *Anne Schwartz*, student

YOU MAKING CONNECTIONS

This book began by making connections. In that spirit, this book ends by asking you to continue the journey by making your own connections between **science** and **poetry** in your classroom and in your personal life. It is my hope and the hope of my science partner that you and your students continue to watch the world *unfold* by writing poetry, like Anne Schwartz, **through the eyes of science**.

Notes on Contributors

The Authors of This Book

Nancy Gorrell (1946–)

Born in Manhattan, New York. Educated at the University of Wisconsin, Madison, Wisconsin (1964–67). Graduated from the State University of New York at Stony Brook, Stony Brook, New York (BA, 1968) with a major in history. She received her Masters Degree in social and intellectual history from the State University of New York at Stony Brook (1970). English teacher at Morristown High School since 1972, she taught, Honors English III, Science Academy English III, humanities, and creative writing and composition electives to grade 11 and 12 students until her retirement in 2007. An award-winning author of numerous articles on the teaching of poetry, writing, and the Holocaust in the National Council of Teachers of English (NCTE) *English Journal*, she was chosen to serve as New Jersey State Teacher of the Year, 1991–1992. In 1993, the National Endowment for the Humanities at County College of Morris recognized her for her innovative, international poetry exchange project, "Poem Pals." Her poetry has been published in *English Journal, Rockford Review, BlueLINE: A Literary Magazine of the Adirondacks, Footwork: Paterson Literary Review, Getting the Knack: Twenty Poetry Writing Exercises, and Reflections of the Gift of a Watermelon Pickle* (2nd edition). In 2001, she was awarded Outstanding English Language Arts Educator by the New Jersey Council of Teachers of English, and she received the gold medallion, the Governor's Award in Arts Education from the State of New Jersey. In 2006 she began collaborating with Erin Colfax in the art of teaching science poetry resulting in the writing of this book. She lives in Bridgewater, New Jersey.

Erin Colfax (1978–)

Born in Warwick, New York. Graduated Elizabethtown College, Elizabethtown, Pennsylvania (BS, 2000), with a major in science education. She received her Masters in Science (2009) at Ramapo College, Mahwah, New Jersey, in educational technology with a concentration in science; she is pursuing a second Masters from Montana State University, Bozeman, Montana, in science education (pending, 2012). Research science teacher at Morristown High School since 2003, she teaches Honors Biology, Research Science, and co-teaches in the Science Academy. In addition, she is a research explorer who has spent the past several years conducting five international research projects while traveling throughout the seven continents. Her original research projects were designed to enlighten her students and enhance their education of science in the field. In Africa, she and her research team tested the effects of high altitude while climbing Mount Kilimanjaro, and in Antarctica, she led a research team to retrace the steps of Sir Ernest Shackleton. She has received numerous scientific grants from scientific institutions and corporations for her expeditions and research. She has presented at the Weston Science Scholars Program at Montclair State University and the Annual Convention for the National Council of Teachers of English. Her honors include Teacher of the Year from the NJCSTE and New Jersey Business / Industry / Science Education Consortium. Her research over the past several years has been published by Laboratory Safety Institute, The New Jersey Education Association, and Leading and Learning with Technology. She lives in Riverdale, New Jersey.

Published Poets and Artists

A. R. Ammons (1926–2001)

Born outside Whiteville, North Carolina. Graduated from Wake Forest University with a major in biology. He received his Masters degree in

English from the University of California at Berkeley. He began teaching at Cornell University in 1964, eventually holding the position of Goldwin Smith Professor of Poetry until his retirement in 1998. Among his major honors are two National Book Awards (1973, for *Collected Poems 1951–1971*, and 1993, for *Garbage*); the Wallace Stevens Award from the Academy of American Poets (1998); and a MacArthur Fellowship in 1981, the year the award was established. His other awards include a 1981 National Book Critics Circle Award for *A Coast of Trees*; a 1993 Library of Congress Rebekah Johnson Bobbitt National Prize for Poetry for *Garbage*; the 1971 Bollingen Prize for *Sphere*; the Poetry Society of America's Robert Frost Medal; the Ruth Lilly Prize; and fellowships from the Guggenheim Foundation and the American Academy of Arts and Letters. Colleague of Roald Hoffmann, Ammons lived in Ithaca, New York.

Alison Hawthorne Deming (1946–)

Born in Hartford, Connecticut. Graduated Vermont College with a Masters in Fine Arts. Nature writer, and poet, she holds the position of Professor of Creative Writing at the University of Arizona. Her honors include the Walt Whitman Award from the Academy of American Poets for *Science and Other Poems* (Louisiana State University, 1994); the Bayer Creative Nonfiction Science Writing Award for *The Edges of the Civilized World* (Picador, 1998); a Wallace Stegner Fellowship from Stanford University (1987–88); two fellowships from the National Endowment for the Arts, and a Pushcart Prize for non-fiction. In addition, the *Washington Post* listed *Science and Other Poems* among its favorite books of 1994, and the *Bloomsbury Review* listed the collection among its Best Poetry books of the past fifteen years. More recent works include *Genus Loci* (Penguin, 2005) and *Rope* (Penguin, 2009). In 1997 she was Distinguished Visiting Writer at the University of Hawai'i in Manoa. A descendant of Nathaniel Hawthorne, Deming lives near Aqua Caliente Hill in Tucson, Arizona.

Robert Frost (1874–1963)

Born in San Francisco, California. Moved to New England at age eleven. Attended Dartmouth College and Harvard University but never graduated. In 1894 the *New York Independent* published his poem, "My Butterfly," and he had five poems privately printed. In 1912, he moved to England where he published his first collection of poems, *A Boy's Will*. It was followed by *North of Boston* (1914), which gained for him international recognition.

After returning to the United States in 1915 with his family, he bought a farm near Franconia, New Hampshire where he launched a career of writing, English teaching, and lecturing. This family homestead served as his summer home until 1938. During the years 1916–20, 1923–24, and 1927–1938, he taught English at Amherst College, in Massachusetts. From 1921 to 1963, he spent nearly every summer and fall teaching at the Bread Loaf School of English of Middlebury College, Vermont. In 1921 Frost accepted a fellowship teaching post at the University of Michigan, Ann Arbor, where he resided until 1927. While there he was awarded a lifetime appointment at the university as a Fellow in Letters. Among the honors Frost received were four Pulitzer Prizes for his books of poetry (1924, 1931, 1937, 1943), and tributes from the U.S. Senate (1950), the American Academy of Poets (1953), New York University (1956), and the Congressional Gold Medal (1962). Considered the unofficial poet laureate of the United States in the 1960s, he participated in the inauguration of President John F. Kennedy by reciting two of his poems.

Robert Graves (1895–1985)

Born in Wimbledon, South London. Graduated Oxford University. Graves was a poet, a professor, a literary scholar, and writer of historical novels. During his long and prolific career, he produced more than 140 works. At the outbreak of World War I, he immediately enlisted in the Royal Welch Fusilliers (RWF). His landmark autobiography, *Goodbye to All That* (1929), reflect his war experiences. He earned his living from writing, particularly popular historical novels such as *I Claudius* and *The Golden Fleece*. In 1934, he was awarded the James Tait Black Memorial Prize for both *I, Claudius* and *Claudius the God*. In addition to his prose, he was regarded primarily as a poet. He published 55 collections of poetry and was professor of poetry at Oxford from 1961–66. In 1968 he received the Queen's Gold Medal for Poetry. He lived on the island of Majorca, at first with fellow poet Laura Riding, and later with his second wife Beryl Hodge.

Steven N. Handel (1945–)

Born in Brooklyn, New York. Steven N. Handel, PhD, holds the position of Professor of Ecology and Evolution at Rutgers University, New Brunswick, New Jersey. He studies the restoration of plant communities in urban habitats, adding ecological services and biodiversity. He is an Aldo Leopold Leadership Fellow of the Ecological Society of America, an Honorary

Member of the American Society of Landscape Architects, and won their 2009 National Award of Honor for Research. He serves as editor-in-chief of the professional journal, *Ecological Restoration*. He has worked with landscape architecture teams on the design of urban parks, including the Brooklyn Bridge Park in New York, and the 1,450 acre Orange County Great Park in California. He lives in Bridgewater, New Jersey.

Roald Hoffmann (1937–)

Born in Zloczow, Poland (now the Ukraine) to a Jewish family. He survived the war in hiding with the help of his Ukrainian neighbors. In 1949, he came to the United States with his mother, one of the few from his immediate family to survive. He studied chemistry at Columbia (BA, 1958) and Harvard Universities (PhD, 1962). Since 1965, he has been a professor of chemistry at Cornell University, teaching both undergraduate and graduate courses. In 1974 he became the John A. Newman Professor of Physical Science. Presently, he holds the position of the Frank H. T. Rhodes Professor of Humane Letters Emeritus. His major honors in chemistry include the 1981 Nobel Prize (shared with Kenichi Fukui), the Priestly Medal of the American Chemical Society (1990), and the gold medal from the American Institute of Chemists (2006). Notable at the same time is his scientific writing, teaching, and reaching out to the public. He participated in the production of a PBS series, "The World of Chemistry," shown widely since 1990. As writer, he has united the arts and sciences through several works: *Chemistry Imagined*; *The Same and Not the Same*; *Old Wine, and New Flasks: Reflections on Science and Jewish Tradition*. Influenced by Marc Van Doren at Columbia, he began writing poetry in the mid-1970s, eventually publishing a number of collections: *The Metamict State* (1987), *Gaps and Verges, Memory Effects* (1999), and *Soliton* (2002). He has also co-written a play with fellow chemist Carl Djerassi, entitled *Oxygen*, which has been performed worldwide and translated into ten languages.

Michael Kravit (1981–)

Born Milwaukee, Wisconsin. He studied art at the New York School of Art, the Glasgow School of Art in Scotland, and the Pont-Aven School of Art in France, graduating from Brandeis University (BA, 2003) with a major in studio art. His wide range of artistic work includes exhibiting paintings in galleries in New York City and international venues as well as eco-design for tea companies in the United States. Currently, his artwork can be found on bottles of Honest Tea. He holds the position of Creative Director for Honest Tea in Bethesda, Maryland. In 2010, *Washington Life Magazine* listed him among the "ten green warriors you need to know." He lives in Washington, DC.

Julius Lester (1939–)

Born in St. Louis, Missouri. Graduated from Fisk University (BA 1960) with a major in English. In 1961, he moved to New York City where he had a talk radio show on WBAI FM from 1966–1973 and hosted a television talk show on WNET from 1969–1971. Since 1968, he has published 43 books for children and adults. His books have received the following awards: Newberry Honor Medal, the Lewis Carroll Shelf Award, National Book Award Finalist, National Jewish Book Award Finalist, National Book Critics Circle Award Finalist, Boston Globe/Horn Book Award, and the Coretta Scott King Award. In 1971, he joined the faculty of the University of Massachusetts where he was a professor in the Judaic and Near Eastern Studies Department. He has been honored by the university for his distinguished teaching and in 1988 was named Massachusetts State Professor of the Year. He lives in a small town in western Massachusetts.

Stanley Moss (1925–)

Born in Woodhaven, New York. Educated at Trinity College and Yale University. Moss served in the U.S. Navy during World War II. After the war, he worked on Botteghe Oscure and taught English in Rome and Barcelona. His first book of poems, *The Wrong Angel*, was published in 1966, and since then he has also published *The Skull of Adam* (1979), *The Intelligence of Clouds* (1989), *Asleep in the Garden* (1997), *A History of Color* (2003), *New & Selected Poems* (2006), *Rejoicing: New and Selected Poems* (2009). In 1977 he founded Sheep Meadow Press, a non-profit publishing company that publishes poetry and belles lettres, with a special focus on international poets in translation. He makes his living as a private art dealer, largely in Spanish and Italian Old Masters. He lives in Riverdale and Clinton Corners, New York.

Howard Nemerov (1920–1991)

Born in New York City. Graduated from Harvard University. During World War II, he flew with the Royal Canadian Air Force (1942–44) and then became a first lieutenant in the U.S. Army Air Forces (1942–44). In 1946 he began a life of teaching, ending his 45-year career at Washington University in St. Louis, where he held the position of the Edward Mallinckrodt Distinguished University Professor of English. By the time of his death, he had produced three novels, two collections of short stories, six volumes of criticism and thirteen volumes of poetry. In 1978 he won both the Pulitzer Prize and the National Book award for *The Collected Poems* (1977). He received the Bollingen Prize in 1981. Nemerov was appointed U.S. Poet Laureate twice, in 1963 and 1988. He lived in University City, Missouri.

William Stafford (1914–1993)

Born in Hutchinson, Kansas. Graduated from the University of Kansas (BA 1937). As a registered pacifist, he spent 1942–1946 in work camps and projects for conscientious objectors. In 1947, he received his Master's Degree in English from the University of Kansas. Based on his master's thesis, he published his memoirs of his time spent as a conscientious objector, *Down in My Heart* (1947). In 1948, he went to Lewis and Clark College, where he taught English until his retirement in 1980. His first major collection of poems, *Traveling Through the Dark*, won the National Book Award in 1963. He published more than sixty-five volumes of poetry and prose. Among his many honors and awards were a Shelley Memorial Award, a Guggenheim Fellowship, and a Western States Lifetime Achievement Award in Poetry. In 1970, he became the Consultant in Poetry to the Library of Congress (a position currently known as the Poet Laureate). Among his best-known works are *The Rescued Year* (1966), *Stories That Could Be True: New and Collected Poems* (1977), *Writing the Australian Crawl: Views on the Writer's Vocation* (1978), and *An Oregon Message* (1987). He lived in Lake Oswego, Oregon.

Notes on Teachers and Featured Student Poets*

Students with more than one poem

Jocelyn Burney (1992–)

Born in Morristown, New Jersey. Graduated from Morristown High School (class of 2010). She attends the University of North Carolina at Chapel Hill, North Carolina, where she is majoring in archeology. She is planning a double major in both archeology and religious studies.

Meghan Crippen (1991–)

Born in Morristown, New Jersey. Graduated from Morristown High School (class of 2009). She attends Boston College in Chestnut Hill, Massachusetts, where she is double majoring in biology and psychology with a concentration in neuroscience.

Alex Davis (1990–)

Born in Morristown, New Jersey. Graduated from Morristown High School (class of 2009). He attends Rutgers University, New Brunswick, New Jersey, where he is majoring in biology with a minor in mathematics. He is pursuing a career in scientific research.

Jennifer Furphey (1971–)

Born in Morristown, New Jersey. Graduated *magna cum laude* from Springfield College, Massachusetts, with a Bachelor of Arts degree in English. Received a Masters degree in English. An English teacher at Morristown High School, Morristown, New Jersey, she teaches Advanced Placement English Language and Composition, honors English and Creative Writing electives. She lives in Chester, New Jersey.

David Pitt (1990–)

Born in Morristown, New Jersey. Graduated from Morristown High School (class of 2009). He attends Stanford University, Palo Alto, California, where he is majoring in symbolic systems, a new major combining linguistics, computer science, and neurology. According to David, "college has made me a scientist more than ever. The poet sometimes gets left behind. But not really. Poetic thinking is still useful, in its short metaphorical bursts, to drive home a brilliant analogy that unlocks the solution to a problem."

Sarah Ryan (1991–)

Born in Summit, New Jersey. Graduated from Morristown High School (class of 2009). She attends Skidmore College, Saratoga Springs, New York, where she is majoring in English and Theater Arts. In her senior year at MHS, her poem, "Death of Winter," won New Jersey Council Teachers of English High School Writing Competition, Poetry Division. As a consequence, her poem was chosen for public reading at the 2010 Dodge Poetry Festival held in the

New Jersey Performing Arts Center, Newark, New Jersey. She continues to pursue poetry and creative writing.

Anne Schwartz (1991–)

Born in Morristown, New Jersey. Graduated from Morristown High School (class of 2009). She attends George Washington University, Washington, DC, majoring in international studies with a focus on Middle East and Women's Studies.

Janyce Trampler

Born in Kearny, New Jersey. Graduated from Georgian Court University, Lakewood, New Jersey (Bachelor of Science degree in biology) and (Masters of Science degree in molecular biology). A science teacher at Morristown High School, Morristown, New Jersey, she teaches Advanced Placement Biology, Anatomy and Physiology, and Honors Biology. She lives in Ocean, New Jersey.

Eric Villhauer (1990–)

Born in Denville, New Jersey. Graduated from Morristown High School (class of 2009). He attends the University of Chicago, Chicago, Illinois, where he is majoring in chemistry.

References

Abisdris, Gil and Casuga, Adele (2001) Atomic poetry: Using poetry to teach Rutherford's discovery of the nucleus. *Science Teacher* 68: 58–62. www3.nsta.org/main/news/pdf/tst0109_58.pdf.

Alber, Mark (2001) Creative writing and chemistry. *Journal of Chemistry Education* 78(4): 478–480.

Allman, John (1984) *Curve Away from Stillness*: *Science Poems*. New York: New Directions Publishing Corporation.

Ammons, A. R. (1987) "Cascadilla Falls." *The Selected Poems of A. R. Ammons* 62. New York: W.W. Norton and Company.

Angier, Natalie (2007) *The Canon: A Whirligig Tour of the Beautiful Basics of Science.* Boston: Houghton Mifflin Company.

Bizzaro, Patrick (1993) *Responding to Student Poems*. Urbana, Illinois: National Council of Teachers of English.

Bly, Robert (1972) *Leaping Poetry: An Idea with Poems and Translations*. Boston: Beacon Press.

Bourdon, David (1 July1995) The alchemist at large: The return of Tchelitchew. *Art in America* 63–67 Retrieved on 1 July 2009 from journal archives, highbeam.com/doc/1G1-17309690.htm.

Brady, James E. (1990) *General Chemistry: Principles and Structure.* John Wiley and Sons, Inc.

Brown, Kurt (1998) *Verse and Universe: Poems about Science and Mathematics*. Minneapolis: Milkweed Editions.

Brown, Kurt (2001) *The Measured Word: On Poetry and Science*. Athens, Georgia: University of Georgia Press.

Burnside, John (2006) A science of belonging: Poetry as ecology. Robert Crawford (ed.) *Contemporary Poetry and Contemporary Science* 91–106. Oxford: Oxford University Press.

Cherry, Kelly (2001) The two cultures at the end of the twentieth century. In Kurt Brown (ed.) *The Measured Word: On Poetry and Science* 24–37. Athens, Georgia: University of Georgia Press.

Coed Kills Herself to Spare Pet Dog Doomed by Father (1968) *New York Times* 7 February 1968: 29.

Coletta, W. John and Tamres, David H. (1992) Robert Frost and the poetry of physics. *The Physics Teacher* 30(6): 360–365.

Collini, Stefan (2007) C. P. Snow *The Two Cultures* (10th Canto edition) vii–lxxi. Cambridge, UK: Cambridge University Press.

Collins, Billy (1988) "Earthling." In *The Apple That Astonished Paris* 37. Fayetteville: University of Arkansas Press.

Crawford, Robert (2006) *Contemporary Poetry and Contemporary Science*. Oxford: Oxford University Press.

Csikszentmihalyi, Mihaly (1996) *Creativity: Flow and the Psychology of Discovery and Invention*. New York: Harper Collins Publishers.

Deming, Alison Hawthorne (1989a) "Essay on Intelligence: One." *The Monarchs: A Poem Sequence* 21. Baton Rouge: Louisiana State University Press.

Deming, Alison Hawthorne (1989b) "Essay on Intelligence: Three." *The Monarchs: A Poem Sequence* 34–35. Baton Rouge, Louisiana: Louisiana State University Press.

Deming, Alison Hawthorne (1989c) "Genetic Sequence" (originally titled "26"). *The Monarchs: A Poem Sequence* 32. Baton Rouge: Louisiana State University Press.

Deming, Alison Hawthorne (1994) "Mt. Lemmon, Steward Observatory, 1990." *Science and Other Poems* 53–56. Baton Rouge: Louisiana State University Press.

Deming, Alison Hawthorne (2001) Science and poetry: A view from the divide. In Kurt Brown (ed.) *The Measured Word: On Poetry and Science* 181–197. Athens, Georgia: University of Georgia Press.

Diehl, Edwin (November 1953) "How We Made the A-Gun Shell" *The Saturday Evening Post* 19–21, 98–101.

Dillard, Annie (1974) *Pilgrim at Tinker Creek*. New York: Harper Collins.

Dove, Rita (1998) "The Fish in the Stone." In Kurt Brown (ed.) *Verse and Universe: Poems about Science and Mathematics* 145. Minneapolis: Milkweed Editions.

Dunning, Stephen and Stafford, William (1992) *Getting the Knack: 20 Poetry Writing Exercises*. Urbana, Illinois: National Council of Teachers of English.

Eiseley, Loren (1998) "Notes of an Alchemist." In Kurt Brown (ed.) *Verse and Universe*: *Poems about Science and Mathematics* 135–137. Minneapolis: Milkweed Editions.

Felstiner, John (2009) *Can Poetry Save the Earth? A Field Guide to Nature Poems*. New Haven: Yale University Press.

Fleischman, Paul (1988) *Joyful Noise: Poems for Two Voices*. New York: Harper and Row.

Frost, Robert (1969) "The Secret Sits." In Edward Lathem (ed.) *The Poetry of Robert Frost* 362. New York: Henry Holt and Company, Inc.

Garfield, Eugene (1983) The poetry-science connection. *Essays of an Information Scientist* 6(29): 223–228.

Gibson, Dan (22 August 1995) Audio CD. *Solitudes: Journey with the Whales: Exploring Nature with Music*. http://www.silverlakemusic.com/art/agibson.html.

Gleick, James (1987) *Chaos: The Making of a New Science*. New York: Viking.

Goodall, M. C. (1965) *Science and the Politician*. Cambridge, UK: F. Schenkman.

Gorrell, Nancy (1989) Let found poetry help your students find poetry. *English Journal* 78(2): 30–34.

Gorrell, Nancy (1990) Poetry to engage the person. In Patricia Phelan (ed.) *Literature and Life: Making Connections in the Classroom* 35–43. Urbana, Illinois: National Council of Teachers of English.

Gorrell, Nancy (1993) Publishing the poetry chapbook: Defining a public self. *English Journal* 82(2): 42–46.

Gorrell, Nancy (27 December 2007) Interview with Steven Handel.

Gorrell, Nancy (5 April 2008) Interview with Roald Hoffmann.

Gorrell, Nancy (17 February 2009) Interview (email) with Lei Bao.

Graves, Robert (2003) "In Broken Images." In Beryl Graves (ed.) *The Complete Poems of Robert Graves* 296. London: Penguin Books. Retrieved on 1 July 2009 from http://www.xs4all.nl/~ace/Literaria/Poem-Graves.html.

Guillen, Michael (1995) *Five Equations that Changed the World: The Power and Poetry of Mathematics*. New York: Hyperion.

Hitchcock, George (ed.) (1969) *Losers and Weepers: Poems Found Practically Everywhere*. San Francisco: Kayak Books.

Hoffmann, Roald (21 March 1988a) How I work as poet and scientist. *The Scientist* 10. Retrieved on 1 July 2009 from http://www.roaldhoffmann. com/pn/modules/Downloads/docs/How_I_Work.pdf.

Hoffmann, Roald. (28 Sept.1988b) "Fluorite." *The Sciences* 30. Retrieved on 19 December 2007 from http://www.roaldhoffmann.com/pn/modules/ Downloads/docs/How_I_Work.pdf.

Hoffmann, Roald (1991) "Giving In." *The Paris Review* 33(121): 189. Retrieved on 1 July 2009 from http://www.roaldhoffmann.com/pn/ modules/Downloads/docs/Giving_In.

Hoffmann, Roald (2002a) On Poetry and the Language of Science. *Daedalus*, Spring: 137–140. Retrieved on 21 August 2008 from http://www. roaldhoffmann.com/pn/modules/Downloads/docs/On_Poetry_and_the_ Language_of_Science.pdf.

Hoffmann, Roald (2002b) "Tsunami." *Soliton* 3. Kirksville, Missouri: Truman State University Press.

Hoffmann, Roald (3 July 2008) Biography Retrieved on 1 July 2009 from www.roaldhoffmann.com.

Hoffmann, Roald and Torrence, Vivian (1993) *Chemistry Imagined* Washington, D.C.: Smithsonian Institution Press.

Holden, Jonathan (2001) Poetry and mathematics. In Kurt Brown (ed.) *The Measured Word: On Poetry and Science* 90–104. Athens, Georgia: The University of Georgia Press.

Holub, Miroslav (2001) Poetry and science: The science of poetry/ the poetry of science. In Kurt Brown (ed.) *The Measured Word: On Poetry and Science* 47–68. Athens, Georgia: University of Georgia Press.

Holub, Miroslav (2006) Rampage or science in poetry. In Robert Crawford (ed.) Contemporary Poetry and Contemporary Science 11–24. Oxford: Oxford University Press.

Isaacson, Walter (2007) *Einstein: His Life and Universe*. New York: Simon and Schuster.

Jacobs, Lucky (1977) Three approaches to the teaching of poetry writing. *English Education* 8(2): 161–166.

Jones, Adrian (2006) *Rocks and Minerals: Get to Know the Natural World.* Collins Wild Guide. New York: Harper Collins.

Kuhn, Thomas C. (1962) *The Structure of Scientific Revolutions*. Chicago: University of Chicago Press.

Kunitz, Stanley (1995) "The Wellfleet Whale." *Passing Through: The Later Poems New and Selected* 133–138. New York: W.W. Norton and Company.

Lehrer, Jonah (2007) *Proust was a Neuroscientist*. New York: Houghton Mifflin.

Lester, Julius (1969) "Parents." *Search for a New Land: History of Subjective Experience* 3. New York: Dial Press.

Long, Leon (2008) Letter to the Editor. *New York Times*, 23 April 2008.

MacDiarmid, Hugh (1978) "In Memoriam James Joyce." In Michael Grieve and William Russell Aitken (eds.) *Complete Poems: 1920–1976,* Vol. II: 782. London: Martin, Brian and O'Keefe.

Michael, Pamela (2005) Helping children fall in love with the Earth: Environmental education and the arts. In Michael K. Stone and Zenobia Barlow (eds.) *Ecological Literacy: Educating our Children for a Sustainable World* 111–125. San Francisco: Sierra Club Books.

Michael, Pamela (2008) *River of Words: Young Poets and Artists on the Nature of Things*. Minneapolis: Milkweed Editions.

Morgan, Edwin (1999) "Submarine Demon." *Demon* 7. Glasgow: Mariscat Press.

Morgan, Edwin (2006) Poetry and virtual realities. In Robert Crawford (ed.) *Contemporary Poetry and Contemporary Science* 27–47. Oxford: Oxford University Press.

Morris, Adalaide (2006) The act of the mind: Thought experiments in the poetry of Jorie Graham and Leslie Scalapino. Robert Crawford (ed.) *Contemporary Poetry and Contemporary Science* 146–166. Oxford: Oxford University Press.

Moss, Stanley (2009) "Tsunami Song." *Rejoicing: New and Collected Poems* 49. London: Anvil Press Poetry Ltd.

Moss, Stanley (2009) "Elegy for the Ancient Tree." *Rejoicing: New and Collected Poems* 80–81. London: Anvil Press Poetry Ltd.

Muller, Gilbert H. (2006) The McGraw-Hill Reader: Issues Across the Disciplines (9th edition). New York: McGraw Hill Inc.

Nabhan, Gary Paul (2004) *Cross-Pollinations: The Marriage of Science and Poetry*. Minneapolis: Milkweed Editions.

NCTE (15 February 2008) Toward a definition of 21st-century literacies. NCTE Executive Committee. Urbana, Illinois: National Council of

Teachers of English. Retrieved on 6 October 2008 from www.ncte.org/announce/129117.htm.

Nemerov, Howard (1977a) "Figures of Thought." *The Collected Poems of Howard Nemerov* 472. Chicago: University of Chicago Press.

Nemerov, Howard (1977b) "Learning the Trees." *The Collected Poems of Howard Nemerov* 486. Chicago: University of Chicago Press. Retrieved on 16 November 2008 from http://www.poemhunter.com/poem/learning-the-trees/.

Oldershaw, Cally (2004) *Guide to Gems.* Firefly Books Ltd.

Orr, David (2005) Foreword In Michael Stone and Zenobia Barlow (eds.) *Ecological Literacy: Educating our children for a Sustainable World* ix–xi. San Francisco: Sierra Club Books.

Padel, Ruth (2009) *Darwin: A Life in Poems* London: Chatto & Windus.

Padgett, Ron (2000) *Teachers and Writers Handbook of Poetic Forms* (2nd edition). New York: Teachers and Writers Collaborative.

Perrine, Laurence (1982) *Sound and Sense: An Introduction to Poetry* (6th edition). New York: Harcourt Brace Jovanovich, Inc.

Peters, Robert L. and Hitchcock, George (eds.) (1967) *Pioneers of Modern Poetry*. San Francisco: Kayak Books.

Platt, John R. (1964) Strong inference. *Science* 146(3642): 347–352.

Proust, Marcel (1982) "The Captive." In *Remembrance of Things Past*, Vol. III (trans. Scott Moncrieff) 259–160. New York: Vintage Books.

Revard, Carter (1998) "This is your Geode Talking." In Kurt Brown (ed.) *Verse and Universe: Poems about Science and Mathematics* 138–139. Minneapolis: Milkweed Editions.

Reznikoff, Charles (1965) *Testimony: The United States (1885–1890)*. New York: New Directions.

Rogers, Pattiann (1998) "Fossil Texts on Canyon Walls." In Kurt Brown (ed.) *Verse and Universe: Poems about Science and Mathematics* 146. Minneapolis: Milkweed Editions.

Ruef, Kerry (2005) The loupe's secret: Looking closely, changing scale. In Michael K. Stone and Zenobia Barlow *Ecological Literacy: Educating our Children for a Sustainable World* 206–212. San Francisco: Sierra Club Books.

Rule, Audrey (January 2004) Using poetry to teach minerals in earth science class. *Journal of Geoscience Education*. Retrieved on 19 December 2007 from http://findarticles.com/p/articles/mi_qa4089/is_200401/ai_n9389082/print.

Stafford, William (1978) *Writing the Australian Crawl*. Ann Arbor, Michigan: University of Michigan Press.

Stafford, William (1987) "What If We Were Alone?" *An Oregon Message* 115. New York: Harper and Row.

Snow, C. P. (2007) *The Two Cultures* (10th edition). Cambridge, UK: Cambridge University Press.

Stevens, Wallace (2004) "Thirteen Ways of Looking at a Blackbird." Retrieved 1 July 2009 from http://www.english.upenn.edu/~afilreis/88/stevens-13ways.html.

Stone, Michael K. and Barlow, Zenobia (2005) *Ecological Literacy: Educating Our Children for a Sustainable World*. San Francisco: Sierra Club Books.

Swanger, David (1974) *The Poem as Process*. New York: Harcourt Brace Jovanovich, Inc.

Tchelitchew, Pavel (1940–1942) *Hide-and-Seek*. New York: Museum of Modern Art (www.MoMa.org).

Thier, Marlene (2002) *The New Science Literacy: Using Language Skills to Help Students Learn Science*. Portsmouth, New Hampshire: Heinemann.

Tobin, Daniel (2001) A. R. Ammons and the poetics of chaos. In Kurt Brown (ed.) *The Measured Word: On Poetry and Science*. 127–155. Athens, Georgia: University of Georgia Press.

Waddington, Conrad H. (1965) *Behind Appearance*. Edinburgh: Edinburgh University Press.

Waldvogel, Jerry A. (2004) Writing poetry to assess creative and critical thinking in the sciences. In Marvin Druger, Eleanor D. Siebert and Linda M. Crow (eds.) *Teaching Tips: Innovations in Undergraduate Science Instruction* 58–59. Arlington, Virginia: National Science Teachers Association Press.

Waldvogel, Jerry A. (2006) Mating Darwin with Dickinson: How writing creative poetry in biology helps students think critically and build personal connections to course content. In Joel J. Mintzes and William H. Leonard (eds.) *Handbook of College Science Teaching* 185–194. Arlington, Virginia: National Science Teachers Association.

Watts, Mike (2001) Science and poetry: Passion v. prescription in school science? *International Journal of Science Education* 23(2): 197–208.

Whitman, Walt (2005) "When I Heard the Learn'd Astronomer." In Margaret Ferguson, Mary Jo Salter Mary Jo Salter and Jon Stallworthy (eds.) Jon

Stallworthy (eds.) *Norton Anthology of Poetry* (5th edition) 1071. New York: W.W. Norton and Company.

Whitman, Walt (2005) "A Noiseless Patient Spider." In Margaret Ferguson, Mary Jo Salter, Jon Stallworthy (eds.) *Norton Anthology of Poetry* (5th edition) 1085. New York: W.W. Norton and Company Retrieved 1 July 2009 from http://www.poets.org/viewmedia.php/prmMID/16158.

Wilson, Edward O. (1998) *Consilience: The Unity of Knowledge*. New York: Alfred A. Knopf.

Young, Art, Connor-Greene, Patrick, Paul, Catherine and Waldvogel, Jerry A. (2003) Poetry across the curriculum: Four disciplinary perspectives. *Language and Learning Across the Disciplines* 6(2): 14–44.

Ziegler, Alan (1989) Midwifing the craft–Teaching revision and editing. In Joseph M. Moxley (ed.) *Creative Writing in America: Theory and Pedagogy* 209–225. Urbana, Illinois: National Council of Teachers of English.

Appendix A

Recommended "Timely" Course Design

Note to All Teachers

Be sure to read Chapter 5, "How to Teach Science Poetry: The Teacher as 'Chemical Artist'," either before or after Section One, for pedagogical tips, strategies, and handouts. Be sure to read Chapter 12, "How to Assess Student Science Poetry: The Art of Response," for methods and strategies for responding, assessing and grading.

In addition, my science partner and I encourage science teachers to explore with their students appropriate activities in Chapter 2, "What is Poetry?" Science teachers should consider having their students try writing a *science found poem* as a creative way to read and engage with their science textbooks. Similarly, my science partner and I encourage English teachers to explore with their students appropriate activities in Chapter 3, "What is Science?" In particular, English teachers should explore methods for dispelling the anti-science mindset through engagement with Walt Whitman's poem, "When I Heard the Learn'd Astronomer" and Robert Graves' poem, "In Broken Images."

FOR THE ENGLISH TEACHER HARD PRESSED FOR TIME

STRATEGY #1: FOR THE ENGLISH TEACHER (2 BASIC LESSONS)

- Integrate science poetry reading and writing as part of any **poetry unit** you are teaching.
- Begin with Chapter 2, "What is Poetry?" Complete Part One, Getting Started, Activities #1 and #2. Complete Activity #3 for students needing background in understanding *what is poetry*?
- Introduce Robert Frost's "The Secret Sits" (see Introduction).
- Proceed to Chapter 4, "What is Science Poetry?" Complete Activity #1, A Lesson in Definition. Have students write their first science poems responding to the model science poem, "Tsunami."
- Essay Writing Assignment: Write a critical essay comparing and contrasting the science poem, "Tsunami," with the lyrical poem, "Tsunami Song."

STRATEGY #2: FOR THE ENGLISH TEACHER (3 BASIC LESSONS)

Integrate science poetry reading and writing as part of any **non-fiction unit** you are teaching that includes science and nature essays.

- Begin with Chapter 1, "Hide and Seek." Complete Activity #1 (a painting), Activity #2 (Annie Dillard's nature essay), and the closure science poem, "Learning the Trees."
- Proceed to Chapter 2, "What is Poetry?" Complete Part One, Getting Started, Activities #1 and #2. Complete Activity #3

for students needing background in understanding *what is poetry?*

- Introduce Robert Frost's "The Secret Sits" (see Introduction).
- Proceed to Chapter 4, "What is Science Poetry?" Complete Activity #1, A Lesson in Definition. Have students write their first science poems responding to the model science poem, "Tsunami."
- After students do their required readings, have them write science poems on similar topics and themes inspired from their science and nature readings (see Chapters 9 and 10 for model student poems).

STRATEGY #3: FOR THE ENGLISH TEACHER (3 BASIC LESSONS)

Integrate science poetry reading and writing into a **fiction, autobiographical fiction, or historical fiction** unit you are teaching on the subject of science or nature. This strategy may be ideal for required curricula that include fiction about science, scientists, or scientific themes, or nature, naturalists, and naturalistic or environmental themes.

- Begin with Chapter 1, "Hide and Seek." Complete Activity #1 (a painting), Activity #2 (Annie Dillard's nature essay), and the closure science poem, "Learning the Trees."
- Proceed to Chapter 2, "What is Poetry?" Complete Part One, Getting Started, Activities #1 and #2. Complete Activity #3 for students needing background in understanding *what is poetry?*
- Proceed to Chapter 4, "What is Science Poetry?" Complete Activity #1, Chapter 4, A Lesson in Definition. After students understand what science poetry is, give them the opportunity to respond in a science poem inspired by the

subjects, characters, and themes presented in their fiction reading.

STRATEGY #4: FOR THE AP ENGLISH TEACHER (4 ADVANCED LESSONS)

- Integrate science poetry reading and writing into your AP curriculum by adopting either strategy #1, 2, or 3. AP English Language and Composition teachers should consider adopting strategy #2, for non-fiction literature; AP English Literature teachers should consider adopting strategy #1 or #4 for poetry and fiction reading.
- Begin with Chapter 1, "Hide and Seek." Complete Activity #1 (a painting), Activity #2 (Annie Dillard's nature essay), and the closure science poem, "Learning the Trees."
- Proceed to Chapter 2, "What is Poetry?" Complete Part One, Getting Started, Activities #1 and #2. Complete Activity #3 and Activity #4, writing a science found poem.
- Proceed to Chapter 4, "What is Science Poetry?" Complete Activity #1, Chapter 4, A Lesson in Definition. After students understand what science poetry is, give them the opportunity to respond in a science poem inspired by the subjects, characters, and themes presented in their fiction reading.
- After completing Chapter 4, a Lesson in Definition, skip to Section Three, advanced science poetry writing. Read the Section Overview: Our Guiding Metaphor, *Fusion*, which explains the distinguishing characteristics of the advanced science poem. Then complete appropriate activities, based upon your students and curriculum readings, from the advanced science poetry writing activities in Chapter 9, "Writing from Awe, Wonder, Reverence, and Empathy," and/or Chapter 10, "Writing from Outrage, Protest, Perplexity, and Speculation."

STRATEGY #5: FOR THE COMPOSITION TEACHER
(3 BASIC LESSONS)

- Integrate science poetry writing as part of any composition unit you are teaching.
- Use science poems as models for the rhetorical patterns of description, narration, exposition, persuasion, process, definition, cause and effect, as well as reflection and speculation prevalent in the personal essay.
- Suggest to your students to write a model essay demonstrating a rhetorical pattern and then respond in kind in a science poem. Encourage students to practice blending more than one rhetorical pattern in a poem (see Chapters 5 and 6 on rhetorical patterns and stance blending strategies and model poems).
- Begin with Chapter 4, "What is Science Poetry?" Complete Activity #1, Chapter 4, A Lesson in Definition. Develop prompt ideas relevant to the essays in your students' readers.
- Proceed to Chapter 6 and/or Chapter 7. Complete Activities # 1 and #2 in each chapter. Have students respond in science poems demonstrating a variety of rhetorical patterns and stances.
- Proceed to Chapter 10, "Writing from Outrage, Protest, Perplexity, and Speculation." Complete Activity #1. Have students respond with their own science poems of protest and persuasion.

STRATEGY #6: FOR THE CREATIVE WRITING TEACHER
(5 LESSONS)

- Begin with Chapter 1, "Hide and Seek" and the multiple ways of seeing a single subject, *trees*, through the eyes of the artist, naturalist, scientist, and science poet. The four activities in this chapter provide the background foundation for developing creativity skills and multiple perspectives essential for poetry writing in general, and science poetry writing in particular.

- Proceed to Chapter 2, "What is Poetry?" Introduce your students to the poetic genre of found poetry and writing science poetry from naturalistic texts.
- Proceed to Chapter 4, "What is Science Poetry?" Complete Activity #1, A Lesson in Definition. Have students respond with their first science poems.
- Proceed to one of the basic, fundamental activities suggested in either Chapter 6 (earth science poems) or Chapter 7 (biology or botany poems). Complete one of the hands-on activities most relevant for your level of students.
- Proceed to the advance level activities in Section Three. Complete the advanced level activities in either Chapter 9, "Writing from Awe, Wonder, Reverence, and Empathy," or Chapter 10, "Writing from Outrage, Protest, Perplexity, and Speculation."

FOR THE SCIENCE TEACHER HARD PRESSED FOR TIME

Use science poetry reading and writing as an anticipatory set for any science lesson, as a tool to facilitate science instruction and lectures, and as a creative approach to closure, reviewing, reinforcing, and synthesizing material at the end of science lessons and units. These strategies will engage your arts and poetry-minded students while fostering the development of creative, imaginative, and analytical thinking for your science students. Most importantly, science teachers hard-pressed for time should integrate poetry reading and writing activities relevant for their specific areas of science and required courses of study.

STRATEGY #1: FOR THE GENERAL SCIENCE TEACHER (3 BASIC LESSONS)

- Begin with Chapter 3, "What is Science?" Complete Activity #1, Science Awareness Poll to assess students' attitudes towards science and scientific literacy. Complete Activities #2 and #3 for a creative introduction to exploring attitudes toward science and the scientific method.
- Proceed to Chapter 4, "What is Science Poetry?" Complete Activity #1, A Lesson in Definition. Have your students respond by writing their first science poems.
- Proceed to either Chapter 6 or Chapter 7, depending upon your particular students. Choose one of the basic and fundamental activities in either Chapter 6, "It's a Gem!" or Chapter 7, "What's Buggin' You?" The professional and student models in these chapters will provide students with sufficient poetic strategies and inspiration to prompt their poetic responses.

STRATEGY #2: FOR THE PHYSICAL SCIENCE TEACHER (3 BASIC LESSONS)

- Begin with Chapter 3, "What is Science?" Complete Activity #1, Science Awareness Poll to assess students' attitudes towards science and scientific literacy. Complete Activities #2 and #3 for a creative introduction to exploring attitudes toward science and the scientific method.
- Proceed to Robert Frost's physics-related poem, "The Secret Sits" (see Introduction).
- Proceed to Chapter 4, "What is Science Poetry?" Complete Activity #1, A Lesson in Definition, focusing on Roald Hoffmann's "Tsunami," a physical science-related poem. Have students write their first science poems.

• Proceed to Chapter 10. Complete Activity #1, Roald Hoffmann's "Giving In," a physical-science related poem. Have students respond in kind with their own science poems.

STRATEGY #3: FOR THE LIFE SCIENCE TEACHER (5 BASIC LESSONS)

• Begin with Chapter 1, "Hide and Seek." Complete Activity #1 (a painting), Activity #2 (Annie Dillard's nature essay), Activity #3 (Interview with botanist, Steven Handel), and the closure science poem, "Learning the Trees."
• Proceed to Chapter 3, "What is Science?" Complete Activity #1, Science Awareness Poll, to assess students' attitudes towards science and scientific literacy. Complete Activities #2 and #3 for a creative introduction to exploring attitudes toward science and the scientific method.
• Proceed to Chapter 4, "What is Science Poetry?" Complete Activity #1, A Lesson in Definition.
• Proceed to Chapter 7, "What's Buggin' You?" The professional and student models in these chapters will provide your students with poetic strategies to prompt biology and botany-inspired poems.
• Proceed to Chapter 9. Complete Activity #1, Stanley Kunitz's "The Wellfleet Whale." This chapter is highly relevant to biology and ecology students.

STRATEGY #4: FOR THE RESEARCH, ENVIRONMENTAL, OR ECOLOGY TEACHER (3 BASIC LESSONS AND A FIELD EXPERIENCE)

• Begin with Chapter 1, "Hide and Seek." Complete Activity #1 (a painting), Activity #2 (Annie Dillard's nature essay),

Activity #3 (Interview with botanist, Steven Handel), and the closure science poem, "Learning the Trees."

- Proceed to Chapter 4, "What is Science Poetry?" Complete Activity #1, A Lesson in Definition. Have students write their first science poems.
- Proceed to Chapter 8, "Into the Field, It's Only Natural." Adapt the Icelandic Expedition Model to your own subject area and curriculum needs. Take your students to an environmental locale in your community for scientific research and poetic response. Or, gather your own sensory or scientific data for your students' poetic response.
- And/or proceed to Chapter 11, "Walking in this World with Our Students and Colleagues." Adapt the urban field expedition models for your own subject area or curriculum needs during school vacation time or during the summer.
- Optional: Have your students participate in the River of Words (ROW) International Poetry Contest in support of watersheds.

STRATEGY #5: FOR THE AP SCIENCE TEACHER (5 ADVANCED LESSONS)

- Begin with Chapter 1, "Hide and Seek." Complete Activity #1 (a painting), Activity #2 (Annie Dillard's nature essay), Activity #3 (Interview with botanist, Steven Handel), and the closure science poem, "Learning the Trees."
- Proceed to Chapter 3, "What is Science?" Complete Activity #1, Science Awareness Poll, to assess students' attitudes towards science and scientific literacy. Complete Activities #2 and #3 for a creative introduction to exploring attitudes toward science and the scientific method.
- Proceed to Chapter 4, "What is Science Poetry?" Complete Activity #1, A Lesson in Definition. Have students write

their first science poems inspired by "Tsunami," a poem related to the physical sciences.

- Choose one fundamental poetry writing activity relevant to your particular area of science: Chapter 6, earth science; Chapter 7, the life sciences; or Chapter 8, research science or environmental science.
- Choose one, advanced poetry writing activity relevant to your particular area of science. Select model poems in Chapter 9 and Chapter 10 that relate to your particular area of science. For example, Chapter 9, "The Wellfleet Whale" (biology); In Chapter 10, "Giving In" (chemistry); "Cascadilla Falls" (physics and earth science).
- Optional: Proceed to Chapter 11, "Walking in This World with Our Students and Colleagues." Take your students on science poetry writing expedition.

Appendix B

Recommended Two-Week Unit Plan

Note to All Teachers

Whether you are a science or English teacher, be sure to read Chapter 5, "How to Teach Science Poetry Writing: Teacher as 'Chemical Artist'," either before or after Section One, for pedagogical tips, strategies, and handouts. Be sure to read Chapter 12, "How to Assess Student Science Poetry: The Art of Response," for methods and strategies for responding, assessing, and grading.

This two-week unit plan is designed and recommended for <u>both</u> science and English students. My science partner and I encourage interested teachers from both disciplines to create imaginative course designs relevant to the unique needs of their particular students and curriculums. With science poetry, there is a universe of possible course designs.

A TWO-WEEK UNIT PLAN

The following sequence of lessons builds science and English students' understanding, appreciation, and science poetry writing skills. Each lesson may take more than one class period or day depending upon the number of activities you choose to do with your students as well as the amount of time you want to devote to discussion, writing poetry in class, hands-on activities, as well as sharing and conferencing over science poetry. For best results, allow two weeks to complete the unit plan, devoting more than one class period to particular lessons based upon your students' response, your curriculum needs, and your school's schedule.

The following plan delineates a two-week unit lesson plan with two optional lessons designated as closure and enrichment activities. My science partner and I recommend concluding the unit with at least one field trip experience, based on either Chapter 8 or Chapter 11. We encourage you to reserve time in the unit plan for assessment, conferencing, and sharing of science poems among students in reading circles.

DAY ONE: THE FOUNDATION, CHAPTER 1 (ANTICIPATORY SET)

Preparatory Lesson: "Hide and Seek: Multiple Ways of Seeing Trees."

Activities: Choose to complete at least two activities relevant to your discipline and students. English teachers should teach Activities #1 and #2 along with Howard Nemerov's science poem: "Learning the Trees." Science teachers should teach Activities #1 and #3 along with Howard Nemerov's science poem, "Learning the Trees."

DAY TWO: THE FOUNDATION, CHAPTER 2 (ASSESSING LITERACY)

Preparatory Lesson: "What is Poetry? Developing the Poetic Eye."

Activities: Choose to complete the Poetry Awareness Poll and/or any other activities relevant to your discipline and students. English and science teachers should teach the science found poem activity to engage students with a creative way to read scientific articles and textbooks.

DAY THREE: THE FOUNDATION, CHAPTER 3 (ASSESSING LITERACY)

Preparatory Lesson: "What is Science? Developing the Scientific Eye."

Activities: Choose to complete the Science Awareness Poll and/ or any other activities relevant to your discipline and students. English and science teachers should complete Activities #2 (science memories) and #3 (Robert Graves' poem) to assess students' attitudes toward science and the scientific method.

DAY FOUR: THE FOUNDATION, CHAPTER 4 (LESSON IN DEFINITION)

Read with students Robert Frost's "The Secret Sits" (see Introduction).

Signature Lesson: "What is Science Poetry?" Read with students the model science poem "Tsunami," by Roald Hoffmann. Have students respond with their first science poems.

DAY FIVE: THE FUNDAMENTALS, CHAPTER 6 (BASIC SCIENCE POEMS)

Basic Lesson: "It's a Gem!" Have students practice with the basics of writing science poetry by completing Activity #1: Practice Gem Poetry Exercise. Then read with students the model science poem "Fluorite" by Roald Hoffmann. Have students respond by writing "gem" science poems.

Activities: For English and creative writing teachers, this lesson offers the basics in poetry writing, including the five poetic stances. For earth science teachers in particular, this lesson offers an ideal, creative approach to mineral, rock, and gemstone instruction.

DAY SIX: THE FUNDAMENTALS, CHAPTER 7 (BASIC SCIENCE POEMS)

Basic Lesson: "What's Buggin' You?" Have students practice with the basics of writing science poetry by completing Activity #1: Practice Insect Poetry Exercise. Then read with students the model science poem, "Genetic Sequence," by Alison Hawthorne Deming. Have students respond by writing insect science poems.

Activities: For English and creative writing teachers, this lesson offers the basics in poetry writing, including the five poetic stances. For biology and botany teachers in particular, this lesson offers an ideal, creative approach to insect, animal, and plant instruction.

DAY SEVEN: FUSION, CHAPTER 9 (ADVANCED SCIENCE POEMS)

Advanced Lesson: "Writing from Awe, Wonder, Reverence, and Empathy." Read with students the model poem, "The Wellfleet Whale," by Stanley Kunitz. Have your students respond with their own inspired science poems.

Activities: Complete the activities and the advanced science poem exercises relevant to your discipline and students. For English and creative writing teachers, Kunitz's poem offers a rare opportunity to inspire poetic response in students. For biology, ecology, and environmental science teachers, Kunitz's poem offers a rare opportunity to inspire scientific ethical issues.

DAY EIGHT: FUSION, CHAPTER 10 (ADVANCED SCIENCE POEMS)

Advanced Lesson: "Writing from Outrage, Protest, Perplexity, and Speculation." Read with students the model poems, "Giving In" by Roald Hoffmann, "Cascadilla Falls" by A. R. Ammons, and "What If We Were Alone?" by William Stafford.

Activities: Complete the activities and the advanced science poem exercises relevant to your discipline and students. For English and creative writing teachers, Hoffmann's and Stafford's poems offer students the opportunity to write persuasion and protest in the form of the science poem. For physics and chemistry teachers, Hoffmann's and A. R. Ammons' poems offer the opportunity for instruction and engagement with scientific moral and ethical issues.

DAY NINE: FUSION, CHAPTER 8 (INTO THE FIELD)

Field Lesson: "Into the Field, It's Only Natural." Have your students gather field data to prompt and inspire science poems back in the classroom.

Activities: Conduct a mini-field trip with your students on school grounds or an all day field trip experience off school grounds to gather data in the field for science poetry writing. For English and creative writing teachers, this activity is ideal for teaching descriptive writing skills as well as the science poem. For biology, ecology, and environmental science teachers, this activity is ideal as a laboratory experience.

DAY TEN: VISIONS AND VOICES (CLOSURE LESSON)

Visions: Use this time to conference, peer edit, and assess poems.

Voices: Use this time for in-class reading circles or performance of poems in progress or completion.

OPTIONAL LESSON: FUSION, CHAPTER 11 (WALKING IN THIS WORLD)

Closure Lesson: "Walking in this World with Your Students."

Activities: Conduct a science poetry writing expedition with your students over a period of several days to conclude the unit. Have students keep field journals and respond with in-the-field science poems.

OPTIONAL LESSON: PUBLIC READING OR PERFORM-ANCE OF SCIENCE POEMS

Closure Lesson: Have students visit and voice their science poems in appropriate science and English classes throughout the school. Or, have students do a science poetry reading in the school library or atrium during an appropriate time or to raise awareness for a particular issue (Earth Day or Poetry Month in the U.S.A. or local or national environmental causes).

Appendix C

Science Poetry Resources for the Teacher

WEBSITES

www.poetryandscience.co.uk Liverpool University Centre for Poetry and Science.

www.artscatalyst.org An arts organization that actively makes connections between art and science through commissions and strategic projects.

www.firstscience.com/site/poems.asp An eclectic selection of science and nature poems.

www.scienceeducationreview.com/poetarticle.html "This article considers some potential benefits of providing poetic learning experiences within a science curriculum and provides practical classroom techniques and resources to support the strategy."

www.roaldhoffmann.com/pn/index.php Personal website of applied theoretical chemist and writer, Roald Hoffman.

www.ericdigests.org/2003-1/poetry.htm An article, some information, resources and links, compiled by Davi Walders.

www.sff.net/people/Geoffrey.Landis/poetry.htp An article which compares poetic and scientific uses of metaphor.

www.the-private-eye.com Offers classroom based kits for developing interdisciplinary habits of the mind.

www.bioneers.org An organization of self-described "biological pioneers" who are working with nature to help heal nature and sustain our ecological systems; an inclusive, interdisciplinary organization with a Bioneers Youth Initiative component.

www.riverofwords.org Offers curriculum guides for teachers K–12 in environmental education: *River of Words Watershed Explorer Curriculum Educator's Guide*.

www.asle.org/site/publications/isle Site for ISLE: Interdisciplinary Studies in Literature and the Environment; the official site for the journal of the Association for the Study of Literature and the Environment (ASLE).

CENTERS AND WEBLOGS

www.mcn.org/ed/CUR/cw/Science_Poetry/Poetry.html The Science Poetry Centre, a space for students to post science poems. Students grades K–12.

ahappening.typepad.com/qarrtsiluni/science_as_poetry/index.html A weblog for artistic collaboration with a section dedicated to science as poetry.

http://qarrtsiluni.com/category/science-as-poetry/index.html *Qarrtsiluni* is an online literary magazine with a section dedicated to science as poetry.

http://www.sciencenews.org/sn_arc97/75th/poetry.htm Science poetry by Science News readers.

CONTESTS AND COMPETITIONS FOR STUDENTS

http://riverofwords.org/contest/index.html International poetry (and art) contest for youth on the theme of *Watersheds*; the contest is designed to help youth explore the natural history of the place they live and to express through poetry what they discover; for all ages.

www.bc.edu/schools/lsoe/poetry The Massachusetts Science Poetry Contest, for students K–8.

www.scienceeducationreview.com/poetcomp.html The online journal's International Science Poetry Competition for students ages 9–15+.

http://www.sciencemetropolis.com/category/poetry/poetry-contest Science Metropolis, Boston conducts a summer science poetry online contest; posts superior science poetry archive by students.

http://www.stonehill.edu/x17064.xml Stonehill College Science Poetry Contest, founded by Professor Roger Denome; open to high school and college students.

Appendix D
Further Reading for the Teacher

BOOKS AND CHAPTERS

Ackerman, Diane. *A Natural History of the Senses* (Random House, 1990).

Brenson, Michael. *Visionaries and Outcasts* (New Press, 2001).

Bronowski, Jacob. *The Ascent of Man* (Little, Brown, 1973).

Bronowski, Jacob. *The Visionary Eye: Essays in the Arts, Literature, and Science* (MIT Press, 1981).

Brown, Kurt. *The True Subject: Writers on Life and Craft* (Graywolf Press, 1993).

Csikszentmihalyi, Mihaly. *Creativity: Flow and the Psychology of Discovery and Invention* (Harper Collins, 1996).

Deming, Alison Hawthorne. *Writing the Sacred into the Real* (Milkweed, 2001).

Deming, Alison Hawthorne. *The Edges of the Civilized World* (Picador USA, 1998).

Dillard, Annie. *Teaching a Stone to Talk: Expeditions and Encounters* (Harper and Row, 1982).

Dillard, Annie. *The Writing Life* (Harper Perennial, 1989).

Doty, Mark. *Still Life with Oysters and Lemon* (Beacon Press, 2001).

Eiseley, Loren. *The Immense Journey* (Random House, 1957).

Eiseley, Loren. *The Invisible Pyramid* (Simon and Schuster, 1970).

Felstiner, John. *Can Poetry Save the Earth? A Field Guide to Nature Poems*. New Haven: Yale University Press, 2009.

Gleick, James. *Chaos: The Making of a New Science* (Viking, 1987).

Gould, Stephen Jay. *Ever Since Darwin*. (W.W. Norton, 1973).

Guillen, Michael. *Bridges to Infinity: The Human Side of Mathematics* (Tarcher, 1985).

Hawking, Stephen. *A Brief History of Time*. (Bantam, 1988).

Hayles, N. Katherine. *Chaos Bound: Orderly Disorder In Contemporary Literature and Science* (Cornell University Press, 1984).

Holmes, Richard. *The Age of Wonder*. New York: Vintage Books, 2008.

Holub, Miroslav. "The Impact of Science on the Poet's Soul." In *The True Subject* edited by Kurt Brown (Graywolf Press, 1993).

Nabhan, Gary Paul, and Stephen Trimble. *The Geography of Childhood: Why Children Need Wild Places* (Beacon Press, 1994).

Pyle, Robert Michael. *Walking the High Ridge: Life as a Field Trip* (Milkweed, 2000).

Richards, I. A. *Science and Poetry* (Kegan Paul, 1926).

Slovic, Scott. *Seeking Awareness in American Nature Writing: Henry David Thoreau, Annie Dillard, Edward Abbey, Wendell Berry, Barry Lopez* (University of Utah Press, 1992).

Snyder, Gary. "Nature Writing." In *The True Subject* edited by Kurt Brown (Graywolf Press, 1993).

Wilson, Edmond O. *Biophilia* (Harvard Press, 1984).

POETRY COLLECTIONS

Ackerman, Diane. *The Planets: A Cosmic Pastoral* (Morrow, 1976).

Ackerman, Diane. *Jaguar of Sweet Laughter: New and Selected Poems* (Random House, 1991).

Armitage, Simon. *Selected Poems* (Farber and Farber, 2001).

Burns, John M. *BioGraffiti: A Natural Selection* (W.W. Norton, 1975).

Burnside, John. *Selected Poems* (Cape, 2006).

Fulton, Alice. *Sensual Math* (W.W. Norton, 1995).

Gander, Forrest. *Science and Steepleflower* (New Directions, 1995).

Goldbarth, Albert. *Across the Layers: Poems Old and New* (University of Georgia Press, 1993).

Hahn, Kimiko. *Toxic Flora.* (W.W. Norton, 2010).

Holub, Miroslav. *The Rampage.* (Farber and Farber, 1997).

Morgan, Edwin. *Collected Poems* (Carcanet, 1990)

Morgan, Edwin. *Virtual and Other Realities* (Carcanet, 1997).

Rogers, Pattiann. *Firekeeper: New and Selected Poems* (Milkweed, 2005).

Sullivan, Anne McCary. *Ecology II: Throat Song from the Everglades.* Cincinnati: WordTech Editions, 2009.

REFERENCE WORKS AND ANTHOLOGIES

Collins Dictionary of Science: Science Defined and Explained (Harper Collins, 2003). Includes an invaluable list of science resources and sites on the Internet.

Collins Dictionary of Human Biology: Human Biology Defined and Explained (Harper Collins, 2006). Includes an invaluable list of human biology resources and sites on the Internet.

The Norton Book of Nature Writing edited by Robert Finch and John Elder (W.W. Norton, 2002). Includes inspirational and provocative essays to prompt science poetry.

General Index

Index of Poems

Index of Poems by Author and Title

Index of Student Poems by Author and Title